THE
Joseph Smith Translation

THE RESTORATION OF PLAIN AND PRECIOUS THINGS

RELIGIOUS STUDIES CENTER PUBLICATIONS

BOOK OF MORMON SYMPOSIUM SERIES

The Book of Mormon: The Keystone Scripture
The Book of Mormon: First Nephi, the Doctrinal Foundation
The Book of Mormon: Second Nephi, the Doctrinal Structure
The Book of Mormon: Jacob Through Words of Mormon, To Learn with Joy
The Book of Mormon: Mosiah, Salvation Only Through Christ
The Book of Mormon: Alma, The Testimony of the Word
The Book of Mormon: Helaman Through 3 Nephi 8, According to Thy Word
The Book of Mormon: 3 Nephi 9–30, This Is My Gospel

MONOGRAPH SERIES

Nibley on the Timely and the Timeless
Deity and Death
The Glory of God Is Intelligence
Reflections on Mormonism
Literature of Belief
The Words of Joseph Smith
Book of Mormon Authorship
Mormons and Muslims
The Temple in Antiquity
Isaiah and the Prophets
Scriptures for the Modern World
The Joseph Smith Translation: The Restoration of Plain and Precious Things
Apocryphal Writings and the Latter-day Saints
The Pearl of Great Price: Revelations From God
The Lectures on Faith in Historical Perspective
Mormon Redress Petitions: Documents of the 1833–1838 Missouri Conflict
Joseph Smith: The Prophet, the Man

SPECIALIZED MONOGRAPH SERIES

Supporting Saints: Life Stories of Nineteenth-Century Mormons
The Call of Zion: The Story of the First Welsh Mormon Emigration
The Religion and Family Connection: Social Science Perspectives
Welsh Mormon Writings from 1844 to 1862: A Historical Bibliography
Peter and the Popes
John Lyon: The Life of a Pioneer Poet
Latter-day Prophets and the United States Constitution

OCCASIONAL PAPERS SERIES

Excavations at Seila, Egypt

THE Joseph Smith Translation

THE RESTORATION OF PLAIN AND PRECIOUS THINGS

Edited by
Monte S. Nyman and Robert L. Millet

VOLUME TWELVE
IN THE RELIGIOUS STUDIES CENTER
MONOGRAPH SERIES

Religious Studies Center
Brigham Young University
Provo, Utah

Copyright © 1985 by
Religious Studies Center
Brigham Young University

All rights reserved

Library of Congress Catalog Card Number: 85–70372
ISBN 0–88494–976–1

2nd Softcover Printing, 1995

Produced and Distributed by
BOOKCRAFT, INC.
Salt Lake City, Utah

Printed in the United States of America

RELIGIOUS STUDIES CENTER
BRIGHAM YOUNG UNIVERSITY

General Director: Robert L. Millet
Associate General Director: Donald Q. Cannon
Associate Director (Publications): Kent P. Jackson

Area Directors

Book of Mormon: Monte S. Nyman
Electronic Texts: Keith W. Perkins

Advisory Board

Robert L. Millet
Clayne L. Pope
Randall L. Jones

Dedication

As a witness for the Lord Jesus Christ and Joseph Smith his Prophet, Elder Bruce R. McConkie was powerful and eloquent. He taught from the scriptures and took literally the Lord's declaration that "this generation shall have my word through" Joseph Smith (D&C 5:10). He rejoiced in the light and divine understanding that is made available through the Joseph Smith Translation of the Bible. He used the JST in his writings and did much to bring this revelatory work to the attention of Church members.

One of his last public discourses on the JST is included herein. We therefore affectionately dedicate this volume to his memory.

Contents

	Preface	ix
1	The Doctrinal Restoration .... Elder Bruce R. McConkie	1
2	Joseph Smith's Translation of the Bible: A Historical Overview .... Robert L. Millet	23
3	Insights into the Book of Genesis................ George A. Horton, Jr.	51
4	Insights into Exodus, Leviticus, Numbers, and Deuteronomy .... George A. Horton, Jr.	71
5	The Contribution of the JST to the Old Testament Historical Books .... Monte S. Nyman	89
6	Joseph Smith and the Poetic Writings............ Joseph F. McConkie	103
7	The Contribution of the JST to Understanding the Old Testament Prophets .... Monte S. Nyman	121
8	The JST and the Synoptic Gospels: Literary Style... Robert L. Millet	147
9	The Sermon on the Mount in the JST and the Book of Mormon .... Robert A. Cloward	163

10	Looking Beyond the Mark: Insights from the JST into First-Century Judaism 201
	Robert L. Millet
11	The JST and the New Testament Epistles 215
	Clyde J. Williams
12	The JST on the Second Coming of Christ 237
	Keith W. Perkins
13	Insights from the JST into the Book of Revelation.. 251
	Gerald N. Lund
14	Major Doctrinal Contributions of the JST 271
	Robert J. Matthews
15	The JST: Retrospect and Prospect—A Panel 291
	Moderated by Robert J. Matthews
	Subject Index 307
	Scripture Index 313

Preface

Joseph Smith the Prophet recorded the following in his journal for 1 December 1831: "I resumed the translation of the Scriptures, and continued to labor in *this branch of my calling* with Elder Sidney Rigdon as my scribe" (*History of the Church*, 1:238; emphasis added). Joseph Smith's work of restoration of many plain and precious truths of the Bible was one of his greatest contributions towards giving this generation the word of the Lord (see D&C 5:10); it stands as a dynamic witness of his prophetic call. This contribution, however, has gone unnoticed or at least unappreciated by the vast majority of the members of the Church of Jesus Christ.

Because of the growing awareness of the Joseph Smith Translation (JST) in recent years, a symposium was held on the subject on 2–3 November 1984. This was sponsored by the BYU Religious Studies Center under the direction of Monte S. Nyman and Robert L. Millet, but with the guidance of Robert J. Matthews, the General Director of the center. The highlight of the symposium was the presence and major address of Elder Bruce R. McConkie of the Council of the Twelve. Thirteen other papers were presented by nine different contributors from Brigham Young University and from the seminaries and institutes of the Church Educational System. The symposium was concluded with a question-answer panel discussion involving these nine men. The views expressed in the various papers do not necessarily represent the position of The Church of Jesus Christ of Latter-day Saints or of Brigham Young University: each author takes sole responsibility for the ideas and conclusions presented in his paper.

Because of his lifetime of labor in bringing to light much of the historical and doctrinal significance of the JST, we express a special appreciation to Robert J. Matthews, professor and dean of Religious Education at Brigham Young University.

It is sincerely hoped that this volume will do much to build faith and enlighten the members of the Church with regard to this critical "branch" of the Prophet's calling.

Monte S. Nyman
Robert L. Millet

1

The Doctrinal Restoration

Elder Bruce R. McConkie

May I say in all sincerity that I am both pleased and honored to meet and counsel with the cream of the teaching crop of the Church.

Here at Brigham Young University we have assembled gospel teachers of scholastic renown and spiritual insight. It is their privilege to be the model teachers of the Church; to be a leavening influence upon all others who teach the words of eternal life; to be lights and guides and patterns for all of the teachers in the earthly kingdom.

May I remind you of the high status of those who teach the gospel by the power of the Spirit. As Paul expressed it, "God hath set some in the church, first apostles, secondarily prophets, thirdly teachers, after that miracles, then gifts of healings, helps, governments, diversities of tongues" (1 Corinthians 12:28).

Note the order of priority. In the true Church apostles are first; they hold the keys of the kingdom, receive revelation for the Church, and regulate all of its affairs in all the world as they are guided by the power of the Holy Ghost. President Spencer W.

Kimball presides over the Church today because he is the senior apostle of God on earth.

Next to the apostles stand the prophets, every prophet ministering in his own place and sphere. The gift of prophecy is the gift of testimony, for, as the angel said to John, "the testimony of Jesus is the spirit of prophecy" (Revelation 19:10).

And it is this gift of prophecy, this gift of testimony, this gift of knowing "by the Holy Ghost . . . that Jesus Christ is the Son of God, and that he was crucified for the sins of the world" (D&C 46:13)—it is this gift of personal revelation that is the rock foundation upon which the Church is built.

Upon this rock—the rock of personal revelation—the Lord builds his Church. Without it there would be no Church, no kingdom of God on earth, no gospel light in the souls of men. Manifestly, in the true Church, it is next in importance to the very apostolic keys and powers.

After apostles and prophets come teachers. Every teacher is expected to be a prophet and to know for himself of the truth and divinity of the work. Indeed, in the true sense, a teacher is greater than a prophet, for a teacher not only has the testimony of Jesus himself, but he bears that testimony by teaching the gospel.

What is the teacher's divine commission? It is "to preach the word of truth by the Comforter, in the Spirit of truth." And if he teaches in "some other way"—meaning by the power of the intellect rather than the power of the Spirit—even though his words are true they are "not of God." (D&C 50:17–18.) Such is the language of the revelation.

Hence in "the law of the Church"—speaking as though from the burning fires of Sinai—the Lord commands: "The . . . teachers of this church shall [it is mandatory!] teach the principles of my gospel, which are in the Bible and the Book of Mormon, in the which is the fulness of the gospel. . . . And . . . these shall be their teachings, as they shall be directed by the Spirit."

Then, with the fires of testimony burning in the hearts of the teachers, and the thunders of Sinai prepared to carry their message to the ends of the earth, the Lord issues this decree—call it the law of the teacher, if you will—"And the Spirit shall be given unto you by the prayer of faith; and if ye receive not the Spirit ye shall not teach."

Thus saith the Lord: "Receive my Spirit and be enlightened thereby; and unless this is the case—Thou shalt not teach my gospel."

"And all this ye shall observe to do as I have commanded concerning your teaching, until the fulness of my scriptures is given." At that time they had only the imperfect King James Version of the Bible and the near-perfect Book of Mormon. These were their only scriptural sources for the principles of the gospel.

When the Joseph Smith Translation of the Bible—included in this revelation under the designation "fulness of my scriptures"—came forth, then teachers were to use it and the various additional direct revelations. This, then, is a command to teach the changes and additions now found in the so-called Inspired Version.

"And as ye shall lift up your voices by the Comforter," the Lord says to his teachers, "ye shall speak and prophesy as seemeth me good." (D&C 42:12-16.)

This, then, is what is expected of us as teachers. We are to teach the restored gospel, the restored truths, the restored doctrines of salvation. And it is of this doctrinal restoration—the revealing anew of the great reservoir of eternal truth—that I shall speak.

Peter, the senior apostle of God on earth in the meridian of time, is the source of one of the greatest pronouncements ever made about the restoration of all things, the restoration which was destined to occur in the last days. He and John, on their own motion and by virtue of their own faith, healed a man lame from his mother's womb.

It was a dramatic occasion of great renown. The crippled alms-seeker was commanded in the name of Jesus Christ of Nazareth to rise up and walk. "Immediately his feet and ankle bones received strength." He arose; he walked; he leaped; he praised God and showed himself to the assembled hosts in the temple. They were amazed; they marvelled; and, greatly wondering, they surged together in Solomon's porch, where Jesus had often taught, to see and learn what great thing had happened in Israel.

Peter had his congregation. It was as when his Master had opened the eyes of the man born blind in order to gain a congregation to whom he could declare himself as the Good Shepherd, the Lord Jehovah, the Promised Messiah who would give his life for the sheep.

Peter's message was that, though they had "killed the Prince of life," God had raised him from the dead, and that his was the only "name under heaven given among men," whereby they could be saved.

But, because their hands dripped with the innocent blood of the sinless Son of God, Peter held out to them, not a hope of immediate salvation, but of some merited reward in a future day of judgment.

"Repent ye therefore, and be converted," he said; that is, believe my witness even though you are not yet ready for baptism; and, God willing, perhaps "your sins may be blotted out, when the times of refreshing shall come from the presence of the Lord."

That is: After you have paid the penalty for your sins, there may be some hope for you in the Millennial day when the earth will be renewed and receive its paradisiacal glory; there may be some hope in that great day of refreshing and regeneration when there will be a new heaven and a new earth whereon dwelleth righteousness.

That is: There may be some hope for you when the Lord "shall send Jesus Christ, which before was preached unto you," when the Son of Man shall come in his glory to rule among the sons of men.

And of this very Jesus, who came once and was by you rejected, know this: Him "the heaven must receive until the times of restitution of all things, which God hath spoken by the mouth of all his holy prophets since the world began." (Acts 3:1–21.)

In other words: Christ must abide in heaven, he cannot dwell again on earth until the age of restoration, the age that ushers in the Millennial day. And in that age of restoration, known as the times of restitution, the Lord will restore all that has been spoken by every prophet in every age, from Adam to that paradisiacal day.

This holy word does not say the Lord will restore all things before the Second Coming; it says all things will be restored in the age of restoration, which age or period or era or time will begin shortly before the return of the Lord Jesus in all the glory of his Father's kingdom.

That this age of restoration will continue during the Millennium is seen from these revealed words: "When the Lord shall come, he shall reveal all things—Things which have passed, and hidden things which no man knew, things of the earth, by which it was made, and the purpose and the end thereof—Things most precious, things that are above, and things that are beneath, things that are in the earth, and upon the earth, and in heaven." (D&C 101:32-34.)

This age of restoration is the one spoken of by Paul in these words: "In the dispensation of the fulness of times" God shall "gather together in one all things in Christ, both which are in heaven, and which are on earth; even in him" (Ephesians 1:10).

What are all the things which God hath spoken by the mouth of all his holy prophets since the world began? And how and in what way will the Lord restore them?

Clearly in the times of restitution—which had their beginning in the spring of 1820, when Elohim the Father and Jehovah the Son stood personally in the Sacred Grove, and will continue on into the Millennial Era, when the returning Christ will reveal all things—clearly in this age of restoration, the promised giving anew of what was known and had anciently will have two aspects.

For one thing the Lord will restore all things, both temporally and spiritually, as they once were. All of the holy prophets, in one degree or another, knew of the promised restoration. All of the prophets knew that Christ would come in the meridian of time to work out the infinite and eternal atonement, and that he would come again to deliver his Saints and reign personally among them on a renewed earth.

We know these things and they knew them. How could any

people have the truths of salvation without a knowledge of the Atonement and without a knowledge of the eventual triumph of truth?

Thus the restoration of all things includes such things as the following:

This earth will return to its Edenic state. As we sing in one of the W. W. Phelps hymns:

> This earth was once a garden place,
> With all her glories common,
> And men did live a holy race,
> And worship Jesus face to face,
> In Adam-ondi-Ahman.

And as our tenth article of faith testifies: "We believe . . . that the earth will be renewed and receive [again!] its paradisiacal glory." Truly, there will be a new heaven and a new earth—a Millennial earth, like unto the Edenic earth—whereon dwelleth righteousness.

In that day—it is part of the restoration of all things—the Lord "shall command the great deep, and it shall be driven back into the north countries, and the islands shall become one land; And the land of Jerusalem and the land of Zion shall be turned back into their own place, and the earth shall be like as it was in the days before it was divided" (D&C 133:23–24).

In that day Enoch's city—the City of Zion, the perfect pattern for the Millennial Zion—will return.

> We read that Enoch walked with God,
> Above the power of Mammon,
> While Zion spread herself abroad,
> And Saints and angels sang aloud,
> In Adam-ondi-Ahman.
>
> Her land was good and greatly blest,
> Beyond all Israel's Canaan,
> Her fame was known from east to west,
> Her peace was great, and pure the rest
> Of Adam-ondi-Ahman.

And thanks be to God, all this shall come again in this age of renewal, of refreshment, of restoration.

> Hosanna to such days to come,
> The Saviour's second coming,
> When all the earth in glorious bloom
> Affords the Saints a holy home,
> Like Adam-ondi-Ahman.
> (*Hymns,* no. 389)

In the day of restoration the bodies of men will be renewed, freed from disease, and be akin to what they were in the primeval day. Once men lived for nearly a thousand years; soon they will begin to live to the age of a tree.

In the day of restoration the two kingdoms of Israel shall become one. As a united people they shall dwell upon the mountains of Israel, in the land of Palestine. They shall build up the ancient cities and reclaim the wasted land, which shall then blossom as the rose as springs of water burst forth from the dry and arid desert.

In the day of restoration the earthly Church and kingdom of God is to be set up among men. Apostles and prophets, holding priesthood and power and keys, are again to roam the earth teaching and testifying of the risen Lord. Gifts and miracles as of old are to be manifest. The blind will see, the deaf hear, and the spirits of men, having departed this life, will be called back to reanimate corpses that would otherwise rot away in graves dug by men.

All these things and ten thousand others are destined to be restored in this glorious age of restoration. All this is or should be well known among us. But there is something that underlies it all; something that is the bedrock upon which it is built; something without which none of these glorious things could occur; something that we either overlook or take for granted.

That something is the doctrinal restoration. It is the restoration of the principles of the gospel. It is the restoration of the truths of salvation. It is the restoration of that knowledge without which men could not have faith like the ancients and thus prepare themselves to receive and be participants in the other restored events of which we speak.

Unless and until men believe the doctrines of the restoration they can never—never, never, never—worlds without end, prepare themselves to abide the day of our Lord's return; to dwell with Enoch and his fellows in the returning Zion; to stand with the elect of Israel in building up their ancient homeland; to perform miracles; to glory in the gifts of the Spirit; and to find full fellowship with the Saints of that God who has bought us with his blood.

It is a knowledge of the truth—restored to us so we can gain faith like the ancients—that will enable us to receive the promised blessings.

Until the doctrine of the Abrahamic covenant was restored, who would have even imagined that celestial marriage is the gate to eternal life?

If the doctrine setting forth the nature and kind of being God is had not been restored we would be worshipping cows or crocodiles or cedar posts or unknown spirit essences—all to no avail.

As members of the kingdom—possessing the gift of the Holy Ghost, having the canonized word, receiving guidance from those called and endowed from on high—it is surely our privilege to receive and understand the doctrines of salvation as they are being restored to us in this great day of restoration.

And as teachers, it is surely our privilege to persuade others to gain like knowledge so they will be inheritors of like blessings with us and with our forebears.

Having all these things in mind; believing that God is no respecter of persons; and knowing that a soul is just as precious in our day as it was in the days of Enoch and Elijah—let us turn our attention to the doctrinal restoration.

How and in what way is the Lord in process of restoring the ancient word, the word that perfected Enoch and his people, the word that will prepare us for fellowship with them when they return?

Let us try, if we may, to put ourselves in the position of devout Christians in the day appointed for the beginning of the doctrinal restoration. To begin with, none of us would have any idea whatever that there is to be a doctrinal restoration. Having the Bible we would think it contains all things necessary for salvation, and it would never enter our minds that any ancient people knew anywhere near as much as we think we know.

A doctrinal restoration! Why, the very thought is almost blasphemous! So we would think. Can we improve upon what Jesus and Paul taught? Surely there would not be more than a score in each legion of our self-styled and self-appointed Christian community who would be open-minded enough to believe that an unchangeable God who spoke anciently, and is the same yesterday, today, and forever, might speak again.

Why, if such an unthinkable thing should happen it might well destroy the whole body of our Christianity, based as it is on the mystical traditions of our fathers.

And yet thoughtful persons among us—remember we are placing ourselves in the position of Christians generally who know nothing of the promised age of restoration—thoughtful persons among us would know that something may be amiss.

Yes, we would have the Holy Bible. But what is the Bible? Most of our priests and ministers have told us it is a book of scripture, a perfect book, one containing verbal revelation, which men must believe to be saved.

As we know, it is a collection of various books, poems, and letters, supposedly written by inspired men. But can we be sure, at this late date, that any of the books were even written by those to whom they are attributed?

How is it, we wonder, that the post-apostolic fathers each had their own differing lists of canonical books?

What persons or councils, we wonder, had the inspiration to approve favored writings, classify some as apocryphal or pseudepigraphic, and discard others entirely?

Where, we wonder, are the various lost books, such as the book of Gad the Seer—all mentioned with approval in the Bible itself?

Some of us might even think—

Isn't it a little strange that there is no book of Adam or Enoch or Noah; no book of Andrew, Philip, or Nathanael?

Can it be that the books in our present Bible are there more by historical accident than by divine design?

And then as we know there is the matter of the accuracy and

purity of the text. There is no such thing as an original manuscript. The best we have are documents that are copies of copies of copies through long generations of time, each preserving and adding to the errors of its predecessors.

One study by biblical scholars counted more than thirty thousand textual differences in extant manuscripts covering a small portion of the Bible. They postulated that if such a study were enlarged to include the whole Bible the textual variations would number in the hundreds of thousands.

Added to all of this there is the matter of translation. Who is able to carry from one culture and language to another all of the idioms and shades of meaning found in the parent setting?

What biblical version shall we accept—the Douay, or King James, or one of the ever-changing Lutheran versions?

In all of this we would not have even mentioned the greatest of all the biblical shortcomings. This we shall do shortly. But for the present we simply ask:

How would we know the Bible is true? If it is true, is it as complete and perfect as it should be? And if it is not, how, and by whom, and in what manner will it be perfected and made whole?

Now, if we were in the position I have here postulated, and had been wise enough to know there was to be a restoration of all things, I think we would have looked for that restoration to come to pass through the perfection and enlargement of the Bible.

And as a matter of fact the Lord had this very thing in mind. But it was not to take place until after a foundation had been laid.

It was his design and purpose to bring forth the Book of Mormon as a new and added witness of the Lord Jesus Christ. Then he would endow his prophets with keys and power and give them direct revelation as to how and in what manner his earthly kingdom should be established anew among men.

After this—as a crowning achievement—he would begin the perfection of the Bible, a work destined to be greater and have more significance than any of us have yet realized.

The Book of Mormon teaches and testifies of Christ and recites in plainness and purity the true doctrines of the gospel. Nowhere else do we receive such profound insights into the

Atonement, into faith and repentance, baptism and the gift of the Holy Ghost, miracles and the gifts of the Spirit, the place of Israel in the eternal scheme of things, and a host of other doctrines.

The Book of Mormon restores many truths lost from the Bible or found in it only in a partial and perverted way. It contains within its covers the proof of its own divinity. All who read, ponder, and pray—in faith—are promised that they shall know by the power of the Holy Ghost that the Book of Mormon is the mind and will and voice of the Lord, to all men everywhere, from this day onward as long as the earth shall stand.

But the Book of Mormon does something more. It announces that the Bible is true. It came forth not alone "to the convincing of the Jew and Gentile that Jesus is the Christ, the Eternal God, manifesting himself unto all nations," as Moroni wrote on the title page.

It also came forth "proving to the world that the holy scriptures," meaning the Bible, "are true, and that God does inspire men and call them to his holy work in this age and generation, as well as in generations of old" (D&C 20:11).

What future would there be in restoring and perfecting the Bible unless it is a true book? And with all due respect to the scholars of the world, to the ministers of Christendom, to professing believers everywhere—how can any of them really know the Bible is true? Intellectual approaches reach as many conclusions as there are people involved.

And how could God do better in proving the Bible to be true than to bring forth a new and parallel and conforming volume of scripture; establish by personal revelation that the new scripture is true; and then use it as the standard that proves and testifies to the truth of the biblical word?

But the Book of Mormon does more than prove the Bible is true. It also is the irrefutable witness that Joseph Smith was a prophet of God; that the Lord calls and inspires men today as he did anciently; that living prophets receive revelation in our day and time.

Thus, knowing the Bible is true, and knowing there are prophets on earth who receive revelation, the stage is set for the restoration—by revelation!—of the Bible. It is now possible to bring the Book of Books back to its original state of purity and plainness.

Thus, the doctrinal restoration is destined to come to pass, first, through the Book of Mormon, second, by direct revelation —a re-revelation—of the doctrines known anciently, and third, by the restoration, by revelation, of the Bible, which in spite of its faults has been the most stabilizing force on earth since the day it came into being.

As we consider these three ways and means of doctrinal restoration—the Book of Mormon, so far translated only in part; the direct revelations given to Joseph Smith and others, particularly those in the Doctrine and Covenants; and the just begun and eventually to be completed restoration of the Bible—as we consider them we should be aware of the insidious and devil-directed attack upon them.

Let me speak plainly. Satan hates and spurns the scriptures. The less scripture there is, and the more it is twisted and perverted, the greater is the rejoicing in the courts of hell.

There has never been a book—not even the Book of Mormon —that has been so maligned and cursed and abused as the Bible.

There is not much the world can do about the Book of Mormon. It is here and it is what it is. It cannot be modified or changed. Men have no choice but to believe or disbelieve it. If they disbelieve they can talk about Solomon Spaulding or any other figments of their imaginations that suits their fancies of the moment.

But the Book of Mormon remains secure, unchanged and unchangeable, a firm and steady witness of Christ and his doctrine. The Book of Mormon has been, is now, and will forever remain secure in the hands of the servants of the Lord, for which we are immeasurably grateful.

But with the Bible it was not and is not so. It is now in the hands of intellectuals and unbelievers and ministers whose delight it is to twist and pervert its doctrines and to spiritualize away the plain meanings of all its important parts. And it once was in the sole and exclusive care and custody of an abominable organization, founded by the devil himself, likened prophetically unto a great whore, whose great aim and purpose was to destroy the souls of men in the name of religion.

In these hands it ceased to be the book it once was. Originally "it contained the fulness of the gospel of the Lord." It was sent forth "from the Jews in purity unto the Gentiles, according to the truth which is in God."

Then it came into the hands of "that great and abominable church, which is most abominable above all other churches." They took "away from the gospel of the Lamb many parts which are plain and most precious; and also many covenants of the Lord."

"And all this have they done that they might pervert the right ways of the Lord, that they might blind the eyes and harden the hearts of the children of men."

Then the Bible—with many "plain and precious things . . . taken away"—went forth to the nations of the earth. And, as Nephi said, "because of the many plain and precious things which have been taken out of the book, which were plain unto the understanding of the children of men, according to the plainness which is in the Lamb of God—because of these things which are taken away out of the gospel of the Lamb, an exceedingly great many do stumble, yea, insomuch that Satan hath great power over them." (1 Nephi 13:24–29.)

Special mention is made of the book of Revelation as written by John. When he wrote the truths that are in it, and when they went forth to the world, they "were plain and pure, and most precious and easy to the understanding of all men" (1 Nephi 14:23). Today, as these writings now are, "all men," save those filled with the spirit of prophecy, stumble over John's apocalyptic words.

During the Dark Ages—during the Black Millennium, if you will—even the Bible that now is was kept from the people. Many is the martyr who suffered death by fire for reading or possessing biblical manuscripts. The translation and publication of the scriptural word was opposed with satanic fury in that day.

For the present the devil has lost that round. Today he centers his powers on denying the authenticity of the scriptures and using them to prove such false doctrines as that God is a Spirit or that we are saved by grace alone without works.

This, then, is where we as Latter-day Saints stand. We all believe the Book of Mormon and rejoice in its teachings. Our stand is in sharp contrast to that of the Reorganized Church. I am told they have a position paper which says the Book of Mormon is simply a recapitulation by Joseph Smith, in story form, of the dominant doctrines of the sectarian world in his day. But in any event we believe the Book of Mormon to be the word of God.

As to latter-day revelation, as found in the Doctrine and Covenants and in the Pearl of Great Price, we have no problem. Since the Book of Mormon is true, it follows that Joseph Smith was a prophet, and hence it is easy to believe his revelations.

Where the Bible is concerned, things get a little sticky. Of course we believe it—always specifying the King James Version—but there is the reservation about parts not being translated correctly. And in some minds there seems to be a nagging uncertainty about the so-called Inspired Version. After all, some say, the Prophet did not finish his work, and how can we be sure what he did finish is correct?

May I be pardoned if I say that negative attitudes and feelings about the Joseph Smith Translation are simply part of the devil's program to keep the word of truth from the children of men.

Of course the revealed changes made by Joseph Smith are true—as much so as anything in the Book of Mormon or the Doctrine and Covenants.

Of course we have adequate and authentic original sources showing the changes—as much so as are the sources for the Book of Mormon or the revelations.

Of course we should use the Joseph Smith Translation in our study and teaching. Since when do any of us have the right to place bounds on the Almighty and say we will believe these revelations but not those?

I think much of the prejudice of the past was based on a lack of understanding and has faded away since we have published our new Church edition of the King James Version with its repeated references to the Joseph Smith Translation.

Would it be amiss if we made a brief overview of what the Joseph Smith Translation now is and what it will one day be?

As to its present state—it contains various additions, deletions, and emendations to the King James Version. But most importantly it contains the book of Moses and the twenty-fourth chapter of Matthew as published in the Pearl of Great Price.

These portions have been formally canonized by us, which should establish that any changes made by the Prophet are true and should be used. Does anyone think that the pure revelation found in Genesis 14 about Melchizedek or in Genesis 50 about the Nephites and Joseph Smith and the latter days is any less a revelation than Moses 1? Does anyone think the first chapter of John's Gospel is of any less worth than the twenty-fourth chapter of Matthew's?

True, the Joseph Smith Translation, though completed to the point that the early Brethren were going to publish it at one time, has not been completed in the full and true sense. But for that matter neither has the Book of Mormon. I am as anxious to read and study what is in the sealed portion of the Book of Mormon as I am to give the same attention to those parts of the Bible yet to be revealed.

I am clear in my mind that the sealed portion of the Book of Mormon will not come forth until the Millennium. The same thing is undoubtedly true of the fulness of the Bible, though some additions could well be made before that time.

Of what will the Bible consist when it is perfected?

Surely it will contain the writings of Adam and Enoch and Noah; of Melchizedek and Isaac and Jacob; and certainly Abraham wrote much more than the Prophet found on the Egyptian papyrus. The book of Abraham in our Pearl of Great Price is obviously a restored biblical record.

Does anyone think we have all of the words of Isaiah or Jeremiah or Malachi? And are there not prophets and apostles without number, whose names we do not even know, who have recorded their teachings and testimonies?

The perfected Bible of the future will surely include all that was on the brass plates of Laban. Indeed, Lehi prophesied "that these plates of brass should go forth unto all nations, kindreds, tongues, and people who were of his seed. Wherefore, he said that these plates of brass should never perish; neither should they be dimmed any more by time." (1 Nephi 5:18–19.)

More than five hundred years later Alma testified that they

should "be kept and preserved by the hand of the Lord until they should go forth unto every nation, kindred, tongue, and people, that they shall know of the mysteries contained thereon," and that they would "retain their brightness." (Alma 37:4–5.)

Someday the Lord will raise up a prophet, who will also be a seer and a translator, to whom he will give the brass plates that they may be translated for the benefit and blessing of those in all nations.

Would God that the work might commence at least in our day, though in fact we have no such hope. Why should the Lord give us what is on the brass plates or in the sealed portion of the Book of Mormon when we do not even treasure up and live by what he has already given us?

The Bible that went forth to the gentile nations in the early days of the Christian era, according to the angelic word to Nephi, "contains the covenants of the Lord, which he hath made unto the house of Israel; and it also containeth many of the prophecies of the holy prophets; and it is a record like unto the engravings which are upon the plates of brass, save there are not so many" (1 Nephi 13:23).

Thereafter the many plain and precious parts were taken away by the servants in the house of that great church which is not the Lord's Church.

Thus our present Bible contains only a fraction of the holy word that once was compiled with and included in it as the acceptable word of the Lord.

From various Book of Mormon references we gain a glimpse of what is on the brass plates.

They contain the record of the Jews down to the days of Zedekiah, including the genealogies of the people and the prophecies of the holy prophets, among which are the words of Isaiah and portions of Jeremiah.

They contain, in their perfect form, the law of Moses and the five books of Moses—Genesis, Exodus, Leviticus, Numbers, and Deuteronomy.

They contain the writings of Joseph who was sold into Egypt, than which few have been greater, and on them is found the mysteries of God and the commandments he has given the children of men.

They contain books of holy scripture of which the world does not dream, including the writings of Zenock, Neum, and Zenos.

But what interests us more than the books included on the brass plates is the tone and tenor and general approach to the gospel and to salvation that they set forth. They are gospel oriented and speak of Christ and the various Christian concepts which the world falsely assumes to have originated with Jesus and the early apostles.

For instance, Zenock taught that "the God of our fathers, who were led out of Egypt, out of bondage, and also were preserved in the wilderness by him, yea, the God of Abraham, and of Isaac, and the God of Jacob, yieldeth himself, according to the words of the angel, as a man, into the hands of wicked men, to be lifted up, according to the words of Zenock."

Neum taught that Christ would be "crucified," and Zenos taught that he would "be buried in a sepulchre" in connection with "the three days of darkness, which should be a sign given of his death unto those who should inhabit the isles of the sea, more especially given unto those who are of the house of Israel." (1 Nephi 19:10.)

Indeed, it was Zenos who wrote of the visit of the Lord God to Israel after his resurrection; of the joy and salvation that would come to the righteous among them; of the desolations and destructions that awaited the wicked among them; of the fires, and tempests, and earthquakes that would occur in the Americas; of the scourging and crucifying of the God of Israel by those in Jerusalem; of the scattering of the Jews among all nations; and of their gathering again in the last days "from the four quarters of the earth." (1 Nephi 19:11–17.)

I do not think I overstate the matter when I say that next to Isaiah himself—who is the prototype, pattern, and model for all the prophets—there was not a greater prophet in all Israel than Zenos. And our knowledge of his inspired writings is limited to the quotations and paraphrasing summaries found in the Book of Mormon.

Our understanding of the prophetic word will be greatly expanded if we know how one prophet quotes another, usually without acknowledging his source.

Either Isaiah or Micah copied the prophetic words of the

other relative to the mountain of the Lord's house being established in the last days with all nations flowing thereto. Their ministries overlapped, but we assume that the lesser Micah copied from the greater Isaiah and then appended some words of his own about the Millennial Era.

Some unnamed Old Testament prophet, who obviously was Zenos, as the Book of Mormon testifies, spoke of the day when the wicked would be destroyed as stubble; when the righteous would be "led up as calves of the stall"; when Christ should "rise from the dead, with healing in his wings"; and when the Holy One of Israel would then reign on earth.

Malachi, who lived more than two hundred years after Nephi, uses these very expressions in his prophetic writings. Can we do other than conclude that both Nephi and Malachi had before them the writings of Zenos?

Both Paul and Mormon expounded with great inspiration about faith, hope, and charity, in many verses using the same words and phrases. If there is any difference between them it is that Mormon expounds the doctrines more perfectly and persuasively than does Paul.

It does not take much insight to know that Mormon and Paul both had before them the writings of some Old Testament prophet on the same subjects.

It is perfectly clear that John the Beloved is copying, in the first chapter of the Gospel of John, words written by John the Baptist, a practice with which we have no fault to find.

Once the Lord has revealed his doctrine in precise language to a chosen prophet, there is no reason why he should inspire another prophet to choose the same words in presenting the same doctrine on a subsequent occasion. It is much easier and simpler to quote that which has already been given in perfection. We are all commanded—including the prophets among us—to search the scriptures and thereby learn what other prophets have presented.

The Lord did not reveal anew to Nephi what Isaiah had written. Rather, Nephi was commanded to quote Isaiah's words as they were found on the brass plates. Then he was free to expound them as the Spirit directed.

Everyone is entitled to receive the same revelations and view the same visions. God is no respecter of persons. But if any of us saw the vision of the degrees of glory, there would be no reason for us to write it anew in the words of Joseph Smith. It has already been recorded in the way the Lord designed; and if we were wont to quote it in a book of scripture we were writing, we would do it in the language of the originating prophet.

As a sidelight to our present discussion, it is clearly evident that the Jews in Jesus' day had more Old Testament scriptures than we have.

Jesus reminded the Jews that Abraham saw the day of the coming of the Son of Man, which fact is not in the Old Testament, but has now been restored in Genesis 15.

Jude quoted from the book of Enoch, which book has not yet been restored to us.

Paul has much to say about Melchizedek and the holy priesthood which remained hidden until put again in Genesis 14.

But let us return to our subject—"The Doctrinal Restoration"—and draw some proper conclusions.

1. *Question: What is being restored in this the dispensation of the fulness of times?*

Answer: We are in process of receiving all that God has spoken by the mouths of all his holy prophets since the world began. Only a small portion has come to us so far; we do not, as yet, begin to know what the ancients knew.

That which has come to us anew breaks the shackles of the past and opens up entirely new vistas to us. It is all Christ-centered, gospel-centered, priesthood-centered, church-centered. It lets us know that all of the ancient Saints had the same gospel, the same hope in Christ, the same holy priesthood, the same celestial marriage, the same church, the same apostolic power, the same gifts of the Spirit, the same system of salvation that we have.

Except for a few things relative to salvation for the dead, we have not yet received one syllable of scripture, one trace of truth, one gospel verity, one saving power, that was not had anciently.

The time is yet future—it will be Millennial—when the Lord reveals to us those things which have been hidden from the foundation of the earth and which have never as yet been given to man.

2. *Question: How and in what way is the new knowledge being restored?*

Answer: By revelation. Our doctrine is not handed down, in the sectarian sense; it is revealed. It is revealed directly as in the case of the Doctrine and Covenants; or by the process of translation, as in the case of the Book of Mormon; or by the process of perfecting ancient scriptures, as in the case of the Joseph Smith Translation.

This generation—the generation that shall be until the coming of the Son of Man—is to have the Lord's word through Joseph Smith, and to some degree through his successors.

3. *Question: What are the vehicles of the restoration?*

Answer: First, the Book of Mormon, which was translated by the gift and power of God; second, the Doctrine and Covenants, whose contents are revealed, coupled with such inspired utterances as the King Follett Sermon; and, third, the so-called Translations, which include the book of Abraham, the book of Moses (itself part of the Inspired Version), and the whole Joseph Smith Translation of the Bible.

None of these vehicles have given us their full load. We have only about a third of the Book of Mormon; the field of revelation is without bounds or limits; and the Bible restoration has scarcely been commenced.

4. *Question: When will we receive more of the mind and will of the Lord, and when will the great doctrinal restoration be completed?*

We have a revealed answer as to when we shall receive the sealed portion of the Book of Mormon. What we have so far received is to test our faith. When we repent of all our iniquity and become clean before the Lord, and when we exercise faith in him like unto the brother of Jared, then the sealed portion of the ancient word will be translated and read from the housetops.

The same is certainly true of the brass plates and the lost portions of the Bible. What we have received so far is to test our faith. Why should the Lord give us more of the biblical word if we are indifferent to what he has already revealed? Does anyone think the Lord should give us the words of Zenos when we are ignoring the words of Isaiah?

There are revelations without end that are available to the faithful at any time they are prepared to receive them.

As a matter of practical reality, however, the great doctrinal restoration is to be Millennial. Of that day Nephi said: Then "the earth shall be full of the knowledge of the Lord as the waters cover the sea. Wherefore, the things of all nations shall be made known; yea, all things shall be made known unto the children of men. There is nothing which is secret save it shall be revealed; there is no work of darkness save it shall be made manifest in the light; and there is nothing which is sealed upon the earth save it shall be loosed. Wherefore, all things which have been revealed unto the children of men shall at that day be revealed; and Satan shall have power over the hearts of the children of men no more, for a long time." (2 Nephi 30:15–18.)

5. Perhaps these are some of the final great questions we should ask: *Is the restored word true? Is it the mind and will and voice of the Lord? Does the Joseph Smith Translation, as it now stands and without more, have divine approval, and should we use it?*

By way of answer let us ask: Is the Book of Mormon true and should we use it? We all know it is true, even though there is more of it to come.

Is the divine word in the Doctrine and Covenants true? Of course, even though new revelations lie ahead.

Is the book of Abraham true? Yes, but it is not complete; it stops almost in midair. Would that the Prophet had gone on in his translation or revelation, as the case may be.

Yes, the Inspired Version is inspired. Yes, the Joseph Smith Translation of the Bible is holy scripture. In one sense of the word it is the crowning part of the doctrinal restoration. At least it sets the pattern and marks the way as to how the doctrinal rivers of the past shall yet flow into the ocean of the present, as shall surely be in the fulness of times.

Having so testified may I leave you with these words to ponder:

Thus saith our God: "Thou fool, that shall say: A Bible, we

have got a Bible, and we need no more Bible? Have ye obtained a Bible save it were by the Jews?"

Is it a perfect Bible? Or have many of its plain and precious parts been lost? Does it set forth the covenants and doctrines of the Lord as they were revealed to his ancient covenant people?

"Wherefore murmur ye, because that ye shall receive more of my word?" saith the Lord.

Now, my attempt, in these somewhat rambling remarks, has been to place the Joseph Smith Translation of God's Holy Word in its proper relationship to the great doctrinal restoration.

In the very nature of things this includes the evidence, proof, and witness that one of the great contributions—perhaps the greatest contribution—of this inspired work is to open the doors of our understanding to the marvelous reality that Christ and his gospel, with all its gifts, powers, and graces, has been had among men, in divers dispensations, from the days of Adam to this present hour.

I have not dwelt upon specifics but have chosen rather to unveil the whole broad panorama. Many of you have greater expertise than I do where these specifics are concerned. My good friend Robert Matthews is of course the world authority on the Joseph Smith Translation.

But I am pleased to say in closing that this inspired work by the great Prophet of the Restoration is one of the great evidences of his divine calling.

One of the reasons we know he was the mighty Prophet of the Restoration is the inspired translation and revision of the Holy Bible.

God grant us the wisdom to walk in the light of that great beacon of understanding that he lighted for our benefit and blessing.

In the name of the Lord Jesus Christ, Amen.

Elder Bruce R. McConkie, a member of the Council of the Twelve of The Church of Jesus Christ of Latter-day Saints, passed away on April 19, 1985, shortly before the publication of this book.

2

Joseph Smith's Translation of the Bible: A Historical Overview

Robert L. Millet

Moses the ancient lawgiver was given prophetic direction: "And in a day when the children of men shall esteem my words as naught and take many of them from the book which thou shalt write, behold, I will raise up another like unto thee; and they shall be had again among the children of men—among as many as shall believe" (Moses 1:41). Through the opening of the heavens in modern times, Joseph Smith, Junior, was called as a prophet, a seer, a revelator, and a modern lawgiver. In addition, he was commissioned as a *translator,* the means whereby the mind and word of God were made known to a generation in the midst of spiritual calamity. (See D&C 1:17.) To the young prophet-leader the Lord explained: "This generation shall have my word through you" (D&C 5:10).

PREPARATION FOR THE NEW BIBLE TRANSLATION

A number of events seem to have been critical in the preparation of Joseph Smith for his labor as Bible translator. As early as

1820 young Joseph recognized that salvation was not to be found within the covers of the Bible alone; confusion and uncertainty were the obvious results of unillumined minds and undirected study, even when the object of study was the Holy Bible. Seeking for both personal fulfillment and the one system of religious practice which would lead him back to the divine presence, Joseph Smith discovered that not all of the answers were to be found within the Bible.

A further lesson was taught to the seventeen-year-old Prophet by the angel Moroni in the year 1823. Moroni quoted numerous passages of scripture to Joseph, particularly Malachi 4, though "with a little variation from the way it reads in our Bibles" (JS-H 1:36). Whether Moroni gave detailed instructions concerning specific passages of scripture, or whether he taught Joseph how to interpret biblical verses, is unknown. The young prophet did learn, however, that the King James Version of the Bible was not the only authorized translation of the scriptures.

Joseph Smith had learned early in his translation of the Book of Mormon that theological darkness and spiritual stumblings in the Judeo-Christian world were due in large measure to a wilful tampering with some of the earliest Bible texts. Approximately six hundred years before Christ's coming, Nephi prophesied of a time when the Bible—identified as a record which proceeded out of the mouth of a Jew (1 Nephi 13:23)—would fall into the hands of designing individuals who would "take away" or "keep back" plain and precious truths, and many covenants of the Lord. As a result of such corruption, "an exceedingly great many do stumble, yea, insomuch that Satan hath great power over them." (1 Nephi 13:26-34.) Joseph Smith further became aware of the fact (through Nephi's prophetic vision) that through the restoration things would be made known once again to those willing to receive them. (1 Nephi 13:35-40.) The Prophet was to observe many years later: "I believe the Bible as it read when it came from the pen of the original writers. Ignorant translators, careless transcribers, or designing and corrupt priests have committed many errors."[1]

While still engaged in the translation of the Book of Mormon (probably in 3 Nephi), Joseph Smith and Oliver Cowdery, on 15 May 1829, "went into the woods to pray and inquire of the Lord respecting baptism for the remission of sins," which was mentioned in the Nephite record (JS-H 1:68). John the Baptist appeared and delivered the keys and powers associated with the Aaronic Priesthood, and gave instructions concerning the baptism and priesthood ordination of Joseph and Oliver. The Prophet Joseph remarked that immediately upon coming up out of the waters of baptism both men enjoyed a rich endowment of the Holy Ghost, and each had the spirit of prophecy and revelation. Joseph further explained: "Our minds being now enlightened, *we began to have the scriptures laid open to our understandings, and the true meaning and intention of their more mysterious passages revealed unto us in a manner which we never could attain to previously, nor ever before had thought of*" (JS-H 1:74; emphasis added). No doubt such spiritual understanding would have given to the Prophet not only the ability to grasp "true meaning and intention," but also the divine perspective to recognize and correct faulty biblical texts.

On 8 October 1829 Joseph Smith and Oliver Cowdery purchased a large pulpit-style edition of the King James Bible (containing the Old and New Testaments and Apocrypha) from E. B. Grandin in Palmyra, New York, for $3.75. The Bible was printed in 1828 by the H. and E. Phinney Company at Cooperstown, New York. It was this Bible which was used in the translation.

THE PROCESS OF TRANSLATION

There was nothing particularly unusual about a new translation of the Bible in the 1830s. Religious revivalism reached a peak in the New York area in the early nineteenth century, and with it came a heightened awareness of the need for the Bible as a divine standard for living. In fact, New England was not the only section of the country which manifested an intense interest at this time in a study and scrutiny of the biblical record; from 1777 to 1833 more than five hundred separate editions of the Bible (or parts thereof) were published in America. Many of these represented new translations or "modern translations," often with an attempt to prepare paraphrased editions or alternate readings based upon comparisons with Hebrew and Greek manuscripts.[2]

Joseph Smith's translation of the scriptures was, however, highly unusual. The Prophet had no formal training in ancient languages until some years later, when he did study Hebrew with a number of the leaders of the Church. Nor did he work with manuscripts written in the biblical languages in undertaking his study. What, then, was the nature of this "translation," and how was it effected? Many in our own day, including some Latter-day Saints, are eager to point out that Joseph's work with the Bible was not a *translation* per se, but rather represented something of a rewording or a biblical targum or midrash. We will deal more specifically with the nature of the translation at the end of this presentation. For the present, however, it is essential that we recognize that Joseph Smith himself called the labor a translation, the members referred to the labor as a translation, and (perhaps most important) the Lord himself made frequent reference to his servant's work as a translation. As indicated earlier, the Prophet was divinely called and appointed as a "seer, a revelator, a translator, and a prophet, having all the gifts of God which he bestows upon the head of the church" (D&C 107:92).

Joseph's mission as translator was not terminated when he had completed the Book of Mormon. In his serious study of the Bible, he sought to harmonize himself with the Spirit of God (and surely with the mind and intentions of the ancient writers) so as to recognize and correct faulty translations, as well as deficient or ambiguous passages of the Bible which had suffered the long and painful process of transmission of texts. In one sense, Joseph Smith was translating the Bible in attempting to interpret it by revelation, to explain it by the use of clearer terms or a different style of language. In another sense, Joseph was translating the Bible inasmuch as he was restoring in the English language ideas and events and sayings which were originally recorded in Hebrew or Greek. The Prophet translated the King James Bible by the same means he translated the Book of Mormon—through revelation. His knowledge of Hebrew or Greek or his acquaintance with ancient documents was no more essential in making the JST than a previous knowledge of Reformed Egyptian or an access to more primitive Nephite records was essential to the translation of the Book of Mormon. Not infrequently the Lord chooses and calls the unlearned, the "weak things of the world," to bring about his purposes (see 2 Nephi 27:15–20).

June of 1830 is the earliest date of translation given in any of the Prophet's records. From his own journal history we have the following entry: "I will say . . . that amid all the trials and tribulations we had to wade through, the Lord, who well knew our infantile and delicate situation, vouchsafed for us a supply of strength, and granted us 'line upon line of knowledge—here a little and there a little,' of which the following was a precious morsel."[3] Joseph then recorded some "selections from the book of Moses" (Moses 1), containing "the words of God, which he spake unto Moses at a time when Moses was caught up into an exceedingly high mountain." The translation of the book of Genesis continued for many months, and major doctrinal truths were revealed concerning premortal existence, the Creation, the Fall, and the Atonement. In December of 1830 the following is contained in the Prophet's journal:

> It may be well to observe here, that the Lord greatly encouraged and strengthened the faith of His little flock, which had embraced the fulness of the everlasting Gospel, as revealed to them in the Book of Mormon, by giving some more extended information upon the Scriptures, a translation of which had already commenced. Much conjecture and conversation frequently occurred among the Saints, concerning the books mentioned, and referred to, in various places in the Old and New Testaments, which were now nowhere to be found. The common remark was, "They are *lost books*"; but it seems the Apostolic Church had some of these writings, as Jude mentions or quotes the Prophecy of Enoch, the seventh from Adam. To the joy of the little flock . . . did the Lord reveal the following doings of olden times, from the prophecy of Enoch.[4]

The Prophet then recorded his inspired translation of Genesis 7 (also known to us as Moses 7), containing many of the remarkable details of the ministry and eventual translation of Enoch and his city.

Work on the Old Testament continued until 7 March 1831. On that date, Joseph Smith received the revelation known to us as Doctrine and Covenants 45, in which he was told the following: "And now, behold, I say unto you, it shall not be given unto you to know any further concerning this chapter [the Savior has been speaking at length concerning the signs incident to his second coming], until the New Testament be translated, and in it all these things shall be made known; Wherefore I give unto you that ye may now translate it, that ye may be prepared for the things to come. For verily I say unto you, that great things await you." (D&C 45:60–62.) The manuscript of the work with the first chapter of Matthew is dated 8 March 1831. To that point a translation of the Old Testament had progressed through Genesis 19:35.[5]

For a period of about one month, work with Matthew and Genesis was undertaken concurrently, but by early April the Old Testament was put aside temporarily in order that the New Testament might receive full attention. During the months that followed, Joseph the Prophet continued the translation of the New Testament, and labored as time would permit. As was so often the case, the problems associated with a growing church, as well as providing the necessities of life for his own family, precluded more frequent work with the Bible. At this point (by 7 April) the translators had progressed through Genesis 24:42a and Matthew 9:2.[6]

Worthy of note at this point is the fact that major revelations (now recorded in our Doctrine and Covenants) were being received concurrently with the translation of the Bible; in fact, it is critical to recognize that such sections as 76 (the vision of the glories), 77 (insights into the Revelation of John), 91 (information concerning the Old Testament Apocrypha), and 132 (eternal and plural marriage) were received as a direct outgrowth of the Prophet's work of Bible translation. In addition, matters in the Doctrine and Covenants pertaining to the Creation, the Fall, and the Atonement (e.g., D&C 29) were matters also being revealed through the inspired translation of Genesis (e.g., Moses 2–6).

In December 1830 the translation of the Bible revealed many great things pertaining to the ancient city of Enoch, the scriptural prototype for the people of God in all ages. Joseph learned that the Lord "called his people Zion, because they were of one heart and one mind, and dwelt in righteousness; and there was no poor among them" (Moses 7:18). In February of 1831—only two months later—the Lord began to make known through revelation the plan by which his people in the latter days could establish a society of the pure in heart, and could build economic and spiritual equality in a modern Zion society (see D&C 42). In summary, one Latter-day Saint writer has explained:

> The Prophet's work with the Bible was a primary source for much of the doctrinal content and the instructional information of the D&C. Consequently, one could not adequately understand either the background or the content of those parts of the D&C without an acquaintance with the history and content of the JST. The two volumes, when placed in tandem, enable the student to gain a clearer picture of how the gospel was restored in this dispensation, and gives the reader an insight as to how divine revelation comes.[7]

Early in 1833 the Mormon leader wrote: "I completed the translation and review of the New Testament, on the 2nd of February, 1833, and sealed it up."[8] At this point, work with the Old Testament resumed. By 8 March 1833 the translators had moved through the Old Testament as far as the Prophets (D&C 90:13). On the very next day, 9 March, Joseph inquired of God concerning the Apocrypha and received what is now Doctrine and Covenants 91. Joseph Smith's journal entry for 2 July 1833 is as follows: "We are exceedingly fatigued, owing to a great press of business. *We this day finished the translating of the Scriptures, for which we returned gratitude to our Heavenly Father.*"[9]

The Work of Joseph Smith's Scribes

Joseph the Prophet was assisted in his translation of the Bible by a number of persons who served as scribes. It may be that his wife, Emma Smith, labored for a short time as scribe. In a revelation given to Emma in July of 1830 she was instructed: "And thou shalt go with him at the time of his going, *and be unto him for a scribe,* while there is no one to be a scribe for him, that I may send my servant, Oliver Cowdery, whithersoever I will"

(D&C 25:6; emphasis added). The Book of Mormon had been published in March of 1830, and so this directive could not have had reference to further work with the Nephite record. Oliver Cowdery would serve for a period of time in the work of translation, but would have his scribal activities interrupted by a call to serve on a preaching mission (see D&C 28, 32). John Whitmer also worked in the role of scribe for a time. He later was given an assignment to assist the Prophet in transcribing and recopying the Bible translation (see D&C 47:1). The bulk of the scribal activity was accomplished by Sidney Rigdon. Sidney entered the Church in Ohio and joined Joseph Smith and the Saints in New York in December of 1830. He became involved immediately in the work with the Bible, and labored consistently until the formal work of translation ceased in July of 1833.

The work of the scribe seems to have consisted in writing on sheets of paper that which was dictated by Joseph Smith. Joseph would read directly from the Bible and through the spirit of inspiration note the need for a revision of a text. An examination of the manuscripts reveals different approaches or methods to the work of translation. For example, the biblical text is written out in full (longhand) on the manuscripts for Genesis 1–24 and Matthew 1–John 5. A shorter method was also employed, whereby only the passages to be revised were noted by the scribe on the manuscript pages. Of equal importance in the process of translation was Joseph's marking of the large Bible. Before or after many of the passages to be altered, one may note a check or an X or some other symbol. Additional marks in the Bible (e.g., dots, slanted lines, circled words, or lined-out words) were discovered to be essential (in conjunction with the manuscripts) in discerning exactly what Joseph Smith intended with regard to particular passages.[10]

We should note at this point that the Prophet's translation of the Bible was made up of four documents: two Old Testament manuscripts and two New Testament manuscripts. A total of 464 manuscript pages constitute the entire JST. For a detailed study of the history, development, and transmission of the JST manuscripts, one should consult Robert J. Matthews's book *"A Plainer Translation": Joseph Smith's Translation of the Bible, A*

History and Commentary (1975), the standard and definitive work on the subject.

THE NEW TRANSLATION: 1833–1844

The Prophet's interest or involvement did not cease when he had made his way through the King James Bible in July of 1833. Joseph spent his remaining years (until the time of his death in 1844) reviewing and revising the manuscripts—seeking to find appropriate words to convey what he had come to know by revelation. Robert Matthews has written concerning revisions in the original manuscripts:

> In the face of the evidence it can hardly be maintained that the exact words were given to the Prophet in the process of a revelatory experience. Exact words may have been given to the mind of the Prophet on occasion, but the manuscript evidence suggests that generally he was obliged to formulate the words himself to convey the message he desired. Consequently, he might later have observed that sometimes the words were not entirely satisfactory in the initial writings. They may have conveyed too much or too little. Or they may have been too specific or too vague, or even ambiguous. Or the words may have implied meanings not intended. Thus through (1) an error of recording, (2) an increase of knowledge, or (3) an inadequate selection of words, any passage of the New Translation might be subject to later revision.[11]

Some of the revisions were written directly on the original manuscripts, while others were separate sheets of paper pinned to the original manuscripts.

Portions of the JST were published before the martyrdom of the Prophet,[12] although the entire translation was not made available until 1867, when the RLDS Church printed the first edition of the JST. Some of the New Translation was available through the *Evening and Morning Star* in Independence, Missouri (1832–33). In the *Lectures on Faith,* a collection of seven theological lectures delivered by the Prophet to the School of the Prophets in Kirtland (1834–35), Joseph quoted a number of scriptural passages according to the New Translation. The *Lectures on Faith* was contained in the first edition (1835) of the

Doctrine and Covenants. In addition, what is now known as Joseph Smith-Matthew (the JST of Matthew 24) was published sometime between 1832 and 1837, while the visions of Moses (Moses 1) was published in the *Times and Seasons* in 1843.

One thing is extremely clear regarding the JST during Joseph Smith's lifetime: the Prophet had every intention of publishing the entire translation, and of making the valuable truths contained therein accessible to the Latter-day Saints. Inasmuch as a person is saved no faster than he gains knowledge,[13] Joseph the Prophet was eager to make known to the people the marvelous insights that had come to him through his work with the Bible. Both the Prophet and the people viewed the labor of translation and certainly the product as matters of profound gravity. In a revelation given to Frederick G. Williams in January of 1834 the Lord explained: "Now I say unto you, *my servant Joseph Smith Jr. is called to do a great work and hath need that he may do the work of translation for the salvation of souls.*"[14] Thus on numerous occasions throughout the closing years of Joseph Smith's ministry the Prophet himself and the Twelve made frequent requests of the Saints for financial assistance, in order that Joseph might "devote himself exclusively to those things which relate to the spiritualities of the Church," one thing in particular being the New Translation.[15]

In July of 1840 the First Presidency and the Twelve appointed two men to go throughout the Church to seek donations and offerings for the printing of various Church books, including the JST. An editorial in the *Times and Seasons* noted: "The authorities of the church here, having taken this subject into consideration, and viewing the importance of Publishing a Hymn Book, and a more extensive quantity of the Books of Mormon, *and also the necessity of Publishing the new translation of the scriptures, which has so long been desired by the Saints;* have appointed and authorized Samuel Bent and Geo. W. Harris, as traveling agents, to make contracts and receive monies &c. for the accomplishment of this glorious work."[16] On 19 January 1841 the Lord gave specific directions and promises to William Law, as now contained in section 124 of the Doctrine and Covenants: "If he will do my will let him from henceforth hearken to the counsel of my servant Joseph, and with his interest support the cause of the poor, *and publish the new translation of my holy word unto the inhabitants of the earth.* And if he will do this I will bless him with a multiplicity of blessings, that he shall not be forsaken, nor his seed be found begging bread." (D&C 124:89–90; emphasis added.) The pleadings of the leaders of the Church in this regard were not heeded, and the Prophet Joseph Smith was murdered before the JST was printed in full.

The question of the "completeness" of the JST is an important one. In short, did Joseph Smith actually complete his work with the Bible? In one sense the Prophet completed his task in that he moved from Genesis to Revelation—that is, made his way through the King James Version of the Bible. As we noted earlier, Joseph recorded in his journal for 2 July 1833: "*We this day finished the translating of the Scriptures,* for which we returned gratitude to our Heavenly Father."[17] If, however, we are asking whether Joseph Smith made every change in the King James Version that could have been made, we are dealing with another matter entirely, so far as completeness is concerned.

One of the strongest evidences of the incomplete status of the JST is to be found in Joseph Smith's sermons from 1833 to 1844. On numerous occasions the Prophet clarified and corrected biblical passages, which alterations were not reflected in his earlier inspired translation of the scriptures. For example, the second verse of the King James Bible describes the state of things in the morning of creation: "And the earth was without form, and void" (Genesis 1:2). The JST of this verse is exactly the same as the KJV. In a sermon delivered on 5 January 1841 in Nauvoo, however, Joseph Smith taught that the words "without form and void" should be translated "empty and desolate."[18] In his epistle to the Corinthians, the apostle Paul explained that "no man can say that Jesus is the Lord, but by the Holy Ghost" (1 Corinthians 12:3). In an address to the Relief Society in the latter part of April in 1842 Joseph explained that no man can *know* that Jesus is the Lord but by the Spirit.[19] Just five months before his death the Prophet clarified another biblical passage which had received no alteration in the JST.

> The question is frequently asked, "Can we not be saved without going through with all those ordinances?" I would answer, No, not the fulness of salvation. Jesus said, There are

many mansions in my Father's house, and I will go and prepare a place for you. *House* here named should have been translated kingdom; and any person who is exalted to the highest mansion has to abide a celestial law, and the whole law too.[20]

Other examples could be given to further illustrate this point,[21] but the preceding seem to be sufficient to establish the ultimate incompleteness of the JST.

There is another very significant angle from which to view the matter of completeness of the JST: the Saints' and the world's readiness to receive all that might have been given through the Prophet Joseph Smith. According to a conversation held in the Salt Lake City School of the Prophets in 1868, "George A. Smith testified that he had heard Joseph say before his death that *the new translation was not complete, that he had not been able to prepare it, and that it was probably providentially so.*"[22] President George Q. Cannon observed regarding the JST: "Joseph did not live to give to the world an authoritative publication of these translations. But the labor was its own reward, bringing in the performance a special blessing of broadened comprehension to the Prophet and a general blessing of enlightenment to the people through his subsequent teachings." President Cannon also noted: "We have heard Brigham Young state that the Prophet before his death had spoken to him about going through the translation of the scriptures again and perfecting it upon points of doctrine *which the Lord had restrained him from giving in plainness and fulness at the time of which we write.*"[23]

Joseph Fielding Smith wrote in 1914 that the Prophet "revised, as it is, *a great deal more than the world can, or will, receive.* In the 'translation' of the scriptures, *he gave to the world all that the Lord would permit him to give, and as much as many of the members of the Church were able to receive. He therefore finished all that was required at his hands, or, that he was permitted to revise,* up to July, 1833, when he discontinued his labors of revision."[24] Elder Bruce R. McConkie has also written: "In many passages all necessary changes were made; in others he was 'restrained' by the Spirit from giving the full and clear meaning. As with all revealed knowledge, the Lord was offering new truths to the world, 'line upon line, precept upon precept. . . .' *Neither the world nor the saints generally were then or are now prepared for the fulness of Biblical knowledge."*[25]

THE JST: 1844 TO THE PRESENT

The Bernhisel Manuscript (1845)

After the death of the Prophet, the manuscripts of the New Translation were held by Joseph's widow, Emma, and thus eventually came into the possession of the Reorganized Church of Jesus Christ of Latter Day Saints.[26] Not long after the death of Joseph Smith, however, Dr. John M. Bernhisel, a trusted friend of the Prophet and Emma, was given an opportunity to examine the original manuscripts. In describing the occasion (in the spring of 1845) when he was able to obtain the manuscripts, L. John Nuttall has recorded:

> Elder John M. Bernhisel called at the request of Pres. Taylor and explained concerning his manuscript copy of the New Translation of the Bible as taken from the Manuscript of the Prophet Joseph Smith. Bro. Bernhisel stated: "I had great desires to see the New Translation, but did not like to ask for it; but one evening, being at Bro. Joseph's house about a year after his death, Sister Emma to my surprise asked me if I would not like to see it. I answered, yes. She handed it to me the next day, and I kept it in my custody about three months. She told me it was not prepared for the press, as Joseph had designed to go through it again. I did not copy all that was translated leaving some few additions and changes that were made in some of the books. But so far as I did copy, I did so as correctly as I could do. The markings in my Bible correspond precisely with the markings in the Prophet Joseph's Bible, so that all the books corrected in his Bible so far as I now know are marked in my Bible: but as I stated, the additions are not all made in my Manuscript of those books that I did not copy."[27]

The limitations of what has come to be known as the Bernhisel Manuscript are clear from John Bernhisel's own words: the copy made by him is incomplete, and thus inadequate in representing exactly what the Prophet Joseph Smith and his scribes recorded.

The following are some errors that were committed unintentionally by Dr. Bernhisel:[28]
1. In some cases, Bernhisel did not copy *all* of the corrections noted on the original manuscripts. Joseph altered 3,410 verses; Bernhisel noted only 1,463.
2. In a sense, Bernhisel's copy is interpretive, in the sense that he seems to be thinking for himself, rather than simply copying from Joseph's manuscripts.
3. Sometimes Bernhisel recorded *more* than he should have; that is, he anticipated corrections that were not there.

It is no doubt the case that had Bernhisel known in the spring of 1845 that the original manuscripts would be unavailable to the LDS Church for such a long period (about 125 years), he would have taken greater care to record everything that Joseph had recorded. His was intended as a personal copy, and was never envisioned by him as becoming an official document. John Bernhisel arrived in the Salt Lake Valley on 24 September 1848, and it is assumed that he brought his manuscript with him. A copy of this manuscript was made by direction of the First Presidency in 1879. The original Bernhisel Manuscript is now available in the Church Historian's Library in Salt Lake City. The Bernhisel Manuscript is significant as a historical relic, and its early date of 1845 does much toward verifying the present accuracy of the original JST manuscripts.

The Pearl of Great Price (1851)

In 1850 Elder Franklin D. Richards of the Council of the Twelve succeeded Elder Orson Pratt as president of the British Mission. One of the first things Richards noticed about the state of things in his mission was the paucity of Church reading material. Few of the Saints even had copies of the standard works. Knowing of the necessity of regular reading of good books (particularly the scriptures), President Richards compiled and published a mission tract, a booklet made up of a number of "gems" of doctrinal and historical worth, many of which were revelations and writings of the Prophet Joseph Smith. This booklet, which came to be known as the Pearl of Great Price, and which was first printed in 1851, contained such items as Joseph's translations of the Egyptian materials (Abraham's writings and the facsimiles); several revelations from the Doctrine and Covenants (e.g., all or part of sections 20, 27, 77, 87, and 107); excerpts from Joseph Smith's history of the Restoration (Joseph Smith-History); the Articles of Faith, as given in the Wentworth Letter; and a poem by John Jaques, a British convert, called "Oh Say, What Is Truth?" In addition, the first edition of the Pearl of Great Price contained the following items from Joseph Smith's translation of the Bible (as given in the table of contents of that first edition):

> Extracts from the Prophecy of Enoch, containing also a Revelation of the Gospel unto our father Adam, after he was driven out from the Garden of Eden. Revealed to Joseph Smith, December, 1830 [Moses 6:43–7:69]
>
> The words of God, which he spake unto Moses at the time when Moses was caught up into an exceeding high mountain, and he saw God face to face, and he talked with him, and the glory of God was upon Moses; therefore Moses could endure his presence. Revealed to Joseph Smith, June 1830 [Moses 1:1–5:16, part; Moses 5:19–40; Moses 8:13–30]
>
> An extract from a Translation of the Bible—being the twenty-fourth chapter of Matthew, commencing with the last verse of the twenty-third chapter. By the Prophet, Seer, and Revelator, Joseph Smith [Joseph Smith-Matthew]

As can be seen, not all of the Moses material was contained in the 1851 Pearl of Great Price. President Richards seems to have been drawing upon the JST materials which we would identify as coming from Old Testament Manuscript 2 and New Testament Manuscript 1, as those materials would have been published earlier in the *Evening and Morning Star* and the *Times and Seasons*.[29]

The First Printing of the JST (1867)

At the April 1866 conference of the RLDS Church, plans were made to publish the Prophet Joseph Smith's translation of the Bible. A committee approached Emma Smith Bidamon on 3 May 1866 regarding the use of the original manuscripts, and Emma turned the manuscripts over to them. She wrote later to her son, Joseph III: "Now as it regards the Ms of the New Translation if you wish to keep them you may do so, but if not I would like to have them. I have often thought the reason our house did not burn down when it was so often on fire was because of them, and I still feel there is a sacredness attached to them."[30]

An RLDS publication committee had the manuscript ready for publication by 1 July 1867, and the first shipment of the printed edition (five hundred copies) of the JST arrived in Plano, Illinois, on 7 December 1867. The book was called The Holy Scriptures. Subsequent editions followed, including a 1936 Teacher's Edition, the first edition to have the words *Inspired Version* as a part of the title of the book. In 1944 a New Corrected Edition was published, in which 352 corrections were made to the original (1867) edition. In 1970 a parallel-column edition of the JST was introduced in which the student could compare the King James Version with the JST at a glance. The 1974 printing of the New Corrected Edition is by far the most accurate printing to be released to date.

The 1867 edition of the JST is important not only because of its historical value (as the apparent realization of the Prophet's desires that the entire New Translation be accessible to all of the members), but also because it was the source upon which Orson Pratt drew in his production of the second (American) edition of the Pearl of Great Price in 1878.[31] Though it would have been marvelous for the Utah Church to have access to the original manuscripts much sooner in our history, we do owe a debt of gratitude to the RLDS Church for printing the Prophet Joseph Smith's translation of the Bible.

The Work of Robert J. Matthews

Interest in the JST or Inspired Version of the Bible continued in both the LDS and RLDS churches. Studies in the history of the JST,[32] comparisons between the King James Version and the Joseph Smith Translation,[33] and major textual analyses[34] were undertaken from 1940 to 1969. The spirit of inquiry and the desire to discover and probe the meaning and significance of Joseph Smith's work with the Bible prompted and directed theses, dissertations, articles, and books in this area for many years.

In the summer of 1944 Robert J. Matthews listened to a radio address over station KSL delivered by President Joseph Fielding Smith.[35] In that sermon President Smith quoted John 1:18, "No man hath seen God at any time," and indicated that the King James translation was incorrect. He then quoted from the Joseph Smith Translation: "And no man hath seen God at any time, *except he hath borne record of the Son; for except it is through him no man can be saved*" (JST John 1:19).* Robert Matthews was at this time only eighteen years of age, and had never before heard of the JST. Suddenly, however, he was struck on this occasion with a deep sense of significance regarding what President Smith had just done, and at the same time gained a desire to know more about this phase of the Prophet's ministry.

Copies of the Joseph Smith Translation were scarce in his hometown, and even more scarce was any person who knew much about the work. Those who did know anything at all were negative towards it, indicating on the one hand that Joseph Smith had never finished the translation, and on the other that the printed edition was unreliable, inasmuch as it had been changed by the Reorganized Church. Finally Brother Matthews was able to obtain a 1947 printing of the Joseph Smith Translation from N. B. Lundwall of Salt Lake City, a man who had formerly belonged to the RLDS Church and who was also known for numerous important compilations and publications in the LDS book market. From 1947 to 1950 Matthews compared the KJV and the JST, quoted from it frequently in talks or lessons, but was often told by people in his ward and at BYU that the Church did not accept the book and that he was in error for even citing it.

The introduction in 1944 of the New Corrected Edition confirmed in the minds of many Latter-day Saints that surely the

---

*Italics are used throughout this book to indicate wording in the Joseph Smith Translation or the Book of Mormon that is not found in corresponding verses in the King James Version. Where noted, italics are also used for emphasis.

RLDS Church had been guilty of tampering with Joseph Smith's original manuscripts. Such attitudes heightened Robert Matthews's desire to examine the manuscripts to check for accuracy of the printed editions. After learning that the manuscripts were in the hands of the RLDS Church, Brother Matthews began to inquire of the leaders of that church as to the possibility of examining the original documents. He continued his requests for fifteen years before permission was finally granted in 1968. Matthews had also learned that a partial copy of the manuscripts —the Bernhisel Manuscript—was held by the LDS Church in Salt Lake City. Largely through the efforts of Reed C. Durham and the graciousness of President Joseph Fielding Smith, the Bernhisel Manuscript became available for research in 1965. In 1960 Robert Matthews did a master's thesis at BYU on the four Gospels in the JST, but in that study he did not have access to the original manuscripts. In 1968 he completed a Ph.D. at BYU, his doctoral dissertation examining the printed sources of the JST and the Bernhisel Manuscript. This study opened the way for the RLDS Church to permit him to have access to the original manuscripts, beginning in 1968. In 1975 he published his book, *"A Plainer Translation,"* and therein discussed the historical and doctrinal significance of the JST, in this work drawing not only upon printed JST sources but also upon the original manuscripts.

Among many of the critical contributions of Robert J. Matthews's work with the original documents, the following points were discovered or confirmed:

1. The Prophet's corrections were not made on the pages of the Bible but on sheets of paper.
2. Various scribes labored for the Prophet in recording the corrections.
3. Some passages were corrected more than one time, with additional information being provided each time. This helped to demonstrate how revelation comes.
4. Use of the manuscripts made available key dates, which served to give a clearer indication of the time when the Prophet was translating certain chapters. Such findings established the doctrinal relationship of the JST to the Doctrine and Covenants.

5. Through access to the dates on the manuscripts it became clear that the work of Bible translation was a major activity of the Prophet, and a significant matter in LDS Church history and in the unfolding of truth in this dispensation.
6. Finally, a most significant contribution of Matthews's work is that it substantiates and verifies the text of the printed JST, giving evidence that readers may feel comfortable with what they now find in print; in almost all instances the printed text follows the manuscripts in content and meaning.

The LDS Edition of the King James Bible (1979)

In 1972 President Harold B. Lee organized a Bible Aids Committee to prepare an edition of the Bible which would provide doctrinal and historical helps for Latter-day Saint students of the scriptures. Among the first matters proposed in the preparation of the LDS edition of the Bible was that significant changes from the Prophet Joseph Smith's translation of the Bible be included. As progress went forward on this new LDS edition, it became clear that such a project would lead naturally to a consideration of the status of the triple combination as well. The Bible Aids Committee became the Scriptures Publications Committee, and consisted finally of Elders Thomas S. Monson, Boyd K. Packer, and Bruce R. McConkie. These three members of the Council of the Twelve were assisted primarily by three members of the BYU Religious Education faculty: Ellis T. Rasmussen, Robert C. Patch, and Robert J. Matthews. In addition, literally hundreds of members of the Church Educational System aided in producing the Topical Guide and an extremely complex cross-referencing system between all four books within the standard works.

There is much to recommend the 1979 LDS Edition of the King James Bible as one of the literary masterpieces of our day. Most important, as Elder Packer observed in 1982, this Bible project (in conjunction with the 1981 triple combination) "will be regarded, in the perspective of history, as the crowning achievement in the administration of President Spencer W. Kimball." Continuing, Elder Packer taught:

With the passing of years, these scriptures will produce successive generations of faithful Christians who know the Lord Jesus Christ and are disposed to obey His will.

The older generation has been raised without them, but there is another generation growing up. The revelations will be opened to them as to no other in the history of the world. Into their hands now are placed the sticks of Joseph and of Judah. They will develop a gospel scholarship beyond that which their forebears could achieve. They will have the testimony that Jesus is the Christ and be competent to proclaim Him and to defend Him.[36]

One of the profound strengths of the new LDS Edition of the Bible is the marvelous light which is shed by the addition of JST changes either at the bottom of the page or at the end of the book. This factor alone—over six hundred JST alterations within our presently accepted and recommended Bible—should do much toward removing fears or hesitations toward Joseph Smith's translation of the Bible. Recently Elder Bruce R. McConkie spoke to a group of Church educators and said:

For historical and other reasons there has been, among some members of the Church in times past, some prejudice and misunderstanding of the place of the Joseph Smith Translation. I hope this has now all vanished away. Our new Church Bible footnotes many of the major changes made in the Inspired Version and has a seventeen-page section which sets forth excerpts that are too lengthy for inclusion in the footnotes.

Reference to this section and to the footnotes themselves will give anyone who has spiritual insight a deep appreciation of this revelatory work of the Prophet Joseph Smith. It is one of the great evidences of his prophetic call.[37]

WHAT IS THE JST?

Unfortunately, Joseph Smith never seems to have taken the time to explain the nature of his inspired translation of the King James Bible. Just as we are uncertain as to exactly how it was that he translated the Book of Mormon, we are not informed by the Prophet himself exactly what he was doing as he studied and pondered upon the biblical text. The following have been suggested[38] as possibilities in explaining exactly what the JST represents:

1. Portions of the JST may represent what might be called "inspired prophetic commentary" by the Prophet Joseph Smith, insights provided by Joseph to assist a latter-day world to better understand a former-day message. This might be similar to what Nephi referred to as likening the scriptures unto us (see 1 Nephi 19:23–24; 2 Nephi 11:8). Prophetic documents may be interpreted and explained by prophets, and it is to Joseph Smith that we owe a deep debt of gratitude in this regard.

2. Portions of the JST may represent a harmonization of doctrinal concepts that were revealed to Joseph Smith independently of his work with the Bible, but proved to be the means whereby he came to recognize a biblical inaccuracy.

3. A third possibility as to what the JST really represents (and one, in my opinion, which has received far too little serious attention) is a restoration of content material, ideas and events and sayings once recorded by the biblical authors but since deleted from the collection. I believe that in a very real sense we question the honesty and integrity of Joseph Smith when we question too strongly the proposition that much of the JST is a restoration of content. Some months ago while making a presentation on the Sermon on the Mount, I referred frequently to the JST additions in the King James text. One man in the group was particularly vocal in his reactions: "Oh, come on now! You don't really believe that Jesus actually said those things, do you? Isn't the Prophet simply reading nineteenth-century Mormonism back into the first century?" I have encountered similar reactions throughout the years, and have given the matter a great deal of thought.

In the Prophet's translation of two of the Gospels, he changed the titles of the works to read "The Testimony of St. Matthew" and "The Testimony of St. John." Such an alteration is not without significance. Joseph Smith was extremely serious about his work with the Bible, and I have great difficulty imagining him playing "fast and loose" with the King James text—adding words to the Savior's sermons, creating discussions between Jesus and the Twelve, and producing settings and re-creating events of which we have no other record—except as those words and events were once part of the testimonies of the Gospel writers. Would it not suggest dishonesty (or pride or haughtiness) to insert or create or conjure up episodes or dialogue which have no basis in historical fact? The words of Joseph Smith himself are poignant in regard to pretending to a divine work:

> After the foregoing was received [D&C 67], William E. M'Lellin, as the wisest man, in his own estimation, having more learning than sense, endeavored to write a commandment like unto one of the least of the Lord's, but failed; *it was an awful responsibility to write in the name of the Lord.* The Elders and all present that witnessed *this vain attempt of a man to imitate the language of Jesus Christ,* renewed their faith in the fulness of the gospel, and in the truth of the commandments and revelations which the Lord had given to the Church through my instrumentality; and the Elders signified a willingness to bear testimony of their truth to all the world.[39]

My personal conviction is certain as to the integrity of Joseph Smith. I do not doubt but that many of the JST alterations represent commentary or harmonization. At the same time, I believe that as a divinely called translator and restorer, Joseph Smith also (1) restored that which was once recorded but later removed intentionally; or perhaps even (2) reconstituted that which occurred or was said anciently but never recorded by the ancient writers. To doubt either the Prophet's intentions or abilities with regard to the Bible is to open the door unnecessarily to other questions relative to the books in the canon of scripture. Joseph the translator of the Book of Mormon and recipient of the revelations in the Doctrine and Covenants was the same man called and empowered as a translator of the Bible.

Some are hesitant to recognize or utilize the JST as a true restoration because the changes often do not reflect the readings or more obvious meanings in some of our oldest extant texts. Of all people, the Saints should use caution in avoiding improper or superficial assumptions regarding the oldest available manuscripts. Textual variants through the centuries are of two kinds—unplanned and planned. The former are frequently the unintentional ones, resulting from human error; they are in some ways the simplest to deal with and the ones to which a sincere textual critic might devote a lifetime of study. The latter—the planned variants—result when a sincere scribe begins to think for himself, or when a more devious scribe seeks to alter, take away, or keep back valuable truths. Even these latter types of errors could be corrected if we had access to original or even earlier (untampered) documents. But we do *not* have such documents.

Nephi's prophetic vision deals with intentional, dramatic alterations to the earliest texts. One Mormon writer has observed: "As we read the words of the angel [in 1 Nephi 13], we discover that the world has never had a complete Bible, for it was massively, even cataclysmically, corrupted *before* it was distributed."[40] It requires no greater faith to suppose that the Prophet Joseph Smith saw well beyond the great texts (now available) to an earlier or more complete text (or perhaps even to an episode or statement not previously recorded), than it does to accept the fact that he translated golden plates which contained a language known only to the Nephites (see Mormon 9:34). In short: "The plain and precious missing parts have not yet been made known through manuscripts and scholars, but are available only through the Book of Mormon, the Joseph Smith Translation, and modern revelation through the instrumentality of a prophet."[41]

CONCLUSION

In looking carefully at the history of the Joseph Smith Translation of the Bible we are able to see the hand of the Lord in a significant way: not only did the Lord direct the labors of his noble servant, Joseph Smith, in the translation itself, but he also opened doors and intervened where necessary, in order that a monumental work might be delivered intact to modern Israel. In short, the production and transmission of the JST reflect the hand of Providence, and further testify of the place of this particular branch of Joseph's calling in the breaking forth of the light of the Restoration.

The attitude with which Joseph Smith approached his assignment of Bible translation is evident in statements by the Prophet. For example, in a letter to W. W. Phelps, Joseph explained: "We have finished the translation of the New Testament great and marvilous glorious things are revealed, we are making rapid strides in the old book and in the strength of God we can do all things according to his will." [sic][42] That Joseph and his scribe recognized that the work of Bible translation was far more than a mental exercise is apparent in a simple entry at the top of page 1 of the manuscript of Matthew: "A translation of the New Testament translated by the power of God."[43] In a revelation to Sidney Rigdon, the principal scribe for the translation, Jesus Christ gives to us His own perception of the nature and scope of the JST: "And a commandment I give unto thee—that thou shalt write for him; and *the scriptures shall be given, even as they are in mine own bosom, to the salvation of mine own elect*" (D&C 35:20; emphasis added).

In 1832 the Lord warned the Saints that unless they took seriously the "new covenant"—the Book of Mormon—the Church would remain under condemnation (see D&C 84:54–57). In 1831 Joseph Smith had taught in a similar manner concerning his Bible translation: "God had often sealed up the heavens because of covetousness in the Church. said that the Lord would cut his work short in righteousness and *except the Church receive the fulness of the Scriptures that they would yet fall*." [sic][44] There is so much beauty and depth of doctrine and insight to be had within the Joseph Smith Translation of the Bible that it is foolish to study and teach without it; to do so is tantamount to being choosy about what we will receive from the Lord and what we will not. Such an attitude is certainly foreign to the genuine truth-seeker. Those who love and revere the name and labors of Joseph Smith should be pleased and enthusiastic to receive whatever God has chosen to reveal through his modern seer and lawgiver.

It should be obvious that we live in a day wherein the effects of the removal of precious truths are being felt in the religious world. But in harmony with the glorious prophecy of Moses, God has indeed raised up in our day a modern Moses, one through whose instrumentality the truths of heaven are "had again among the children of men—among as many as shall believe" (Moses 1:41).

Robert L. Millet is assistant professor of Ancient Scripture at BYU.

NOTES

1. Joseph Smith, *History of The Church of Jesus Christ of Latter-day Saints,* 7 vols. (Salt Lake City: Deseret Book Co., 1957), 6:57. Hereafter cited as *History of the Church.*

2. See Margaret T. Hills, *The English Bible in America* (New York: The American Bible Society, 1961); cited in Robert J. Matthews, *"A Plainer Translation": Joseph Smith's Translation of the Bible, A History and Commentary* (Provo: Brigham Young University Press, 1975), p. 9.

3. *History of the Church,* 1:98.

4. Ibid., pp. 131–33.

5. Matthews, *"A Plainer Translation,"* p. 96.

6. Ibid.

7. Robert J. Matthews, "The Joseph Smith Translation: A Primary Source for the Doctrine and Covenants," in *Hearken, O Ye People* (Salt Lake City: Randall Book Co., 1984), p. 90.

8. *History of the Church,* 1:324.

9. Ibid., pp. 368–69 (emphasis added).

10. See Matthews, *"A Plainer Translation,"* chapters 3 and 4.

11. Ibid., p. 86.

12. Ibid., p. 52.

13. *History of the Church,* 4:588.

14. Revelation given to Frederick G. Williams, 5 January 1834, Joseph Smith Collection, Letters 1834, Church Historian's Office, Salt Lake City, Utah (emphasis added).

15. *History of the Church,* 4:137.

16. *Times and Seasons,* vol. 1, no. 9 (July 1840), pp. 139–40 (emphasis added).

17. *History of the Church,* 1:368–69 (emphasis added).

18. See Andrew F. Ehat and Lyndon W. Cook, eds., *The Words of Joseph Smith* (Provo, Utah: BYU Religious Studies Center, 1980), p. 60.

19. Ibid., p. 115.

20. Ibid., p. 319.

21. See Matthews, *"A Plainer Translation,"* pp. 210–13.

22. Journal History of the Church, April–June 1868, Church Historical Department, Salt Lake City, Utah. Entry for 20 June 1868 (emphasis added).

23. George Q. Cannon, *Life of Joseph Smith the Prophet* (reprint ed., Salt Lake City: Deseret Book Co., 1972), p. 148 and note (emphasis added).

24. Joseph Fielding Smith, "Joseph Smith's 'Translation' of the Scriptures," *Improvement Era,* vol. 17, no. 6 (April 1914), p. 595 (emphasis added).

25. Bruce R. McConkie, *Mormon Doctrine,* 2nd ed. (Salt Lake City: Bookcraft, 1966), p. 384 (emphasis added).

26. For a detailed treatment of the transmission of the manuscripts, see Matthews, *"A Plainer Translation,"* chapter 4.

27. Diary of L. John Nuttall, 1:335, Harold B. Lee Library, Brigham Young University, under date of 10 September 1879.

28. See Matthews, *"A Plainer Translation,"* chapter 6.

29. Ibid., pp. 278–79.

30. Letter from Emma Smith Bidamon to Joseph Smith III, 2 December 1867, original in RLDS Auditorium, Department of History, Independence, Missouri.

31. Matthews, *"A Plainer Translation,"* pp. 225, 278–79.

32. James R. Clark, *The Story of the Pearl of Great Price* (Salt Lake City: Bookcraft, 1955); Reed C. Durham, Jr., "A History of Joseph Smith's Revision of the Bible" (Ph.D. diss., Brigham Young University, 1965).

33. Sidney B. Sperry and Merrill Y. Van Wagoner, "The Inspired Revision of the Bible," *Improvement Era,* April–September 1940; Calvin H. Bartholomew, "A Comparison of the Authorized Version and the Inspired Revision of Genesis" (master's thesis, Brigham Young University, 1949).

34. James R. Harris, "A Study of the Changes in the Content of the Book of Moses from the Earliest Available Sources to the Current Edition" (master's thesis, Brigham Young University, 1958); Robert J. Matthews, "A Study of the Doctrinal Significance of Certain Textual Changes Made by the Prophet Joseph Smith in the Four

Gospels of the Inspired Version of the New Testament" (master's thesis, Brigham Young University, 1960); Robert J. Matthews, "A Study of the Text of the Inspired Revision of the Bible" (Ph.D. diss., Brigham Young University, 1968); Richard P. Howard, *Restoration Scriptures* (Independence, Mo.: Herald Publishing House, 1969).

35. The address was delivered on 9 July 1944; cited in *The Restoration of All Things* (Salt Lake City: Deseret Book Co., 1945), p. 57.

36. Boyd K. Packer, in Conference Report, October 1982, p. 75.

37. Bruce R. McConkie, "The Bible—A Sealed Book," Address delivered at CES Symposium on the New Testament, 17 August 1984, p. 12.

38. Matthews, *"A Plainer Translation,"* p. 253.

39. *History of the Church,* 1:226 (emphasis added).

40. From Robert J. Matthews, "The Book of Mormon as a Co-Witness with the Bible and as a Guide to Biblical Criticism," LDS Church Educational System *Symposium on the Book of Mormon* (Salt Lake City: The Church of Jesus Christ of Latter-day Saints, 1982), p. 57.

41. Ibid.

42. Letter to William W. Phelps, 31 July 1832, in Dean C. Jessee, comp., *The Personal Writings of Joseph Smith* (Salt Lake City: Deseret Book Co., 1984), p. 248.

43. See a copy of New Testament Manuscript 1, page 1 (8 March 1831), in Matthews, *"A Plainer Translation,"* p. 267; see also Richard P. Howard, *Restoration Scriptures,* p. 171.

44. From an entry dated 25 October 1831 in Donald Q. Cannon and Lyndon W. Cook, eds., *The Far West Record* (Salt Lake City: Deseret Book Co., 1983), p. 23 (emphasis added).

3

Insights into the Book of Genesis

George A. Horton, Jr.

One afternoon, shortly after the "new" King James Version, LDS Edition came out, I boarded the Wasatch Boulevard Bus going south on State Street in Salt Lake City and found that there was only one seat vacant—right in the middle of the back row. After the bus had gone a few blocks, I noticed the person next to me was reading his Bible. All I knew about him was where he got on and off the bus. His well-worn Bible appeared to be one of the old black-covered Cambridge missionary editions, and he was reading Genesis 14. He finished the chapter, slowly closed the book, and began to gaze out the window.

Risking the possibility that he might not be LDS, I said, "Pardon me, do you mind if I ask you a question?" Looking a little surprised, he said, "No, go ahead."

"Do you mind telling me why you are reading the *old* Bible when the *new* one is available?" Again he looked a little shocked at the challenge, but as he searched for words, he almost unconsciously pulled his book close to him and said, "I just like my old Bible, that's all." Then he added, "And besides, I guess it's the money."

"You can buy a new Bible at the Distribution Center for about seven dollars," I suggested. After a pause, he said, "What's so good about the new one?"

"Well, I happened to notice that you just read Genesis 14. Did you know that you skipped over sixteen complete verses of scripture that you didn't even read?"

"What do you mean?" he questioned.

Reaching into my briefcase, I pulled out my new KJV, LDS Edition. Opening to Genesis 14, and holding the book over where he could see, I pointed to the little superscript "a" at the end of verse 24. "See that little 'a.' Now let's look down to the cross-references. It refers us to JST Genesis 14:25–40. If we go back to the Joseph Smith Translation [hereafter referred to as JST] in the appendix, we will find sixteen more verses of scripture which you did not read." The questioning look on his face was obvious, but before he could even finish his next question, "What does it say?" I had already closed my book and was putting it back in my briefcase. Just then the buzzer rang for his stop, and as he started for the door, he looked back and grinned as if to say "Thanks!"

The man who studies the stories and message of Genesis without the aid of the Joseph Smith Translation is like unto the captain of a ship who, while viewing the tips of many icebergs (doctrines), tries to estimate their true size and shape without considering all information available and the underlying currents which affect their movement. His ship (the good ship *Private Interpretation*) will surely be on a collision course—he will miscalculate, and if he does not make the proper corrections may, like the *Titanic,* sink into the depths of faulty interpretation and misunderstanding from which it is difficult to return.

HOW IS THE BOOK OF MOSES RELATED TO JST GENESIS?

Most of us probably don't fully appreciate or have a true perspective on the value of the JST because we have been using part of it for such a long time (i.e., the book of Moses). We are much like a person who often has steak or some other delicacy for dinner—he probably won't fully appreciate it unless he is suddenly without it.

To gain valuable insights into Genesis, the place to start is with the book of Moses—in fact, chapter 1. The Lord revealed to Joseph Smith the experience Moses had when he (Moses) "was caught up into an exceedingly high mountain, And he saw God face to face, and he talked with him" (Moses 1:1–2). This revelation to the latter-day prophet came at the time when he was being instructed to begin the inspired study, translation, or revision of the Bible.[1]

Our current book of Moses (2:1–8:30) is an almost verbatim copy of JST Genesis 1:1–8:18 (covering King James Version Genesis 1:1–6:13). It was prepared by Orson Pratt in 1878 as he edited the Pearl of Great Price to be presented in the general conference of the Church.[2] Therefore, when we read the book of Moses we are in reality reading the first chapters of JST Genesis. The title of the former seems appropriate since the first book of the Bible in some editions is given as "The First Book of Moses Called Genesis." (See title of Genesis in the King James Version.)

Approaching the study of the JST is a lifetime endeavor to which we each bring different levels of gospel scholarship. Since our individual insights usually come according to the level of spiritual maturity which we bring to the task, you may be able to add to the following basic questions:

1. What is the fundamental message of Genesis?
2. What great gospel themes are better clarified in the JST?
3. What other unique textual contributions are given?
4. What related extra-textual sources are available?

WHAT IS THE FUNDAMENTAL MESSAGE OF GENESIS?

When discussing the Genesis creation story, what teacher has not been pressed with questions such as: How was the earth created? How long did it take? Were there dinosaurs before Adam? Were there pre-Adamites? Did God just place a spirit in man at one point in his evolutionary development from lower forms? What about organic evolution? Was Adam brought from another planet? Where did God come from? Did God's father's father have a father? What is an intelligence? Where did it all begin? And numerous others that you can think of. Is it possible that most of these questions totally miss the mark?

If the Lord intended to reveal the specific details of creation there seems to be a great defect in the present record. In this regard, Elder James E. Talmage said, "The opening chapters of Genesis, and scriptures related thereto, were never intended as a textbook of geology, archeology, earth-science, or man-science."[3]

Instead of trying to squeeze out information that doesn't seem to have been in the Genesis account in the first place (indeed, may not yet be revealed—consider Doctrine and Covenants 101:32-34), let us ask the following: What is the source of the book? Who was the prophet-scribe? When did he write? Where was he at the time? To whom was he writing? What seemed to be the intent of his book?

The Divine Author is easy to recognize, especially in the first part—the premortal Lord Jesus Christ is speaking as the Father by divine investiture of authority.[4] He is the Almighty God of Abraham, Isaac, and Jacob—the great I Am—and Jehovah of the Old Testament. Moses, the eighty-year-old shepherd of Midian, spoke to him "face to face" (Moses 1:2), beheld the world and the end thereof (1:8), was instructed at the time of the burning bush (1:17), received the call to deliver Israel from its long Egyptian bondage (1:6, 26), and was commanded to "write the things which I shall speak" (1:40). That these writings were not only for the Hebrew slaves is revealed in the added note that "in a day when the children of men shall esteem my words as naught and take many of them from the book which thou shalt write, behold, I will raise up another like unto thee; and they shall be had again among the children of men—among as many as shall believe" (1:41). The translation of the Bible through Joseph Smith must be a major part, if not the direct fulfillment, of this prophecy.

Judging from the more complete revelation to Moses (found in JST Genesis), could not ancient and modern Israel conclude that among the most important things they were to know are the following:

1. The Lord God (Jehovah) was their God. (A great contrast to Osiris, Ammon Re, Ptah, Horus, Anubis, Hapi, Sobek, Khnum, Atum, and hundreds of other false deities in the Egyptian Pantheon, not to mention the Canaanite Baal, or the later trinitarian God of the current Christian creeds.)
2. He was their creator and all of creation was good.
3. The Creation was planned and orderly.
4. Every person was created in the image of his Eternal Father and the Only Begotten Son.
5. A gospel of redemption was taught from the beginning.
6. Through personal righteousness, man could gain eternal life.
7. Israel had a great patriarchal lineage going back to Adam.
8. Israel was the covenant people with a divine destiny and the promises made to their fathers would all be fulfilled.
9. They were to receive special blessings.
10. As custodian of the covenant, Israel had the responsibility to share it with all of Adam's other children.

Because Genesis covers a period of history over twice as long as all the other thirty-eight books of the Old Testament combined, obviously it was not intended as a detailed history, but contains things the Lord felt were vital for Israel to know.

Before considering the great gospel themes which become plain in the JST, one other preliminary observation could be made to emphasize the large amount of additional scripture that it makes available. If we organized all the scriptures chronologically (in parallel columns) so the scriptural story could be read as completely as possible, we might be mildly shocked at Genesis 5:21–24 (the Enoch material), when instead of 5 or 10 or even 25 additional verses in the JST, there are 111 consecutive verses with no counterpart in the common edition of Genesis.

WHAT GREAT GOSPEL THEMES ARE BETTER CLARIFIED IN JST GENESIS?

One who is familiar with Genesis in the King James Version (hereafter KJV) is excited when he discovers some almost obscure gospel themes suddenly coming into focus in the JST. Let us con-

sider eight which are either obscure or completely missing in the KJV:
1. The role and mission of Jesus Christ.
2. The role of Satan.
3. The fall of Adam.
4. The nature of man.
5. The gospel of Jesus Christ taught in the beginning.
6. God's ways versus man's ways.
7. The priesthood.
8. Covenants.

The Role and Mission of Jesus Christ

The single most important concept to grasp in a study of Genesis is the role and mission of Jesus Christ (known in his preexistent state as Jehovah). Unfortunately, the KJV adds to the obscurity of this idea because the translators generally rendered the Hebrew tetragrammaton (i.e., *Jod He Vav He*) representing Jehovah (or Yahweh) to read L*ORD* (i.e., large capital *L* and small capitals *ORD*). Therefore, one can read Genesis without recognizing that Jehovah (or Jesus Christ) is on almost every page.

Some of the major facts which cannot be overlooked in the JST are:

He is the Only Begotten Son—creator of heaven and earth.

He was prepared before the foundation of the world—chosen to suffer for men if they would repent.

Men are created in his image.

Men were to make offerings in similitude of his atoning sacrifice.

They are to believe in him, hearken to his word, be baptized in his name, and pray to the Father in his name.

He was the Lord God who spoke to Adam and all the prophets.

With his Father, it is his work and glory to bring to pass the immortality and eternal life of man.

In short, Adam knew of the mission of Jesus Christ, received instruction from him, understood the necessity of exercising faith in him, bore witness of him, and taught these things to his descendants for several generations.

The Role of Satan

To appreciate the contribution of the JST on the adversary's role, we remind ourselves that the word *Satan* occurs only nineteen times in the KJV Old Testament, and its first occurrence does not appear until 1 Chronicles 21:1. The word *Lucifer* occurs only once, at Isaiah 14:12, and the word *devil* does not occur at all. Thus, we see that none of them occur in the common version of Genesis.[5]

We recognize the work of Satan as represented by the serpent in the story of the Fall, but his presence or influence seems to be practically nonexistent in the rest of the Genesis story. Consider the JST Genesis contributions:

Satan wanted to save all mankind and receive God's honor.
He rebelled and sought to destroy man's agency.
He was cast down and became the devil, the father of lies, to deceive, blind, and lead men captive.
He spoke by the mouth of the serpent.
He knew not the mind of God.
Because of his sophistries, many loved him more than God.
Cain's unacceptable offering came only after Satan commanded it.
Satan agreed to submit to Cain's commands in return for Cain's entering into the secret oaths to commit murder.
Thus Satan became the author of secret combinations of darkness.

The Lord Jesus Christ and Satan represent the two great forces vying for man's allegiance in this life—(1) the power of life, truth, love, service and salvation offered by Jesus Christ, or (2) the power of death, error, darkness, and damnation which come by following Satan. We can only wonder to what extent the seeming systematic failure of these topics to be found in the common version of Genesis represents a calculated effort to obscure Satan's struggle for souls. Did Nephi see this in vision?

"For behold, they have taken away from the gospel of the Lamb many parts which are plain and most precious; and also many covenants of the Lord" (1 Nephi 13:26).

The Fall of Adam

In Genesis, the Fall is mentioned primarily as an event only. Most of the Christian world, with the help of a few assumptions, reaches the following conclusions: Adam and Eve both openly rebelled against God and committed a wicked, evil sin—undoubtedly breaking the law of chastity. Also, that by this sin they doomed all mankind to be born already stained with original sin upon their souls into a world of grief, sorrow, and suffering.

By way of contrast, the JST says:

> "The sins of the parents [e.g., Adam and Eve] cannot be answered upon the heads of the children, for they are whole from the foundation of the world" (JST Genesis 6:56/Moses 6:54).

> Man's nature is not fallen to begin with, but "they loved Satan more than God. And men began from that time forth to be carnal, sensual, and devilish." (JST Genesis 4:13/Moses 5:13.)

> The consequences of partaking of the fruit are given and then qualified by "nevertheless, thou mayest choose for thyself" (JST Genesis 2:20-22/Moses 3:17).

> After the Fall, Adam and Eve were taught "the plan of salvation unto all men, through the blood of mine Only Begotten" (JST Genesis 6:65/Moses 6:62).

Contrary to the traditional Christian view of being dejected, conscience-smitten, beaten, hanging their heads in shame, and in a general state of hopelessness, when they comprehended the implications of the Fall, Adam and Eve sort of jumped up and clicked their heels.

> "Because of my transgression," said Adam, "my eyes are opened, and in this life I shall have joy, and again in the flesh I shall see God" (JST Genesis 4:10/Moses 5:10).

> Eve "heard all these things, and was glad, saying: Were it not for our transgression we never should have had seed, and never should have known good and evil, and the joy of our

redemption, and the eternal life which God giveth unto all the obedient" (JST Genesis 4:11/Moses 5:11).

The Nature of Man

According to the generally accepted Christian doctrine, man is born with the taint of original sin upon his soul; therefore, his nature is automatically evil. It would be hard to overestimate the negative psychological impact this false doctrine would have on a person's life when trying to overcome individual weaknesses and gain eternal perfection. Would this not make it possible to rationalize bad behavior by assuming that by nature, man is bad to begin with?

The JST clarifies these fundamental aspects of the nature of man: "The Son of God hath atoned for original guilt, wherein the sins of the parents cannot be answered upon the heads of the children, for *they are whole from the foundation of the world*" (JST Genesis 6:56/Moses 6:54; emphasis added). But, if children are born whole, then how does one account for the wickedness in our society? The scriptures explain by saying that "when they begin to grow up, sin conceiveth in their hearts" (JST Genesis 6:56/Moses 6:55).

"Adam and Eve . . . made all things known unto their sons and their daughters. And Satan came among them, saying: I am also a son of God; and he commanded them, saying: Believe it not; and they believed it not, and they loved Satan more than God. And men began from that time forth to be carnal, sensual, and devilish." (JST Genesis 4:13/Moses 5:12-13.) Enoch reaffirms this teaching: "Behold, Satan hath come among the children of men, and tempteth them to worship him; and men have become carnal, sensual, and devilish, and are shut out from the presence of God" (JST Genesis 6:50/Moses 6:49).

It is clear that "every spirit of man was innocent in the beginning" (D&C 93:38), and can remain that way unless there is failure to yield to "the enticings of the Holy Spirit" (Mosiah 3:19). In most of the passages there is an emphasis on the fact that man *becomes* that way, clearly implying he was not so to begin with.

The Gospel of Jesus Christ Was Taught from the Beginning

The fact that the gospel of redemption was taught from the beginning has to be one of the most exciting insights we encounter in our gospel study. "The Gospel began to be preached, from the beginning, being declared by holy angels sent forth from the presence of God, and by his own voice, and by the gift of the Holy Ghost" (JST Genesis 5:44/Moses 5:58). Thus we see the perfect justice of God in working with his children for their salvation. This reinforces the apostle Paul's statement that "Jesus Christ [is] the same yesterday, and to day, and for ever" (Hebrews 13:8). The principles that will sanctify, save, and exalt men today are the same that applied in every age or dispensation.

Jesus Christ (the Only Begotten Son) was called before the foundation of the world to be the Savior and Redeemer. Therefore, even though men sin, through faith in Christ, true repentance, and baptism, they can be given the gift of the Holy Ghost, and by living in the Lord's way, be justified, sanctified, sealed up to eternal life, and eventually dwell in his presence. Since these blessings are contingent on man's overcoming his personal sins, it is no surprise that the most persistent single injunction in the early record is for men to *repent*. This is in contrast to the KJV where there is no direct call to repent in the entire book of Genesis. In no other place in scripture is the need to repent more consistently emphasized than in the JST.

> Adam was told to repent, and he in turn called upon his sons to repent.
> The Lord called on men everywhere by the Holy Ghost to repent.
> All men must repent.
> One must repent to inherit the kingdom.
> Christ suffered for sins and we will return to him if we repent.

God's Way Vs. Man's Way

The big choice placed before Adam and Eve, their children, and grandchildren is identical to ours. Will we choose to serve the Lord, or, by deliberate choice (or default), serve Satan? The early record provides ample examples of the consequences of such a decision. Adam and Eve taught their children in the ways of the Lord, but Satan prevailed "and they [the children] loved Satan more than God" (JST Genesis 4:12–13/Moses 5:12–13). At Cain's birth, Adam and Eve were filled with great anticipation. Eve said, "I have gotten a man from the Lord" (Genesis 4:1). "But behold, Cain hearkened not, saying: Who is the Lord that I should know him? . . . And Cain loved Satan more than God." (JST Genesis 5:4, 6/Moses 5:16, 18.)

However, not all was lost; his younger brother (Abel) "walked in holiness before the Lord" (JST Genesis 5:11/Moses 5:26), yet another (Seth) offered an "acceptable sacrifice" (JST Genesis 6:4/Moses 6:3), and they began "to call upon the name of the Lord" (JST Genesis 6:5/Moses 5:4). Undoubtedly there were others who chose the path of faith and obedience, but the sacred records reflect that many in Adam's generation did not enthusiastically lean toward spiritual things.

Righteous patriarchs did teach their children "in the ways of God" (JST Genesis 6:12, 22, 43/Moses 6:13, 21, 41), and those who learned to "walk with [the Lord]" and "abide" in him (JST Genesis 6:36/Moses 6:34) became the sons and daughters of God. Those who would not hearken became known as the sons and daughters of men. The JST clearly provides the reason why Noah, his sons, and their wives boarded the boat and were saved, while the rest of their family, friends, and neighbors all went to a watery grave. The JST says: "And Noah and his sons hearkened unto the Lord, and gave heed, and they were called the sons of God" (JST Genesis 8:1/Moses 8:13). This also explains why the Lord was grieved when Noah's daughters accepted marriage proposals from the sons of men (i.e., those who would not hearken). (JST Genesis 8:3/Moses 8:15.)

Lest the value of the JST be missed, consider the conclusion reached in a popular Bible dictionary about the nature of the sons of God and daughters of men referred to in Genesis 6:2: "The text seems to imply that the gods married existing gigantic earthly women and that these marriages produced the mighty men . . . [or] Nephilim (i.e., giants) . . ."[6] Thus the story is further dismissed as simply "saga and legend."[7]

The Priesthood

The only direct reference to priesthood in KJV Genesis is to Melchizedek, priest of the most high God (see Genesis 14:18–20). From this, who could possibly reconstruct the history or operation of the priesthood for approximately twenty-five hundred years—from Adam to Moses?

To Enoch it was revealed that after Adam was baptized and received the Holy Ghost, the Lord said, "And thou art after the order of him who was without beginning of days or end of years, from all eternity to all eternity" (Moses 6:67), thus referring to the Holy Priesthood after the Order of the Son of God, now called the Melchizedek Priesthood (cf. JST Hebrews 7:3; D&C 107:3). After mentioning that Seth was appointed in his murdered brother's stead, the record continues, "Now this same Priesthood, which was in the beginning, shall be in the end of the world also" (JST Genesis 6:7/Moses 6:7). The Lord ordained Noah (see JST Genesis 8:7/Moses 8:19 and cf. D&C 107:52). Melchizedek also, "having been approved of God, he was ordained an high priest after the order of the covenant which God made with Enoch, It being after the order of the Son of God; which order came, not by man, nor the will of man; neither by father nor mother; neither by beginning of days nor end of years; but of God" (JST Genesis 14:27–28). Priesthood functions are also mentioned: "He [Melchizedek] blessed Abram, being the high priest, and keeper of the storehouse of God; Him whom God appointed to receive tithes for the poor" (JST Genesis 14:37–38).

At least one other allusion to priesthood includes the three messengers at the time of Sodom's impending destruction, "which were holy men, and were sent forth after the order of God" (i.e., the order of the Melchizedek Priesthood). (JST Genesis 18:23.)

Covenants

When priesthood is mentioned covenants most assuredly will be there also. References to covenants do appear in Genesis, particularly in chapter 17, but the details are vague.

After mentioning that the gospel had been preached, the JST continues: "And thus all things were confirmed unto Adam, by an holy ordinance" (JST Genesis 5:45/Moses 5:59). Those covenants mentioned directly or indirectly include tithing (Genesis 14:20), priesthood (JST Genesis 6:7/Moses 6:7), and baptism (Moses 6:52). The Lord also covenanted to preserve the patriarchal lineage of Enoch, Methuselah, Noah, and Abraham (JST Genesis 7:58/Moses 7:51; 8:2; JST Genesis 8:23; 9:14, 17, 21–25). However, the covenant is best elaborated in connection with Abraham wherein it is called an "everlasting covenant" (JST Genesis 13:13). He was not the first to receive it, but was counseled that he "should observe to keep all my covenants wherein I covenanted with thy fathers" (JST Genesis 17:12).

Also promised is that one would be raised up in the latter days to once again bring Israel to a knowledge of the covenants (JST Genesis 50:31).

It is clear that reading Genesis without the benefit of the JST would be something like chewing on a T-bone with much of the steak already cut off, or reading the New Testament parables, never realizing that they had a dual meaning and that the one we missed was the most valuable.

Having sampled the main course, let's go back and pick here and there at the relish plate.

WHAT OTHER UNIQUE TEXTUAL CONTRIBUTIONS ARE GIVEN?

Before considering many unique changes, it might be observed that Joseph Smith's work anticipates some of the very elements and themes emerging from recently discovered apocryphal texts, including segments about Adam, Enoch, Melchizedek, Abraham, and Joseph, thereby providing additional evidence of Joseph Smith's prophetic calling.[8]

There are over two hundred changes or added verses in JST Genesis, which in itself suggests the monumental impact that it would have on an understanding of its message. Following are a few small but critical corrections that add to the beauty of the scriptural account:

1. Genesis 1:26–27 (JST Genesis 1:27, 29; Moses 2:26–27). The antecedent given to *us* in "Let us make man" is the Father and the Only Begotten Son in whose image man is made.

2. Genesis 1:30 (JST Genesis 1:32; Moses 2:30). "Every green herb" becomes "every clean herb."

3. Genesis 2:5 (JST Genesis 2:5; Moses 3:5). To the expression "every plant of the field before it was in the earth, and every herb of the field before it grew" is added, "For I, the Lord God, created all things, of which I have spoken, spiritually, before they were naturally upon the face of the earth . . . for in heaven created I them."

4. Genesis 4:1–8 (JST Genesis 4:2–5:13; Moses 5:2–28). Several additions are given: A popular commentary says, "The first son of this [Adam and Eve's] union is named Cain."[9] Not so, for Adam and Eve had many sons and daughters prior to the birth of Cain and Abel. The sons and daughters divided two and two in the land and had children of their own. When commanded to offer sacrifice, Adam did so in complete faith. Adam and Eve mourned because of Cain's rebellion. Another commentary says Cain's wife was a daughter of Adam, "and consequently was a sister to Cain."[10] But it is recorded in the JST that Cain married one of his brother's daughters.

5. Genesis 5:1 (JST Genesis 6:5; Moses 6:5). A book of remembrance was kept with which Adam's children were taught a language which was pure and undefiled.

6. Genesis 5:22–23 (JST Genesis 6:21–7:78; Moses 6:21–7:69). This includes writings of Enoch, some of which have already been cited. Additional information includes: Enoch's speech and vision; the translation of the city of Zion; that many others were later translated before the flood; the great wickedness of Enoch's time surpassed that among the Lord's other creations; the city of Zion and the New Jerusalem are to be joined together; and a millennium of peace is foretold.

7. Genesis 6:6 (JST Genesis 8:15; Moses 8:25). It was Noah, not the Lord, who was sorry (repented) that the Lord had made man.

8. Genesis 14:24 (JST Genesis 14:25–40). Additional details not referred to heretofore (and missed by the man on the bus) include the faith of Melchizedek who had great power to perform many miracles; that men having such faith (including his people) were translated and joined the city of Enoch; Melchizedek was appointed the keeper of the storehouse of God and henceforth was the appropriate one to whom tithes were paid.

9. Genesis 17:17 (JST Genesis 17:23). Abraham "rejoiced" rather than "laughed" when told that Sarah would have a child.

10. Genesis 19:8 (JST Genesis 19:11). The order of events in Lot's interaction with the wicked men of Sodom is changed. "We will have the men, and thy daughters also." The latter was their idea, not Lot's, contrary to the Genesis account.

11. Genesis 19:31–33 (JST Genesis 19:37–39). Lot's incestuous daughters "did wickedly."

12. Genesis 21:33 (JST Genesis 21:31). It was Abimelech and his captain, not Abraham, that planted a grove in Beersheba.

13. Genesis 24:2, 9 (JST Genesis 24:2, 8). The "hand" was involved in making the covenant rather than the "thigh."

14. Genesis 28:22 (JST Genesis 28:22). Instead of the "stone" being the house of God, it is the "place" of the house of God.

15. Genesis 48:5–6 (JST Genesis 48:5–11). Grandsons Ephraim and Manasseh were adopted like sons to Jacob with the same standing as his own twelve sons. Jacob acknowledges that Joseph was to save the house of Israel, and Joseph's children were to be blessed above those of his brethren. They also were to bring salvation to the rest of Jacob's house at a time when they were all bowed down in sin.

16. Genesis 50:24 (JST Genesis 50:24–36). Joseph's prophecies to his children just prior to his death included: the mission of Moses; the calling of a latter-day Joseph and the Restoration; writings which Joseph would be instrumental in bringing forth to be joined with those of Judah to the "confounding of false doctrine," and bringing Israel to a knowledge of their fathers and their covenants.

There are many more exciting contributions to be found, each worth a diligent search.

WHAT RELATED EXTRA-TEXTUAL SOURCES ARE AVAILABLE?

One of the most significant dimensions of this quest for insights is represented by sources that are not actually in the JST itself, but which might be considered an *extension* of it. Robert J. Matthews has pointed out that "most of the revelations dealing with doctrinal subjects [found in the D&C] were revealed to Joseph Smith . . . from June 1830 to July 1833, which was exactly the time he was working on the Bible translation. While engaging in such a concentrated study of the scriptures, it was natural for him to ask questions and ponder on various subjects, inquire of the Lord, and receive divine revelation in answer to his inquiry."[11] Of what consequence could this be to a greater understanding of Genesis? Consider two examples:

1. The Prophet was working on the Genesis portion of the translation on and off during the period of June 1830 to June 1835—the latter date including a period when an additional review was specifically made of Genesis 1 through 5. One will note that Genesis 5 gives the patriarchal line from Adam to Noah, indicating little more than the age of the patriarchs when the sons in the patriarchal line of succession were born. In this regard, we can see a similarity to eighteen verses in Doctrine and Covenants 107.

The section summary for Doctrine and Covenants 107 indicates that portions of that particular revelation were received as early as November 1831 and the remainder is dated 28 March 1835. Compare verses 40 to 57 with Genesis 5 (or Moses 6) about the Patriarchs: "The order of this priesthood [i.e., Melchizedek] was confirmed to be handed down from father to son, and rightly belongs to the literal descendants of the chosen seed, to whom the promises were made. This order was instituted in the days of Adam, and came down by lineage in the following manner: From Adam to Seth, who was ordained by Adam at the age of sixty-nine years, and was blessed by him three years previous to his (Adam's) death, and received the promise of God by his father, that his posterity should be the chosen of the Lord, and that they should be preserved unto the end of the earth; Because he (Seth) was a perfect man, and his likeness was the express likeness of his father, insomuch that he seemed to be like unto his father in all things, and could be distinguished from him only by his age." (D&C 107:40–43.) Then the revelation continues to indicate at what age and by whom each of the patriarchs was ordained, down to and including Noah (see D&C 107:44–52).

Continuing further, the revelation states that "Three years previous to the death of Adam, he called Seth, Enos, Cainan, Mahalaleel, Jared, Enoch, and Methuselah, who were all high priests, with the residue of his posterity who were righteous, into the valley of Adam-ondi-Ahman, and there bestowed upon them his last blessing. And the Lord appeared unto them, and they rose up and blessed Adam, and called him Michael, the prince, the archangel. . . . And Adam stood up in the midst of the congregation; and, notwithstanding he was bowed down with age, being full of the Holy Ghost, predicted whatsoever should befall his posterity unto the latest generation." (D&C 107:53–56.) None of the foregoing information is found in either Genesis or JST Genesis directly, but "These things were all written in the book of Enoch, and are to be testified of in due time" (D&C 107:57).

2. The section summary for Doctrine and Covenants 132 indicates that it was recorded on 12 July 1843, but "it is evident from historical records that the doctrines and principles involved in the revelation had been known by the Prophet since 1831."[12] It is also well known that after his review of Genesis in June of 1835, Joseph continued to make changes in the translation for almost nine additional years, when finally his work was cut short by martyrdom.

The wording of section 132 and its doctrinal nature reflect its connection with JST Genesis. "Verily, thus saith the Lord unto you my servant Joseph, that inasmuch as you have inquired of my hand to know and understand wherein I, the Lord, justified my servants Abraham, Isaac, and Jacob . . . as touching the principle and doctrine of their having many wives and concubines. . . . I am the Lord thy God, and will answer thee as touching this matter." (D&C 132:1–2.) Then follows an explanation of the new and everlasting covenant of marriage. The indications that at least part of this revelation was received while Joseph was studying the lives of these ancient patriarchs is very persuasive. Continuing, the revelation says, "Abraham received all things, whatsoever he received, by revelation and commandment" (v. 29), which brings us back to Genesis.

When introducing the covenant to Abraham, in the King James Version Abraham is instructed to "walk before me, and be thou perfect" (Genesis 17:1). In the JST this is considerably strengthened: "I, the Almighty God, give unto thee a *commandment*; that thou shalt walk uprightly before me, and be perfect" (emphasis added). This seems a most appropriate place to conclude.

SUMMARY

In summary, to gain insights into the book of Genesis, it has been suggested that:
1. Our current book of Moses is taken from JST Genesis.
2. Genesis was given to help raise a benighted people (ancient and modern) from their bondage to a renewed sense of who their creator is, who they are, what their blessings and responsibilities are, and the potential of their divine destiny.
3. Great gospel themes are better clarified in JST Genesis.
4. It provides many unique textual contributions.
5. There are extra-textual sources available to give us additional insights.

However, the search of the dedicated student or teacher will not end here. He will continue to look for valuable insights wherever they may be found, and be persuaded that the most valuable commentary on the scriptures are the scriptures themselves (e.g., Lehi on the fall of Adam, Alma on the tree of life, Paul on a variety of topics relating to the early patriarchs and covenants). Other sources highly relevant to a greater understanding of Genesis include the book of Abraham, *Lectures on Faith,* doctrinal expositions of the First Presidency and the Quorum of the Twelve (e.g., "The Father and the Son"), statements of the First Presidency (e.g., "Origin of Man"), and the sermons and writings of the latter-day prophets (e.g., *Teachings of the Prophet Joseph Smith* and the Conference Reports).

The man who studies Genesis with the aid of the JST is like unto a ship's captain who, while viewing many majestically beautiful icebergs (doctrines) floating in a vast ocean (the everlasting gospel), seeks all the information available (from the standard works and teachings of the modern prophets) as to their true size, shape, and direction. If he applies his knowledge properly, his ship (the good ship *Inspired Interpretation*) will surely sail safely through difficult waters to the blissful shore.

> Blessed Savior, [wilt thou] guide us,
> Till we reach that blissful shore.
> (*Hymns,* no. 188)

George A. Horton, Jr., is associate professor of Ancient Scripture at BYU.

NOTES

1. Joseph Smith, *History of The Church of Jesus Christ of Latter-day Saints,* ed. B. H. Roberts, 7 vols. (Salt Lake City: The Church of Jesus Christ of Latter-day Saints, 1932–51), 1:97.

2. The book of Moses excerpts in the first edition of the Pearl of Great Price (1851) were taken from the *Evening and Morning Star* and the *Times and Seasons.*

3. "The Earth and Man," 9 August 1931. Reprinted in *Deseret News,* 12 November 1931.

4. Joseph Fielding Smith, *Doctrines of Salvation,* 3 vols. (Salt Lake City: Bookcraft, 1954–56), 1:27; "The Father and the Son: Doctrinal Exposition of the First Presidency and Quorum of Twelve," June 30, 1916, quoted in Talmage, *Articles of Faith,* pp. 465–73.

5. James Strong, *The Exhaustive Concordance of the Bible* (Nashville, Tenn.: Abingdon Press, 1955).

6. *The Interpreter's One Volume Commentary on the Bible* (Nashville, Tenn.: Abingdon Press, 1971), p. 7.

7. Ibid.

8. S. Kent Brown, "The Joseph Smith Translation of the Bible: A Panel," in *Scriptures for the Modern World,* ed. Paul R. Cheesman and C. Wilfred Griggs (Salt Lake City: Bookcraft, 1984), pp. 81–83.

9. *The Interpreter's One Volume Commentary on the Bible,* p. 6.

10. C. F. Keil and F. Delitzsch, *Biblical Commentary on the Old Testament,* 25 vols. (Grand Rapids, Mich.: Wm. G. Eerdmans Publishing Company, n.d.), 1:116.

11. *"A Plainer Translation": Joseph Smith's Translation of the Bible, A History and Commentary* (Provo, Utah: Brigham Young University Press, 1975), p. 257; also cf. D&C 76:15ff.

12. Ibid.

4

Insights into Exodus, Leviticus, Numbers, and Deuteronomy

George A. Horton, Jr.

Some years ago a prominent clergyman said, "Were a parchment discovered in an Egyptian mound, six inches square, containing fifty words which were certainly spoken by Jesus, this utterance would count more than all the books which have been published since the first century."[1] If that is so, how great would be the worth of not just fifty, or even a hundred, but several thousand words coming by revelation from the Lord Jesus Christ to a modern prophet.

Is it not true that we have just that in the restored verses of scripture in the Joseph Smith Translation of the Bible? To what degree have we treasured these inspired words and recognized them for what they are?

Recently, university students in some sections of Religion 301 (i.e., Genesis through 2 Samuel) were instructed that the King James Version, LDS Edition was the text for the class and that no other Bible would be acceptable.

A couple of weeks into the semester I noticed that one very good student continued to bring her old Bible to class. It soon became apparent that she was by far the best scripturalist in the group. She had filled a mission while her father had served as mission president, and she was highly imbued with the gospel and a love for the scriptures. Her margins were filled with notes and many verses were carefully marked.

I was determined to persuade her that she should get a new Bible, but no calculated encouragement seemed to have any effect on her. She seldom made comments during class, but would come up to the desk at the end of almost every period with a series of questions. On the day we discussed the latter part of Exodus, as the class left the room, she came to the front, waited her turn, and then opened her book on the desk.

"See right here," she said pointing to Exodus 33:18, "Moses asked the Lord to 'show me thy glory' and then on down here in verse 20 the Lord replies, 'Thou canst not see my face: for there shall no man see me, and live.' Now since we claim that Joseph Smith saw God and lived, how do we explain that verse?"

CAN A MAN SEE GOD AND LIVE?

I felt that this was an opportunity to demonstrate the value of the KJV, LDS Edition, so I opened my Bible and placed it on the desk alongside hers.

"See the footnote to that part of the verse that says no man can see God; it refers us to Moses 1:11, which as you know is part of the Joseph Smith Translation." So we turned to Moses' account where he "saw God face to face, and he talked with him, and the glory of god was upon Moses; therefore Moses could endure his presence" (JST Genesis [preface] A revelation, verse 2/Moses 1:2). Then Moses explains: "But now mine own eyes have beheld God; but not my natural, but my spiritual eyes, for my natural eyes could not have beheld; for I should have withered and died in his presence; but his glory was upon me; and I beheld his face, for I was transfigured before him" (JST Genesis, [preface] A revelation, verse 7; Moses 1:11).

"Now let us look at the next cross-reference which refers us to the JST Ex. 33:20 (Appendix), which is to be found just following the Bible Dictionary in the KJV, LDS Edition. It reads, 'And he said *unto* Moses, Thou canst not see my face *at this time, lest mine anger be kindled against thee also, and I destroy thee, and thy people;* for there shall no man *among them* see me *at this time,* and live, *for they are exceeding sinful. And no sinful man hath at any time, neither shall there be any sinful man at any time, that shall see my face and live.*'

"With regard to the question of whether any man has seen the Lord and lived, let's also look at this cross-reference from Exodus 33:20 which refers us to the Topical Guide subject 'God, Privilege of Seeing.' Notice all of the scriptural instances when a man has seen God and lived. They include the great patriarch Jacob, the nobles of the children of Israel, Moses, Solomon, Isaiah, Nephi and his brother Jacob, King Lamoni, brother of Jared, Joseph Smith, Sidney Rigdon, Oliver Cowdery, Enoch, Abraham, and perhaps many others."

"Well," she said, "I had noticed earlier in chapter 33 that it says, 'And the Lord spake unto Moses face to face, as a man speaketh unto his friend' (Exodus 33:11), and that is another reason why I was a little confused. Anyway, what about these verses over here?" she continued as she pointed to verses 22–23. "'And it shall come to pass, while my glory passeth by, that I will put thee in a clift of the rock, and will cover thee with my hand while I pass by: And I will take away mine hand, and thou shalt see my back parts: but my face shall not be seen.'"

Again we followed the little superscript "c" to the bottom of the page where, following the words "my face shall not be seen" was added *"as at other times; for I am angry with my people Israel"* (JST Exodus 33:23). "Wow!" she said softly. "That makes more sense doesn't it! The scriptures really don't contradict themselves do they? I really like the way the JST clarifies things, and it also means that Joseph Smith's vision of the Father and the Son is in perfect harmony with Moses' experience, doesn't it?"

Without waiting for a response to her question, she pointed to the next chapter. "You remember that Moses smashed the first set of commandments because the people were having a wild party when he came down off the mount. Right here it says, 'And the Lord said unto Moses, Hew thee two tables of stone like unto the first: and I will write upon these tables the words that were in the first tables which thou brakest' (Exodus 34:1). Somewhere in the back of my mind, I have a vague recollection that we Mormons don't believe that is exactly right, but I don't know where to look it up."

WAS THERE A DIFFERENCE BETWEEN THE FIRST AND THE SECOND SETS OF TABLETS?

Again I ran my finger down to the footnotes and cross-references. When her eyes focused on JST Ex. 34:1-2 (Appendix), she sort of whispered to herself, "I should have guessed it." So we read the following: "And the Lord said unto Moses, Hew thee *two other* tables of stone, like unto the first, and I will write upon them also, the words *of the law, according as they were written at the first* on the tables which thou brakest; *but it shall not be according to the first, for I will take away the priesthood out of their midst; therefore my holy order, and the ordinances thereof, shall not go before them; for my presence shall not go up in their midst, lest I destroy them. But I will give unto them the law as at the first, but it shall be after the law of a carnal commandment; for I have sworn in my wrath, that they shall not enter into my presence, into my rest, in the days of their pilgrimage.*"

It was apparent that she was now recognizing the value of the new KJV, LDS Edition and one of its greatest assets—the addition of over six hundred verses of the Joseph Smith Translation to the footnotes and appendix plus references to the book of Moses. Looking over at my book she pointed to the other cross-references related to Exodus 34:1 and said, "Do those others have any exciting additions?"

"Let's look at Deuteronomy 10:1 and its JST footnote. It says about the same thing but in slightly different words: 'And I will write on the tables the words that were in the first tables which thou brakest, *save the words of the everlasting covenant of the holy priesthood.*' Maybe President John Taylor had reference to the inspired revision when he said: 'The first tables of stone, we are informed by the *inspired translators,* contained not only many instructions for the government of the people, but revelations containing the gospel of the Son of God; the principles of the higher law, that were calculated to cause all who obeyed the same, to enter into his rest, which rest was the fulness of his glory.' "[2] Elder Orson Pratt further explained: 'The first law, the higher law of the gospel, contained on the first tables, was destroyed and the covenant broken, and a new law introduced. Incorporated on the second tables . . . were the ten commandments, which pertain to the gospel, which were also on the first tables. In addition to these ten commandments which pertain to the gospel, were many of those carnal laws. . . . By this second code of laws, it was impossible for Israel to enter into the fulness of celestial glory, in other words, they could not be redeemed and brought into the presence of the Father and the Son, they could not enter into the fulness of that rest that was intended to be given to such only as obeyed the higher law of the gospel.' "[3]

This fine student still had several other questions, all except one of which could be answered through the study aids in the KJV, LDS Edition. She was beginning to appreciate what a valuable resource was available in this edition with more than six hundred footnotes to the Joseph Smith Translation.

HOW MUCH REVISION DID JOSEPH DO IN THE PENTATEUCH?

The major changes and additions in the Old Testament were made largely in the book of Genesis. The revelation which appears as introductory to JST Genesis contains twenty-five verses (divided into forty-two in the book of Moses and designated as chapter 1). There are about two hundred verses added or changed in JST Genesis from the common Genesis account. Exodus is next with about sixty-six changes, while Leviticus has six, Numbers has two, and Deuteronomy has seven.

In determining the number of changes, one cannot assume that all differences between the Joseph Smith Translation and the present King James Version are a result of Joseph Smith's revision. This is one of the errors made in the parallel column edition published by Herald Publishing House,[4] otherwise, a fine study tool. A search of H. & E. Phinney's 1828 edition of the Bible[5] used by the Prophet reveals that what at first seem to be JST changes are actually changes in various editions of the King James Version. For example, both the JST and the Phinney edition read "a" at least nineteen times in certain places in the book of Leviticus where the current KJV reads "an." A few other examples of changes that have taken place in the King James Version itself include: "of" to "from," "which" to "where," "am" to "is," "be" to "are," and "to" to "unto."

However, the change of "wot" to "know" (e.g., Exodus 32:1 and Leviticus 22:6) which appears as if it fits in the same category, is actually a JST change.

There are also some spelling changes in the King James Version. An example would be the change from "aught" to "ought" (Exodus 5:11).

For the remainder of this discussion, let us consider some other important questions that are relevant to the quest for insights into the study of Exodus, Leviticus, Numbers, and Deuteronomy:

Who knew the sacred name of Jehovah?
Who hardened Pharaoh's heart?
What other verses have significant changes?
Why "seek ye the priesthood also"?
What insights come from related extra-textual sources?

WHO KNEW THE SACRED NAME OF JEHOVAH?

The casual reader of the Old Testament might easily conclude that for about the first twenty-five hundred years of earthly history (from the fall of Adam to the time of Moses), men did not know the Lord God by his name of Jehovah. This is occasioned by at least two factors.

First, at the time of Moses' confrontation with the Pharaoh of Egypt, the Authorized Version reads, "God spake unto Moses, and said unto him, I am the Lord: And I appeared unto Abraham, unto Isaac, and unto Jacob, by the name of God Almighty, but by my name JEHOVAH was I not known to them" (Exodus 6:1–3).

Second, as you are undoubtedly aware, the King James translators translated the Hebrew tetragrammaton (JHVH or YHWH) to read LORD (i.e., large capital *L* and small capitals *ORD*), and thus it appears throughout the Old Testament 6,823 times (see preface to New World Translation of the Hebrew Scriptures, 1:21). There are a number of additional places where it has been translated to read *God* (Elohim) or *Lord* (Adonai). It appears that the translators did this in deference to the tradition which grew up among the Hebrews that it was sacrilegious to utter the sacred name of Jehovah. The Jews through the centuries have generally substituted the word *Adonai* or a similar appellation.

Whatever the reasons, the King James translators only rendered the sacred name to read *Jehovah* instead of *Lord* in the Old Testament four times (Exodus 6:3; Psalms 83:18; Isaiah 12:2 and 26:4; it also appears at Psalms 68:4 in its shortened form as JAH). Therefore, a student of the scripture could study the Bible diligently for years, and perhaps never realize that, in a sense, beginning with Genesis 2:4, the name *Jehovah* appears in the text on almost every page. Knowing this, it would be obvious that contrary to what it says in Exodus 6:3, the patriarchs from Adam to Moses did know Jehovah by his name. It was Jehovah who "made the earth and the heavens" (Genesis 2:4); it was Jehovah who warned Noah of the impending flood; it was Jehovah who allowed men to be scattered at the time of the tower of Babel; it was Jehovah who instructed Abram to move from Chaldea to Canaan (cf. Abraham 1:16; 2:8); it was Jehovah who revealed that Jacob was to receive the birthright and have his name changed to Israel; and it was Jehovah who was "with Joseph" when he was made "ruler over all the land of Egypt" (Genesis 41:43).

If the "Almighty God" (Genesis 17:1) who appeared unto Abraham is actually the Lord God Jehovah, what can possibly be made out of the Exodus reference which indicates that "but by my name JEHOVAH was I not known to them" (Exodus 6:3)? Fortunately, the JST corrects the problem by making the statement into a question: "And I appeared unto Abraham, unto Isaac, and unto Jacob. *I am the Lord God Almighty; the Lord JEHOVAH. And was not my name* known *unto* them?" (JST Exodus 6:3).

Another JST reference that reinforces the fact that they knew the name of the Lord reads, "For thou shalt worship no other god; for the Lord, whose name is *Jehovah,* is a jealous God" (JST Exodus 34:14).

The foregoing throws a flood of light on the scriptures—helping us realize that Jehovah, the preexistent Lord Jesus Christ, was the God who spoke with and through the great prophets and patriarchs of the Old Testament. As the prophet Isaiah so clearly informs us: "I, even I, am the Lord [i.e., Jehovah]; and beside me there is no saviour" (43:11). "Thus saith the Lord [i.e., Jehovah], your redeemer, the Holy One of Israel . . . the creator of Israel, your King" (43:14–15). All of which remind us of, "For unto us a child is born, unto us a son is given: and the government shall be upon his shoulder: and his name shall be called Wonderful, Counsellor, The mighty God, The everlasting Father, The Prince of Peace" (9:6).

WHO HARDENED THE PHARAOH'S HEART?

Many Old Testament scripture students have long been puzzled by the notion prompted by the King James Version that the Lord God Jehovah called the Midian shepherd Moses to go bring the children of Israel out of Egypt from their long bondage, and no sooner was Moses persuaded to go than the Lord promptly announced, "When thou goest to return into Egypt, see that thou do all those wonders before Pharaoh, which I have put in thine hand: but I will harden his heart, that he shall not let the people go" (Exodus 4:21). And again, "I will harden Pharaoh's heart . . ." (Exodus 7:3). That this intent is actually carried out is reflected when the text indicates that the Lord "hardened Pharaoh's heart, that he hearkened not . . . [and refused] to let the people go" (Exodus 7:13–14). Not only does the Lord seem to do this once, but as Moses pleads, coaxes, and threatens the Pharaoh, the Lord seems to do the same thing seven more times (see Exodus 9:12; 10:1, 20, 27; 11:10; 14:8, 17). As the text reads, "And the Lord hardened the heart of Pharaoh and he hearkened not unto them" (Exodus 9:12).

Opinions among scholars seem to be divided on the implications of these passages. Many seem to feel that it is the Lord's intent to make the task so difficult for Moses that when the

Pharaoh finally lets Israel go, all Israel will know that it is because of the hand of the Lord in their behalf.[6] By this they will know that he is the Mighty God of Israel to whom they owe their freedom from slavery and their redemption. Others, such as Adam Clarke, feel that the text is faulty. He points out that the same words in the Hebrew text used here were also translated "And the heart of Pharaoh was hardened" in Exodus 7:22. Therefore they should be translated the same here, "lest the *hardening*, which was evidently the effect of his own obstinate shutting of his eyes against the truth, should be attributed to God.'"[7] Still other commentaries are completely silent and do not attempt to explain the implications of the passages.[8]

In the King James text, the behavior of the Lord seems to be slightly inconsistent with his attributes and character as reflected in other parts of holy writ. However, a student's suspicion about the passage is not completely without a clue in the Authorized Version, because there are places where it clearly indicates that on occasion the Pharaoh hardened his own heart (e.g., Exodus 8:32; 9:34) or simply that his heart was hardened without attributing it to any outside source (e.g., Exodus 7:14, 22).

The JST reports, "And *Pharaoh* hardened his heart, that he hearkened not unto them" (Exodus 7:13). In fact, the translation is corrected systematically in all nine occurrences in this particular context (cf. JST Exodus 4:21; 7:13; 9:12; 10:1, 20, 27; 11:10; 14:8, 17).

We are left to wonder how many people, because of such passages as this, and others that are similar dealing with causality in life, ascribe actions and responsibility to the Lord that are clearly the result of men exercising their own agency?

WHAT OTHER VERSES HAVE SIGNIFICANT CHANGES?

In the following examples, the JST versification is the same as the KJV unless otherwise specified.

Corrections in the Book of Exodus

The following are not all-inclusive (there being about sixty-six), but these indicate some of the more interesting changes:

1. Exodus 3:2. The "angel of the Lord" who appeared at the burning bush is changed to read "the *presence* of the Lord" which makes the entire conversation that follows with Jehovah (I Am) much more comprehensible.

2. Exodus 5:4. The JST strengthens the Pharaoh's charge from "Wherefore do ye, Moses and Aaron, let the people from their works?" to "Wherefore do ye, Moses and Aaron, *lead* the people from their works?"

3. Exodus 6:30. We are often perplexed by the seeming difference between Stephen's assertion that Moses was "mighty in words" (Acts 7:22) and Moses' own response to his call, "Oh my Lord, I am not eloquent, neither heretofore, nor since thou hast spoken unto thy servant: but I am slow of speech, and of a slow tongue" (Exodus 4:10). A significant insight comes when the JST clarifies another Moses statement that "I am of uncircumcized lips," by rendering it to read "I am of stammering lips, and slow of speech" (JST Exodus 6:29).

4. Exodus 7:1. This passage has Moses becoming "a god to Pharaoh: and Aaron thy brother shall be thy prophet." It is corrected in the JST to read "I have made thee a *prophet* to Pharaoh: and Aaron thy brother shall be thy *spokesman*."

5. Exodus 12:37. The JST simply adds the fact that there were *women* in addition to the six hundred thousand men plus children.

6. Exodus 14:20. The antecedents to *them* and *these* are plainly clarified to be first the Egyptians and in the latter case the Israelites. To the former, what came up before them was a cloud of darkness, but to the Israelites it gave light by night.

7. Exodus 21:20. In the JST, the penalty for murdering a servant is designated as *death,* rather than merely punishment.

8. Exodus 22:18. It is not a "witch" who shall be put to death, but "Thou shalt not suffer a *murderer* to live."

9. Exodus 22:28. "Revile the gods" is corrected to read "Thou shalt not revile *against God.*"

10. Exodus 23:3. The King James text gives us a shock in saying, "Neither shalt thou countenance a poor man in his cause," but fortunately it is a *wicked* man that shalt not be countenanced.

11. Exodus 32:12. Moses takes the Lord to task for his judg-

ments upon Israel, and boldly says, "Turn from thy fierce wrath, and repent of this evil against thy people." Doesn't this seem a little presumptuous for mortal man, prophet or no prophet, to be demanding of the Lord, maker of heaven and earth? The JST corrects it to read, "Turn from thy fierce wrath. *Thy people will* repent of this evil: *therefore come thou not out against them.*"

12. Exodus 32:14. Continuing the thought, the text reads, "And the Lord repented of the evil which he thought to do." What a revolting thought to consider that a perfect God would entertain such evil thoughts that it would be necessary for him to repent. Does that suggest that he could make other mistakes? Heaven forbid! Did not Moses say in other places, "God is not a man, that he should lie; neither the son of man, that he should repent" (Numbers 23:19), and "his work is perfect: for all his ways . . . are without iniquity, just and right" (Deuteronomy 32:4). The inspired revision says, *"And the Lord said unto Moses, If they will repent of the evil which they have done, I will spare them, and turn away my fierce wrath; but, behold, thou shalt execute judgment upon all that will not repent of this evil this day. Therefore, see thou do this thing that I have commanded thee, or I will execute all that which I had* thought to do unto *my* people." (JST Exodus 32:14). Alas, it is men who always have need of repentance.

13. Exodus 32:35. It sounds as if the plagues came on the people not just because they asked for the golden calf, but more particularly because they *worshipped* the calf.

Corrections in the Book of Leviticus:

The basic changes are as follows:

1. Leviticus 12:3–5. There are corrections in these three verses which seem euphemistic. That is, the changes appear to be made in order to read more comfortably in a puritan society. In verse 3, there is a change from "the flesh of his foreskin shall be circumcized" to "the *man child* shall be circumcized." In verses 4 and 5, there is a change from "the blood of her purifying" to "the *time* of her purifying." There is probably no objective way of knowing whether these changes were the Prophet's idea, or whether they came from the Lord.

2. Leviticus 21:1. "There shall none be defiled for the dead" to "There shall none be defiled *with* the dead."

3. Leviticus 21:11. A clarifying word is added in this verse: "Neither shall he go in to *touch* any dead body."

Corrections in the Book of Numbers:

This book contains only two changes:

1. Number 16:10. Discussed hereafter in the section on "Seek Ye the Priesthood Also."

2. Numbers 22:20–22. A strange paradox exists in the Authorized Version. Balaam is being harassed with pleadings and lucrative bribes to curse the advancing Israelites coming into the land of Moab. King Balak sends his emissaries to further persuade Balaam. Then God instructs Balaam, "If the men come to call thee, rise up, and go with them," and then when Balaam does just that the text says, "And God's anger was kindled because he went." Does God vacillate? The corrected version reads, "If the men come to call thee, rise up *if thou wilt,* and go with them; but yet the word which I shall say unto thee, that shalt thou do."

Corrections in the Book of Deuteronomy:

The changes are as follows:

1. Deuteronomy 2:30. KJV reads, "But Sihon king of Heshbon would not let us pass by him: for the Lord thy God hardened his spirit, and made his heart obstinate." The correction here is reminiscent of several Exodus passages. As corrected it reads, "But Sihon king of Heshbon would not let us pass by him: for *he* hardened his spirit."

2. Deuteronomy 10:2. Discussed earlier, in the section dealing with the first and second sets of tablets.

3. Deuteronomy 14:21. This passage gives the impression the Lord has a double standard—one for Israel and another for strangers. "Ye shall not eat of any thing that dieth of itself; thou shalt give it unto the stranger . . . or thou mayest sell it unto an alien" is corrected to read, "Ye shall not eat of anything that dieth of itself; thou shalt *not* give it unto the stranger . . . or thou mayest *not* sell it unto an alien."

4. Deuteronomy 16:22. The JST qualifies the kind of image set up. "Neither shalt thou set thee up any *graven* image; which the Lord thy God hateth."

5. Deuteronomy 34:6. What happened to Moses at the time of his death has been the subject of some speculation. The scripture says, "And he buried him in a valley in the land of Moab, over against Beth-peor: but no man knoweth of his sepulchre unto this day." From statements by ancient and modern prophets, it is clear that Moses was translated. In speaking of Alma it was said, "He was taken up by the Spirit, or buried by the hand of the Lord, even as Moses" (Alma 45:19). Maybe the following from the JST hints more strongly in that direction. *"For the Lord took him unto his fathers"* (JST Deuteronomy 34:6). Josephus also lends credence to the idea of translation, saying, "As he was going to embrace Eleazar and Joshua, and was still discoursing with them, a cloud stood over him on the sudden, and he disappeared in a certain valley, although he wrote in the holy books that he died, which was done out of fear, lest they should venture to say that, because of his extraordinary virtue, he went to God."[9]

SEEK YE THE PRIESTHOOD ALSO?

During the long Israelite sojourn in the wilderness of Paran, times had been hard. Moses had sought for assistance and the Lord responded by calling "seventy men of the elders of Israel" (Numbers 11:10–16), and placed upon them the spirit that was upon Moses.

Not long after this time Korah, who was a Levite (but not of Aaron), and two Reubenites, led 250 leaders of Israel in a rebellion against Moses, charging that he and Aaron "take too much upon you, seeing all the congregation are holy . . . [why] lift ye up yourselves above the congregation" (Numbers 16:3). In his rebuke to Korah and the sons of Levi among the group, Moses says, "Seemeth it but a small thing unto you, that the God of Israel hath separated you from the congregation . . . to bring you near himself to do the service of the tabernacle . . . and to stand before the congregation to minister unto them . . . and seek ye the priesthood also?" (Numbers 16:9–10).

Bible scholars have puzzled over this statement because the Levites in the group already held the Levitical Priesthood which the Lord had restricted to their tribe only. Some have guessed that the group was trying to get the same authority held by the sons of Aaron or Aaron himself,[10] but they have also felt that the problem was in their timing (i.e., it was premature). Others have guessed, "What else was this but the first foregleam of the universal priesthood of all believers,"[11] which they thought would be forthcoming in the Christian dispensation.

We remind ourselves that the higher or Melchizedek Priesthood and its ordinances were taken from the people generally, at the time of the second set of tablets, and was no longer widely available to the Israelites (JST Exodus 34:2; JST Deuteronomy 10:1). Nevertheless, the JST rendering of Numbers 16:10 provides an insight into what the group was seeking after: "And he hath brought thee near to him [the Lord], and all thy brethren the sons of Levi with thee; and seek ye the *high* priesthood also?"

Since there was to be only one high priest, and since many of this group already held the Levitical Priesthood, this seems like a direct reference to the fact they were seeking the higher or Melchizedek Priesthood. This makes sense because this would also accommodate the non-Levites who were part of the group.

Another valuable change in the text is found at Exodus 18:1, which in the Authorized Version refers to "Jethro, the priest of Midian." The correction in the JST is enlightening when we find that Jethro is "the *high* priest." This reference cannot possibly be to the office held by Aaron which was to be in the tribe of Levi only, but for Jethro, who was not a descendant of Jacob, it must have reference to the higher or Melchizedek Priesthood. This strongly suggests there were others living during this period who held the Melchizedek Priesthood. The affirmation of this brings us to another area where one can gain insights into the priesthood during the period of the Pentateuch.

WHAT RELATED EXTRA-TEXTUAL SOURCES ARE AVAILABLE?

As has been suggested before,[12] as the Prophet Joseph worked on the inspired revision, he often inquired of the Lord about the matter he was pondering and received revelations that are integrally related to the Bible—in other words, they could be looked upon as an *extension* of the biblical text. He worked on the books of Exodus, Leviticus, Numbers, and Deuteronomy during the period of 20 July to 22 September 1832. Is it any surprise that he should receive a revelation on priesthood lineage and other matters pertaining to Moses that is dated 22 and 23 September 1832? The Lord speaks of the gathering in the last days and then adds: "For verily this generation shall not all pass away until an house shall be built unto the Lord, and a cloud shall rest upon it, which cloud shall be even the glory of the Lord, which shall fill the house. And the sons of Moses, according to the Holy Priesthood which he received under the hand of his father-in-law, Jethro." (D&C 84:5-6.) Jethro's priesthood line is then traced all the way back to Adam.

Continuing on, the Lord says, "And this greater priesthood administereth the gospel and holdeth the key of the mysteries of the kingdom, even the key of the knowledge of God. Therefore, in the ordinances thereof, the power of godliness is manifest. And without the ordinances thereof, and the authority of the priesthood, the power of godliness is not manifest unto men in the flesh; For without this no man can see the face of God, even the Father, and live. Now this Moses plainly taught to the children of Israel in the wilderness, and sought diligently to sanctify his people that they might behold the face of God; But they hardened their hearts and could not endure his presence; therefore, the Lord in his wrath, for his anger was kindled against them, swore that they should not enter into his rest while in the wilderness, which rest is the fulness of his glory. Therefore, he took Moses out of their midst, and the Holy Priesthood also." (D&C 84:19-25.) This valuable insight is not clearly stated in the Authorized Version of the Old Testament. Neither are some of the related priesthood duties; for example, "And the lesser priesthood continued, which priesthood holdeth the key of the ministering of angels and the preparatory gospel; Which gospel is the gospel of repentance and of baptism, and the remission of sins, and the law of carnal commandments, which the Lord in his wrath caused to continue with the house of Aaron among the children of Israel until John." (D&C 84:26-27.)

While searching for insights in the books from Exodus through Deuteronomy, we might ask whether it is possible that the apostle Paul also, not unlike Joseph Smith in this respect, received some of his revelations while studying the Old Testament record? Paul gives us great insights on the Mosaic period, particularly in Hebrews chapters 3–5 and 7–11. Consider his comment, "If therefore perfection were by the Levitical priesthood, (for under it the people received the law,) what further need was there that another priest should rise after the order of Melchisedec, and not be called after the order of Aaron?" (Hebrews 7:11). He reminds us that the law of Moses gave forth "patterns," "figures," and was "a shadow of good things to come," namely, Jesus Christ, who would be the sacrifice to "bear the sins of many" (Hebrews 9:23–24, 28; 10:1).

SUMMARY

It has been suggested that although the combined JST changes in Exodus through Deuteronomy are less than half those in Genesis, they still provide many useful insights, such as:

1. Mortal man, under certain conditions, can see God and live.

2. Ancient Israel had the full gospel law (cf. Hebrews 3:8; 4:2), the Melchizedek Priesthood, and the higher ordinances associated with it until they forfeited their rights through disobedience.

3. Perhaps they knew the Melchizedek Priesthood had been taken generally, and was only retained by the prophets. In any event, these rebellious Israelites complained because they did not have power and authority like that of Moses.

4. The Lord Jesus Christ was known to the early patriarchs from the time of Adam by his name Jehovah.

5. If a man's heart is hardened, it is the man, not the Lord that is responsible for the condition.

6. A wide variety of small but significant changes add to the internal consistency of the biblical account.

7. There are related extra-textual sources available which provide further insights into the books of Moses.

In conclusion, if we were to hear of a new discovery of even a few authentic words of our Lord Jesus Christ, how much effort would we make to find out what they say? Would it matter whether they came from an Egyptian mound or ancient parchment? If we knew that the Lord prompted a prophet to make even one change in the scriptures (let alone hundreds), to what lengths would we go to find out what it was? Wouldn't we want to know why it was significant enough to warrant a change? The sum and substance of the whole matter is—we ought to consider every JST change as a valuable treasure waiting to be discovered.

Should we not enthusiastically search the scriptures, compare the corrections, seek the Spirit, and ponder the words of the modern prophets, that we may continue to gain greater insights not only into Exodus, Leviticus, Numbers, and Deuteronomy, but into all the words the Lord has seen fit to give for our instruction, blessing, and eternal salvation?

George A. Horton, Jr., is associate professor of Ancient Scripture at BYU.

NOTES

1. Charles A. Callis, *Fundamentals of Religion* (Independence, Mo.: Zion's Printing and Publishing Co., 1945), p. 155.

2. *Journal of Discourses,* 26 vols. (London: Latter-day Saints' Book Depot, 1855–56), 16:152 (emphasis added).

3. Ibid., 15:69.

4. *Joseph Smith's "New Translation" of the Bible* (Independence, Mo.: Herald Publishing House, 1970).

5. H. & E. Phinney's Stereotype Edition, *The Holy Bible, Containing the Old and New Testaments Together with the Apocrypha* (Cooperstown, N.Y.: H. & E. Phinney, 1828).

6. *The Interpreter's One Volume Commentary on the Bible,* (Nashville, Tenn.: Abingdon Press, 1955), p. 493.

7. *The Holy Bible Containing the Old and New Testaments with*

a Commentary and Critical Notes (Nashville, Tenn.: Abingdon Press, n.d.), 1:324.

8. *The Interpreter's One Volume Commentary on the Bible,* pp. 40-45.

9. Flavius Josephus, *Josephus' Complete Works,* trans. William Whiston (Grand Rapids, Mich.: Kregel Publications, 1970), Antiquities 4:8:48.

10. C. F. Keil and F. Delitzsch, *Biblical Commentary on the Old Testament,* 25 vols. (Grand Rapids, Mich.: Wm. B. Eerdmans Publishing Company, n.d.), 3:99.

11. *The Interpreter's Bible,* 12 vols. (Nashville, Tenn.: Abingdon Press, 1953), 2:221.

12. Robert J. Matthews, *"A Plainer Translation": Joseph Smith's Translation of the Bible, A History and Commentary* (Provo, Utah: Brigham Young University Press, 1975), p. 257.

5

The Contribution of the JST to the Old Testament Historical Books

Monte S. Nyman

The Prophet Joseph Smith apparently did not work extensively on the historical books of the Bible. This may sound contradictory when it is known that ninety-four verses have been changed in the twelve books under consideration. However, sixty-seven of those ninety-four verses are in three of the twelve books: twenty-four in 1 Kings, twenty-one in 2 Chronicles, and twenty-two in Nehemiah. Another book, 1 Samuel, has fourteen changes, making eighty-one of the ninety-four verse changes in only four of the twelve books. The other eight books have only thirteen verses changed: 2 Kings has five verses changed, 1 Chronicles and 2 Samuel each have three verses changed. Joshua and Judges have only one verse changed in each, and Ruth, Ezra, and Esther have no changes.

A closer examination shows that the Prophet focused on specific passages within each book and also dealt with a variety of subjects. Of the fourteen verses changed in 1 Samuel, eight are in chapters 15, 16, 18, and 19, and are concerned with only two subjects. The other six changes, all in chapter 28, relate to a single incident. Of the twenty-four verses changed in 1 Kings, eleven are in chapter 3 and the other thirteen verses (in chapters 11, 13, 14 and 15) all relate to the same topic. Of the twenty-two verses changed in Nehemiah, all but four are in chapter 7 and are about the numbers of children in the various families returning from Babylon. The other book containing a large number of verses changed, 2 Chronicles with twenty-one, has more diversity in the types of changes than any of the other historical books, although thirteen of these changes are contained within three chapters. An analysis of each book will disclose the subjects or the incidents which the Prophet corrected or restored. These will here be followed in chronological order rather than by subject.

TRUE ATTRIBUTES OF GOD

The only change in the book of Joshua is the same kind of change that was made repeatedly in the book of Exodus, concerning the Lord hardening a person's heart (see Exodus 4:21; 7:3; 9:12; 10:1, 20, 27; 11:10). The KJV reads, "For it was of the Lord to harden their hearts, that they should come against Israel in battle, that he might destroy them utterly" (Joshua 11:20). The Prophet changed it to read, "For it was of the Lord to *destroy them utterly because they hardened their hearts.*" The context of the verse is Joshua's making war with the inhabitants of the land of Canaan to drive them out as the Lord had commanded. The change shows that it was the *people* who had hardened their hearts and not the Lord. The rest of the verse in the JST is primarily a rearrangement of the phrases, and shows that the reason the Lord commanded them to be driven out was that they had hardened their hearts and come against Israel in battle.

Since this is the only change in the entire book of Joshua, it seems that the Prophet Joseph's attention was drawn to this verse because it deals with the Lord hardening people's hearts. The concept taught in the change which he made in Joshua, however, is different from the concept taught in Exodus. The purpose in Exodus was to clarify the translation of a Hebrew word. The word *chazak* means to be firm or strong. In the Lord's firmness with Pharaoh, he indirectly hardened Pharaoh's heart but it was still the Pharaoh's own choosing. In the words of Brigham Young and Willard Richards, "He [the Lord] manifested Himself in so many glorious and mighty ways, that Pharaoh could not resist the truth without becoming harder."[1] Joseph Smith's role as the Prophet was to make certain the people understood the passage correctly. He apparently made the changes in Exodus to make certain of this. While these changes in Exodus seemingly drew his attention to the verse in Joshua, the change in Joshua corrected the historical record of the people's condition. This further illustrates the role of the Prophet and the diversity evident in his work of translation.

The single change in Judges is another example of previous changes probably drawing the Prophet's attention to this verse. The KJV reads, "For it repented the Lord because of their groanings" (Judges 2:18). In the JST this verse reads, *"For the Lord hearkened* because of their groanings." The Prophet had made several changes in the books of Genesis and Exodus showing that it was the people who repented and not the Lord (see Genesis 6:6; Exodus 32:12, 14). The change in Judges illustrates a change in the Lord's actions based on the condition of the people. This too is a problem of the meaning of the Hebrew word. To repent is to change one's pattern, but repentance also denotes a previous erroneous action. The Lord had indeed changed his pattern, but his previous course had not been erroneous; his decision to "hearken" to the people was based on a change in their condition. Since the same Hebrew word has both meanings, it is obvious that the translators of the KJV selected the wrong one or were not aware of the alternate meaning. Again the Prophet's change was consistent with gospel principles.

The first changes made in 1 Samuel are in chapter 15. There are two changes in this chapter, but both concern the Lord repenting, as discussed in the previous paragraph. The first change (v. 11) is that Saul did not repent after the Lord had made him king, instead of the Lord repenting because he had made Saul king. The second change (v. 35) is that the Lord rent the kingdom from Saul, instead of the Lord repented because he had made him king. This makes the account historically correct in addition to correcting the false concept of the Lord repenting.

THE RELATIONSHIP OF EVIL SPIRITS AND PROPHETS

There are four verses changed in chapter 16 of 1 Samuel, but all four changes are the same. This is the account of King Saul being bothered by an evil spirit. The KJV calls it "an evil spirit from the Lord." The JST corrects the text to read "an evil spirit *which was not of* the Lord" or *"not of God"* (vv. 14, 15–16, 23). God does not send evil spirits. "All things which are good cometh of God; and that which is evil cometh of the devil" (Moroni 7:12). Chapter 18 (v. 10) and chapter 19 (v. 9) each have the same correction. The Prophet apparently observed the error and followed the account until all of the corrections were made.

Chapter 28 of 1 Samuel is another example of the Prophet correcting a doctrinal concept in a historical account. The account is of Saul visiting the witch of En-dor. There are changes in six of the verses in this chapter. The first change (v. 9) is in the woman's response to Saul's request to call up a familiar spirit. At this point, Saul is not recognized by her and she reminds him that Saul has cut off those who followed such practices; she accuses him of laying a snare to cause her death. The words *"also, who hath not a familiar spirit"* are added, which are her denial of being such a practitioner. After an assurance that such will not happen, the KJV records that the woman called up Samuel. The JST text indicates that *"the words of"* Samuel were called up rather than Samuel himself (vv. 11, 12).

In verse 13 of the KJV the woman says, "I saw gods ascending out of the earth." The JST replaces these words with, "I saw *the words of Samuel ascending out of the earth"* but also adds, *"And she said, I saw Samuel also."* Verse 14 has several words changed but they are not significant; they merely make the text read better. The last change in this chapter (v. 15) is the same as previous ones: *"These are the words of Samuel"* replaces the designation of Samuel speaking to Saul. Obviously, it is easier to deceive through mimicking words than by personal appearances. A further significance of these changes is that God does not operate through false mediums, but the devil will attempt to deceive through a means as close to the true principle as possible. In the words of Joseph Smith, "False prophets always arise to oppose the true prophets and they will prophesy so very near the truth that they will deceive almost the very chosen ones."[2]

LIVES OF DAVID AND SOLOMON

There are only three changes in 2 Samuel. The first is the prophet Nathan's reply to king David when David acknowledged that he had sinned before the Lord (see 2 Samuel 12:13). The KJV represents Nathan as responding, "The Lord also hath put away thy sin; thou shalt not die." The JST changes Nathan's reply to, "The Lord hath *not* put away thy sin *that* thou shalt not die." This change is historically consistent with the rest of the scriptures and many subsequent changes in the JST. That David was to die, as indicated in the JST, should be interpreted as spiritual death; he was not put to death physically as the law required, but was given a worse punishment. He was to live to see his wives live with others and his family turn against him (see 2 Samuel 12:11–12). Only after years of weeping and supplication did David receive the promise that his soul would not be left in hell (see Psalms 16:10; cf. Acts 2:27, 31).[3] His wives were taken from him, which in one sense is a spiritual death—he was not to be in the highest glory of the celestial kingdom. Beyond this, the eternal status of David has not been revealed. The JST change is thus consistent with these teachings.

The other two changes in 2 Samuel are in chapter 24 (vv. 16–17). Verse 16 again deals with the Lord repenting, and the JST changes it to be the people who repented. The phrases of the verse are greatly rearranged but it is primarily to show that the Lord does not repent. The only change in verse 17 is the first word. The KJV uses the word, "*And* David spake unto the Lord," while the JST reads, "*For,* David spake unto the Lord." While this may seem insignificant, a careful reading shows the JST change to be consistent with the rearrangement of the phrases in verse 16. It shows that the reason the Lord told the angel not to destroy Jerusalem was because of David's plea to the Lord.

There are eleven verses changed in chapter 3 of 1 Kings. All eleven of these changes are in the first half of the chapter, the first fourteen verses. They clarify and add to the account of

Solomon's reign as king of Israel. The KJV begins by stating that Solomon made affinity with Pharaoh, king of Egypt, and took Pharaoh's daughter and brought her into the city of David. The JST adds at the beginning of the verse that the Lord was not pleased with Solomon for these acts, and further clarifies that Solomon took the Pharaoh's daughter to wife. It further explains that Solomon brought the Pharaoh's daughter to the *house* of David rather than the *city* of David. The end of the verse adds, *"And the Lord blessed Solomon for the people's sake."* Verse 2 has the first word changed from *only* to *and* which makes verse 2 compatible with the addition to the end of verse 1. In other words, in spite of Solomon's sins, the people deserved to be blessed.

Verse 3 in the KJV states that Solomon loved the Lord. The JST additions show that Solomon's love for the Lord was a growth process as a result of the blessings which the Lord poured out upon Solomon because of the righteousness of the people:

KJV 1 Kings 3:3-4

And Solomon loved the Lord, walking in the statutes of David his father: only he sacrificed and burnt incense in high places.

And the king went to Gibeon to sacrifice there; for that was the great high place: a thousand burnt offerings did Solomon offer upon that altar.

JST 1 Kings 3:3-4

And because the Lord blessed Solomon *as he was* walking in the statutes of David, his father, *he began to love the Lord,* and he sacrificed and burnt incense in high places, *and he called on the name of the Lord.*

And the king went to Gibeon to sacrifice there, for *Gibeon was in a* great high place; *and Solomon offered upon that altar, in Gibeon,* a thousand burnt offerings.

Verse 4 is a further amplification of the ending of verse 3. It shows that the reason why Solomon went to Gibeon to sacrifice was that Gibeon was in a great high place, rather than that it was the great high place as stated in the KJV. This takes away the inference of the worship of Baal. The KJV also states that "in Gibeon, the Lord appeared to Solomon in a dream by night." The JST shows that the Lord's appearance was in response to Solomon's calling upon the name of the Lord, which was added to the end of verse 3. It reads, "And the Lord God hearkened unto Solomon, and appeared...."

Verse 6 has a slight change in the middle of it. The KJV quotes Solomon as recognizing that the Lord has "shewed unto thy servant David my father great mercy, according as he walked before thee in truth." The JST states that David was shown "great *things according to thy mercy when* he walked before thee in truth." This qualifying change shows the true character of David, and also illustrates that blessings are dependent upon obedience to law (see D&C 130:20–21).

Verses 7 and 8 must be treated together, since the JST places the last phrase of verse 7 in the beginning of verse 8. The only other change in verse 7 is the adding of *"over thy people"* to Solomon's declaration that he has been made king instead of David his father. In the KJV, Solomon acknowledges his inexperience before the Lord: "I am but a little child: I know not how to go out or come in. And thy servant is in the midst of thy people." The JST clarifies his words in this manner: "And I know not how *to lead them,* to go out, or come in *before them,* and *I,* Thy servant, *am as a little child,* in the midst of thy people." Again we note a fuller and more sensible treatise, although it is of little consequence doctrinally or historically.

Verse 9 adds just one word so that it reads, "This thy *people,* so great a people," rather than, "This thy so great a people," again, a plainer reading. In verse 12, the change is of a similar nature. The plural KJV *words* is singular in the JST and the KJV "none like thee" is rendered, "none *made king over Israel* like *unto* thee." The last change in this chapter (v. 14) deals with the conditional promise extended to Solomon concerning his kingship, but clarifies or corrects the statement about the character of his father, king David:

KJV 1 Kings 3:14

And if thou wilt walk in my ways, to keep my statutes and my commandments, as thy father David did walk, then I will lengthen thy days.

JST 1 Kings 3:14

And if thou wilt walk in my ways to keep my statutes, and my commandments, then I will lengthen thy days, *and thou shalt not walk in unrighteousness,* as did thy father David.

THE CHARACTER OF DAVID

There are thirteen other verses changed in the book of 1 Kings. Most of these changes concern the character of David, king of Israel and father of Solomon. They are primarily in chapters 11 and 15, with one change in each of chapters 13 and 14. Chapter 11 describes the downfall of king Solomon. Verse 4 in the KJV states, "His heart was not perfect with the Lord his God, as was the heart of David his father." The JST corrects this to say, "His heart was not perfect with the Lord his God, *and it became* as the heart of David his father." Verse 6 reverses the last two phrases, which totally reverses the meaning. The KJV reads, "And Solomon did evil in the sight of the Lord, and went not fully after the Lord, as did David his father." The JST rearrangement is, "And Solomon did evil in the sight of the Lord, as did David his father, and went not fully after the Lord."

The end of the chapter has several changes which also clarify the life of David. Verse 33 in the KJV ends with the same phrase, "as did David his father." The JST makes the same correction as above but also adds another concept, *"And his heart is become as David his father; and he repenteth not* as did David his father, *that I may forgive him."* Verse 34 represents the Lord, through the prophet Ahijah, promising that he will not take the kingdom from Solomon for his servant David's sake, because David kept his commandments. The JST adds *"in that day."* This addition merely qualifies a time period when David kept the commandments and implies that it was not all of his life.

Verse 35 gives a promise to Jeroboam, through Ahijah, that the kingdom will be taken from Solomon and the ten tribes will be given unto him. The JST adds the first line of verse 36 to the end of verse 35, which states that one tribe will be given to Solomon's son. Two other insignificant words are deleted from the rest of the verse. Verse 38 promises blessings to Jeroboam if he will keep the commandments "as David my servant did." The JST adds *"in the day that I blessed him,"* again qualifying a time period when David kept the commandments. Verse 39, which was changed in this chapter, shows why the kingdom was taken away. The KJV says the seed of David will be afflicted but not forever. The JST adds, *"And for the transgression of David, and also for the people, I have rent the kingdom,* and for this I will afflict the seed of David." This places the blame on both the king and the people.

Chapter 13 of 1 Kings has a perplexing story about an old prophet instructing a younger prophet to go against the Lord's instructions. In the KJV, it states that the old prophet lied unto the young prophet. The JST adds an additional phrase showing the purpose of the old prophet's escapade and also adds that the old prophet lied not. He invited the young prophet to return to his house to eat bread and drink water *"that I may prove him, and he lied not."* Chapter 14 has only one change (v. 8) and that change is another concerning the character of David, that "he kept *not* the commandments," thus making this chapter consistent with the changes made in chapters 3 and 11 of 1 Kings.

Chapter 15 also has four verses changed regarding the character of David. In verse 3, the KJV compares king Abijam of Judah with David. It reads, "His heart was not perfect with the Lord his God, as the heart of David his father." The JST modifies the last phrase to read, *"As the Lord commanded* David his father." However, verse 5 in the JST confirms the teachings of the Doctrine and Covenants (132:39) concerning David. It also makes the verse compatible with the period of David's repentance.

KJV 1 Kings 15:5	*JST 1 Kings 15:5*
Because David did that which was right in the eyes of the Lord, and turned not aside from any thing that he commanded him all the days of his life, save only in the matter of Uriah the Hittite.	Because David did right in the eyes of the Lord, and turned not aside from all that he commanded him, *to sin against the Lord; but repented of the evil* all the days of his life, save only in the matter of Uriah the Hittite, *wherein the Lord cursed him.*

Verse 11 concerning Asa, king of Judah, has the same change as verse 3, substituting "as did David his father" with "as *he commanded* David his father." Verse 12 states that Asa removed the idols of the land, and the JST adds *"and it pleased the Lord."* Thus, the primary changes of 1 Kings are concerning the character of David.

STORY-CLARIFYING CHANGES

The book of 2 Kings has five verses changed, but four of these are very insignificant changes. In chapter 1, there are four places in three verses where "from heaven" in the KJV is changed to "*out of* heaven" in the JST. In chapter 8, the KJV "go say unto him" is rendered "*thou wilt* go *and* say unto him." The fifth change is in an amusing story, as worded in the KJV, concerning an angel of the Lord smiting one hundred eighty-five thousand Assyrians. The story is also recorded in chapter 37 of Isaiah. The account ends with the statement, "And when they arose early in the morning, behold, they were all dead corpses" (2 Kings 19:35; Isaiah 37:36). This KJV reading sounds as if it is those who were killed that arose. However, the JST in both the 2 Kings and Isaiah account adds "when they *who were left* arose," showing that it was not those who were killed that arose. We see that the book of 2 Kings has only this one important change, but one that is not doctrinally or historically significant.

The book of 1 Chronicles also was not changed significantly by the Prophet Joseph. There are three changes, all of which are, like those in 2 Kings, word changes to make it more readable. One of these changes, however, also corrects the concept of the Lord repenting:

KJV 1 Chronicles 21:15	*JST 1 Chronicles 21:15*
And God sent an angel unto Jerusalem to destroy it: and as he was destroying, the Lord beheld, and he repented him of the evil, and said to the angel that destroyed, It is enough, stay now thine hand. And the angel of the Lord stood by the threshingfloor of Ornan the Jebusite.	And God sent an angel unto Jerusalem to destroy it. And *the angel stretched forth his hand unto Jerusalem to destroy it;* and God said to the angel, Stay now thine hand, it is enough; for as he was destroying, the *Lord beheld Israel, that he repented him of the evil; therefore the Lord stayed* the angel that destroyed, as he stood by the threshingfloor of Ornan, the Jebusite.

Verse 20 of the same chapter rearranges the phrases to make it more readable and easier to understand the sequence, but does not change the story:

Monte S. Nyman 99

KJV 1 Chronicles 21:20

And Ornan turned back, and saw the angel; and his four sons with him hid themselves. Now Ornan was threshing wheat.

JST 1 Chronicles 21:20

Now Ornan was threshing wheat, and his four sons with him; and Ornan turned back and saw the angel, and they hid themselves.

The book of 2 Chronicles is one of the three books having several changes in the JST. Twenty-one changes are grouped as in other books discussed above. Five verses are changed in chapter 2. All of these changes concern Solomon's building a house unto the Lord, but they are of little significance other than making the text more readable. Chapter 18, however, has three significant changes which not only correct the story historically but doctrinally as well:

KJV 2 Chronicles 18:20–22

Then there came out a spirit, and stood before the Lord, and said, I will entice him. And the Lord said unto him, Wherewith?

And he said, I will go out, and be a lying spirit in the mouth of all his prophets. And the Lord said, Thou shalt entice him, and thou shalt also prevail: go out, and do even so.

Now therefore, behold, the Lord hath put a lying spirit in the mouth of these thy prophets, and the Lord hath spoken evil against thee.

JST 2 Chronicles 18:20–22

Then there came out a *lying* spirit, and stood before *them,* and said, I will entice him, Wherewith?

And he said, I will go out, and be a lying spirit in the mouth of all his prophets. And the Lord said, Thou shalt entice him, and thou shalt also prevail; go out, and do even so; *for all these have sinned against me.*

Now therefore, behold, the Lord hath *found* a lying spirit in the mouth of these thy prophets, and the Lord hath spoken evil against thee.

As noted in these verses, the Lord does not send out spirits to tell lies, but does allow them to go forth among those who have sinned against him.

Chapter 20 has five verses changed. All of these are relatively insignificant. In 2 Chronicles 22:2, the KJV states that Ahaziah was forty and two years when he began to reign. The JST changes this to twenty and two, which makes it conform to the parallel account of 2 Kings 8:26. Chapter 24 has two insignificant changes in verses 9 and 22. In 2 Chronicles 25:18, a little parable about the thistle and cedar in Lebanon has the KJV italicized word *was* changed to *grew* in the JST, making it read more sensibly. The last change in the book of 2 Chronicles is in 34:16. "Brought the king word back" in the KJV is changed to "brought the word *of the* king back" a clearer wording. The fact that most of these changes are insignificant suggests that the Prophet did not work much on this book.

The last historical book which the Prophet made changes in was Nehemiah. While there are twenty-two verses changed, seventeen of them are in chapter 7 and concern the numbers of the various families who returned from Babylon. They are changed to conform to the parallel account given in Ezra. Another verse in chapter 7 has a name changed to conform with Ezra's account. It is interesting to note that the sum total of the Ezra and Nehemiah accounts are the same with or without the changes made in Nehemiah.

Two changes in chapter 6 are mainly a better selection of words or a rearrangement of phrases to make the text more readable but have no historical or doctrinal significance.

There is a significant change in chapter 10, verse 29. After listing those who entered into a covenant, the KJV states that they "entered into a curse, and into an oath, to walk in God's law." The JST changed the verse to read, "And entered into an oath, *that a curse should come upon them if they did not* walk in God's law." The end of that verse and verse 30 also have several pronoun changes. *Our* is changed to *their*, and *we* is changed to *they*, making it more specific to whom the verse is referring. All in all, the changes are not very significant, suggesting again that the Prophet Joseph did not spend a lot of time on the book of Nehemiah.

SUMMARY

The Prophet's work on the historical books of the Bible seems to have been based upon four different topics: the true attributes or workings of the Lord; the work and relationship of evil spirits and prophets; the lives of David and Solomon, kings of Israel; and the correlation of contradictory texts within the books. As he worked on these four topics, it seems apparent that he came upon verses which were not very clear; so he rearranged or altered them to make them more understandable. It is obvious there will be much more to do when the time comes for a complete restoration of the text (see D&C 42:56–58). Nevertheless, it should be recognized that what the Prophet accomplished is a great contribution to our understanding, and these types of changes should be kept in mind as these historical books are studied. Also, from the changes which were made, it is obvious that the gospel is consistent and everlasting, and is the anchor to which all study should be tied—not just the historical books. As one studies the Bible, the changes made in the JST, as well as the truths of the Book of Mormon and the Doctrine and Covenants, may serve as guides until the complete restoration is revealed.

Monte S. Nyman is associate dean of Religious Education and professor of Ancient Scripture at BYU.

NOTES

1. Joseph Smith, *History of The Church of Jesus Christ of Latter-day Saints,* ed. B. H. Roberts, 7 vols. (Salt Lake City: The Church of Jesus Christ of Latter-day Saints, 1932–51), 4:264.

2. *Teachings of the Prophet Joseph Smith,* comp. Joseph Fielding Smith (Salt Lake City: Deseret Book Co., 1938), p. 365.

3. Ibid., p. 339.

6

Joseph Smith and the Poetic Writings

Joseph F. McConkie

Most of us are willing to suffer in silence if everyone knows that we are suffering. In the presentations that have been made to this point—and they have all been marvelously insightful and inspiring—my colleagues have lamented that they could tell you but the "hundredth part" of what the Prophet did. My assignment is somewhat different. Whereas they took to themselves those books in which the Prophet did much, they have invited me to speak on those books in which the Prophet did nothing, or at least comparatively little. Yet, I am far too good a sport to even mention that they ate the steak and left me the soup bone. I have no complaints, for the company is good and the soup is good. The handprint of the Prophet is also to be found upon the poetic books, and significant lessons are there to be learned. Where Joseph walked he sowed seeds, and those seeds—nourished with even a modest amount of scholarship and a particle of faith—make what was a desert blossom as a rose.

The books I will review are Psalms, Proverbs, Ecclesiastes, and the Song of Solomon. The latter three of these books merit little more than a passing observation. All scripture is not of equal worth and these books fall far short of the spiritual power contained in some of their companion volumes. We will consider them briefly first and then spend the major portion of our time where it properly belongs—in the Psalms.

PROVERBS AND ECCLESIASTES

Proverbs is an anthology of epigrams, wise sayings, and fatherly advice gathered from both Hebrew and foreign sources over many generations. Ecclesiastes is an attempt to find meaning in a world in which good often goes unrewarded, while evil flourishes. The author of this latter work assumes a position of an aloof observer of human folly while writing in a tone which is at best gloomy. Neither of these books espouses gospel principles or contains so much as a word of prophecy. Other than an occasional proof text for a doctrine that must be established elsewhere or a quotation for a sacrament meeting pep talk, these books go unused. Their relative unimportance is evidenced by the few corrections made in them by the Prophet in the Joseph Smith Translation.

The most significant change made in Proverbs is in the verse which states, "Whoso findeth a wife findeth a good thing, and obtaineth favour of the Lord" (Proverbs 18:22). The Prophet corrected the verse to read, "Whoso findeth a *good* wife hath obtained favor of the Lord." There was only one change in Ecclesiastes (3:1), and it is of little consequence.

THE SONG OF SOLOMON

The Song of Solomon appears to be a collection of erotic love poems. Its story line is unclear as is the matter of which of its characters is speaking in many instances. The book makes no mention of God, nor is it quoted in the New Testament. Notwithstanding the inordinate efforts that have been made to make the light of the Spirit shine through it, the Song of Solomon does not give forth light nor is there a single spiritual truth to be found in it. Those seeking a positive message in the book have found it only by means of allegory: that is, by interpreting everything in it as meaning something other than what it says. Let me illustrate. The story apparently deals with a virtuous young maiden, the daughter of a widowed mother, who loves a young shepherd to whom she is betrothed. She is employed by her brothers in their vineyard, and while on her way there happens into company with the king and his traveling party. The king is so impressed with her beauty that he brings her to his pavillion and eventually takes her to Jerusalem. He surrounds her with the pomp, splendor, and the glory of his court, hoping thereby to win her love. Yet her love for the shepherd boy remains unswayed by royal blandishments. When the king realizes he has failed to gain her favor, he sets her free to marry the shepherd. Now, what have commentators had to say of this work?

The rabbis interpreted the book to be an expression of God's love for the Jews. Christian commentators have claimed it as an expression of God's love for them in preference to the Jews. Other interpretations have included the idea that it is a history of the Jews from the Exodus to the Messiah; that it is a book of consolation for Israel; that it is an occult history; that it represents the union of the spirit with the body; that it is a conversation of Solomon and Wisdom; that it is an expression of thanksgiving on Solomon's part for a peaceful reign; that it is an account of the reconciliation of God and man; that it is a prophecy of the Church from the Crucifixion through the Reformation and the coming of Christ in power; that it is an account of the marriage of Solomon with the daughter of Pharaoh; that it is a prophetic description of the sepulchre of the Savior and his death; that it is a description of Hezekiah and the ten tribes; and of course, according to Roman Catholics, it is the glorification of the Virgin Mary.[1] These interpretations include the idea that the watchmen, vineyard-keepers, shepherds, etc., are the ministers of the gospel, and the wine so often spoken of is a representation of the joys of the Holy Spirit.

None, however, have spoken with greater praise of the Song of Solomon than the famed Rabbi Akiba who argued for its place in the Canon saying, "For in all the world there is nothing to equal the day on which the Song of Songs was given to Israel, for all the Writings are holy, but the Song of Songs is the Holy of Holies."[2] It was, he said, written by God himself on Mount Sinai, and in it was to be found God's description of himself.[3]

In contrast to all of this, the Prophet Joseph Smith, while laboring on the Joseph Smith Translation, simply said: "The Songs of Solomon are not Inspired Writings," and he left them out of his translation of the Bible.[4]

In the Song of Solomon, we have the classic historical illustration that you do not establish doctrine from poetry and that you most assuredly do not establish it from allegory.

One verse from the Song of Solomon, chapter 6:10, finds expression in the Doctrine and Covenants, suggesting the possibility that the author of the Song took it from a scriptural source now lost to us.[5] The verse is in question form: "Who," it asks, "is she that looketh forth as the morning, fair as the moon, clear as the sun, and terrible as an army with banners?" It might be quite romantic to tell your new bride that she is beautiful as the dawn, the morning stars, or even as glorious as moonlight, but I dare say that it will not be well received if you tell her that she is "terrible as an army with banners."

The manner in which the passage is used in the Doctrine and Covenants seems much more natural. It is first used in Doctrine and Covenants 5:10, where it refers to the Church coming forth in the last days "out of the wilderness" of the dark ages. It is used again in Doctrine and Covenants 105:31, where it describes the army of Israel, which army, the Lord said, was to become "very great," "be sanctified," and thus become "fair as the sun, and clear as the moon, that her banners may be terrible unto all nations." The Prophet also used this language in the dedicatory prayer of the Kirtland Temple to describe the Church which had come out of the "wilderness of darkness" to "be adorned as a bride" for that day when the Lord would come (D&C 109:73–74). The language is very reminiscent of that of Isaiah wherein he spoke of that day when the Lord would "cause righteousness and praise to spring forth before all the nations," for both bride and bridegroom would be clothed in "the garments of salvation," and the "robes of righteousness" (Isaiah 61:10–11; D&C 109:76).

PSALMS—A BIBLE WITHIN A BIBLE

The book of Psalms is a collection of one hundred fifty hymns used by ancient Israel in their temple worship. King David is credited with the authorship of seventy-three of these compositions, twelve are ascribed to a temple musician named Asaph (Psalms 50; 73–83), two of them are reputed to have been written by Solomon (Psalms 72, 127), Moses is said to have written one of them (Psalm 90); the authorship of the others remains unknown. The period of their composition may well stretch from Moses to two hundred years past the time of Malachi. Their content ranges from some of the oldest to perhaps the most recent of Old Testament writings. There is no chronology represented in the order in which they have been placed in the Psalter, though they have obviously been divided into five sections or five books within the book, each division closing with a doxology or utterance of praise to God (Psalms 1–41; 42–72; 73–89; 90–106; 107–150). Tradition has it that this was in imitation of the Pentateuch.

In the time period of its composition, the number of its authors, and the breadth of its content, the book of Psalms is easily the most comprehensive book in the Bible. Martin Luther called it the "little Bible" and indeed it is a library within a library, or a Bible within a Bible. As such it provides us with an excellent case study as to how scripture comes into being, how it was perverted in the hands of uninspired men, and its absolute dependency on the spirit of revelation for meaningful understanding. Since no message is more central to the Psalms than the coming of Christ, let us take its messianic prophecies as our illustration.

Suppose, for instance, that we lived in Old Testament times, that this building was our synagogue, and that we had come today to worship. In that day, the system of worship consisted of the reading of scripture and discussion as to its meaning. Suppose further that the text chosen for the day was Psalm 69. Now let us quote from this Psalm written by David at a time of great personal distress and consider what commentary would have been given on it:

Verse 8. "I am become a stranger unto my brethren, and an alien unto my mother's children." (Would the commentary on this verse have announced, as did John [John 7:5], that it applied to Christ, whose brothers—that is, Mary's other sons—would not believe in him?)

Verse 9. "For the zeal of thine house hath eaten me up . . ." (Would this verse have been understood as a prophecy of Christ cleansing the temple? So it was announced again by John [John 2:17].)

Verse 21. "They gave me also gall for my meat; and in my thirst they gave me vinegar to drink." (Would this verse have been seen as a prophecy to be fulfilled by Christ at his crucifixion as testified to by Matthew, Mark, and John [Matthew 27:34, 48; Mark 15:23; John 19:29]?)

Verse 22. "Let their table become a snare before them: and that which should have been for their welfare, let it become a trap."

Verse 23. "Let their eyes be darkened, that they see not; and make their loins continually to shake." (Would these verses have been explained as a prophecy of the wickedness of their nation at the time of Christ, their rejection of him and the subsequent taking of the gospel to the Gentiles as it was explained by the apostle Paul [Romans 11:9–11]?)

Verse 25. "Let their habitation be desolate; and let none dwell in their tents." (Would any have been expected to see in these words Judas' betrayal of Jesus and the necessity of another being called to fill his place among the apostles as explained by Peter [Acts 1:20]?)

Would these verses have been seen as anything more than a recital of David's complaints against his enemies and his hope that they be rewarded according to their works? Could anyone living at that time independent of the spirit of prophecy hear these verses read and know that they were messianic? If we did not have the testimony of the Gospel writers, would any of these verses be clear to us? Thus the book of Psalms, our Bible within the Bible, establishes the principle—it takes prophets to understand prophets and scripture to understand scripture.

Now, the point of the illustration is this: the book of Psalms is as much a book of prophecy for our day as it was for those living before the coming of Christ. That is, it is as much in need of the help of contemporary prophets and contemporary scripture if it is to be understood in our day as it was in days of old. It contains many phrases and verses, and in some instances, entire chapters that prophesy of events of the last days, including the First Vision; the coming forth of the Book of Mormon; the restoration of the gospel; the gathering of Israel; the building of temples; and the establishment of Zion, matters which are as far removed from the understanding of Bible readers today as its messianic prophecies were from the peoples of the Old Testament. The book and its many mysterious passages could only be unlocked by one who rightfully professed "power from on high," and such a one was the Prophet Joseph Smith, and such is the story that we will now briefly tell.

The Gathering and Redemption of Israel

Joseph Smith was still in his teens when he learned of the prophetic significance of the book of Psalms. We can virtually identify the very moment—it was during the night and early morning hours of the 21 and 22 September 1823, when Moroni first visited him. It was Oliver Cowdery who, after a lengthy conversation with the Prophet, preserved this knowledge for us.[6] In the Pearl of Great Price account, Joseph Smith only tells us of a few of the passages of scripture quoted and explained by Moroni, adding that "he quoted many other passages of scripture, and offered many explanations which cannot be mentioned here" (JS-H 1:36–41). In his account of what the Prophet told him, Oliver lists more than two dozen such passages, among which are five of the Psalms. We will briefly examine each. They are Psalms 91:6; 100; 107; 144; and 146:10. Though Moroni's explanation of these passages has not been preserved for us, their interpretation in the context of Moroni's instruction to Joseph Smith will be obvious.

Psalm 91:6. This is a messianic psalm, the introductory verses of which are refrains of praise and rejoicing in the protection afforded Israel through faith in God. The sixth verse speaks of pestilence and of a "destruction that wasteth at noonday." Moroni placed the passage in the same context as Joel's prophecy that the moon would turn to blood and the stars fall from heaven (see Joel 2:31), and Isaiah's prophecy of the earth reeling to and fro as a drunken man (see Isaiah 24:20). Oliver's account records, "The Lord will bring to the knowledge of his people his commandments and statutes, that they may be prepared to stand when the . . . nations tremble, and the destroying angel goes forth to waste the inhabitants at noon-day: for so great are to be the calamities which are to come upon the inhabitants of the earth, before the coming of the Son of Man the second time, that whoso is not prepared cannot abide; but such as are found faithful, and remain, shall be gathered with his people and caught up to meet the Lord in the cloud, and so shall they inherit eternal life."[7] Moroni would obviously have emphasized to Joseph Smith his role in restoring the "commandments and statutes" of the Lord that a people might be prepared to stand when the Lord comes.

Psalm 100. This Psalm begins with the announcement that all the earth must declare the Lord and serve him joyfully. It is an invitation for the worthy of all nations to "come before his presence," which is an Old Testament phrase meaning "to come to the temple." The witness of the Psalmist is that the truths taught therein endure from generation to generation, unchanged. This, we learn from Moroni, was the day for which David longed and often prayed. Further, we are told that David knew that such a day could not come "until the knowledge of the glory of God covered all lands, or all the earth."[8]

Psalm 107. This Psalm speaks of affliction and distress which would come upon Israel because they "rebelled against the words of God." It promised a day when they would be freed from their bondage of "darkness" and gathered from the lands of the "east, and from the west, from the north, and from the south," a time when the Lord would "send his word" and heal them, after which they would be expected to "declare" or testify of "his works with rejoicing." The Psalm also promises that for those so gathered the Lord would turn the "desert into pools of water, and parched earth into springs of water."[9] Here the hungry, it was prophesied, would settle and establish a city to dwell in and be blessed with abundant harvests. Here they were to multiply "greatly," for the promise was that the Lord would make "him families like a flock."

Commenting on this, Oliver wrote: "Most clearly was it shown to the prophet, that the righteous should be gathered from all the earth: He knew that the children of Israel were led from Egypt, by the right hand of the Lord, and permitted to possess the land of Canaan, though they were rebellious in the desert, but he further knew that they were not gathered from the east, the west, the north and the south, at that time; for it was clearly manifested that the Lord himself would prepare a habitation, even as he said, when he would lead them to a city of refuge."[10]

Psalms 144:11-12 and 146:10. Here we again find David praying for that day when Israel will be freed from the hand of foreigners that her sons might be "as plants grown up in their youth" and their daughters "as corner stones, polished after the similitude of a palace." Only then, according to the Cowdery account of Moroni's discourse, will their sons and daughters prophesy, their old men dream dreams, and young men see visions. This was then given as the context of Psalm 46:10, which announces a day when the Lord would reign forever in Zion.

The Joseph Smith Translation and the Psalms

Joseph Smith made changes in almost two hundred verses in the Psalms. Most of these, however, were mechanical or grammatical changes. Let us briefly examine some of the significant doctrinal changes he made.

Psalm 11. This song is an expression of trust in God. It speaks of the wicked who will "privily shoot at the upright in heart." It assures that the Lord will protect his own, while raining "snares, fire and brimstone" upon the wicked. Changes made by the Prophet in this Psalm place it in the context of the last days with the protection afforded the Saints being found in the temple of the Lord, represented by the symbol "my mountain." The private attacks of the wicked, we learn, are directed at the "foundation" of the faith of the righteous, yet we are assured that it is the "foundation" of the wicked that is to be destroyed. "The Lord loveth the righteous," we are told while "the wicked . . . his soul hateth."

Psalm 14. The JST rendering of this Psalm reads like another account of the First Vision. The first verse reads: "The fool hath said in his heart, there is no man that hath seen God. Because he showeth himself not unto us, therefore there is no God. Behold, they are corrupt; they have done abominable works, and none of them doeth good." The second verse has the Lord speaking from heaven to "his servant" asking if there are any who "understand God." The response is that many so profess. In the third verse the Lord says of those so professing that "they are all gone aside, they are together become filthy," and that there are none of them "doing good, no, not one." Continuing in the next verse he says, "All they have for their teachers are workers of iniquity, and there is no knowledge in them." Finally the Psalm concludes with the longing refrain: "Oh that Zion were established out of heaven, the salvation of Israel. O Lord, when wilt thou establish out of heaven, the salvation of Israel? O Lord, when wilt thou establish Zion? When the Lord bringeth back the captivity of his people, Jacob shall rejoice, Israel shall be glad."

Seeing God. Other changes made by the Prophet in the Psalms are consistent in sustaining the idea that he will manifest himself to the righteous. For instance, in Psalm 13:1 to the question "how long wilt thou hide thy face from me?" are added the words "that I may not see thee? Wilt thou forget me, and cast me off from thy presence for ever?" Psalm 42:2 which reads, "My soul thirsteth for God, for the living God," was changed by the Prophet to read, "My soul thirsteth for *to see* God, for *to see* the living God." Psalm 90:13, which refers to how long it will be until the Lord returns, was changed in the Joseph Smith Translation of this verse to ask: "How long wilt thou hide thy face from thy servants?"

That Joseph Smith had in mind the actual appearance of the Lord to men in the flesh in these texts is evident from the manner in which the same phrase is used in the Doctrine and Covenants. Section 84, a great revelation on the priesthood, announces the necessity of Israel of our day obtaining the "power of godliness" that they might "see the face of God, even the Father, and live." Further, we are told that such was the design of Moses, and so he "sought diligently to sanctify his people that they might behold the face of God; But they hardened their hearts and could not endure his presence" (D&C 84:22–24). To modern Israel the Lord has said: "Sanctify yourselves that your minds become single to

God, and the days will come that you shall see him; for he will unveil his face unto you, and it shall be in his own time, and in his own way, and according to his own will" (D&C 88:68). Again in Doctrine and Covenants the Lord assures the obedient that they "shall see my face and know that I am" (D&C 93:1).

Other renderings of the Psalms sustain the emphasis that Joseph Smith placed on the righteous being privileged to see God. For instance, the footnote in our new LDS edition of the Bible for the phrase, "his countenance doth behold the upright" in Psalm 11:7 notes that the verse could have been rendered, "the upright shall behold his face." This is the rendering given it in the American Standard Version. In Psalm 27:8 we read the injunction of the Lord that we seek his face. The language of this text is picked up in the Doctrine and Covenants: "And seek the face of the Lord always, that in patience ye may possess your souls, and ye shall have eternal life" (D&C 101:38).

Psalm 90:13, which reads "Return, O Lord, how long? and let it repent thee concerning thy servants," was corrected to read: "Return us, O Lord. [Note that it is "us" not the Lord who left.] How long wilt thou hide thy face from thy servants?" Clarifying that promised day, Psalm 102:18, which speaks of a people that would be "created" to praise the Lord, is corrected to speak of a people who shall be "gathered" to his praise.

Redeeming the Oppressed. Central themes of the Psalms are the first and second comings of Christ. This message is enhanced and expanded by the Joseph Smith Translation. To that theme is added these words in Psalm 12:1: "In that day thou shalt help, O Lord, the poor and the meek of the earth." It is in the Psalms that we first read the promise that "the meek shall inherit the earth." "For," we are told that those who are blessed of the Lord "shall inherit the earth: and they that be cursed of him shall be cut off. . . . The righteous shall inherit the land [earth], and dwell therein for ever" (Psalm 37:11, 22, 29). By revelation through Joseph Smith, we obtain insight into this promise, repeated by Christ in the Sermon of the Mount (Matthew 5:5), and assumed by virtually all in the sectarian world to be a figurative expression. In the Doctrine and Covenants we are told that this earth will be "sanctified from all unrighteousness," that it will be celestialized, and that the righteous "poor and the meek" of this world will literally inherit it (D&C 88:17–20).

To Psalm 24, which speaks of Christ as the king of glory, the Prophet added these words: "And he will roll away the heavens; and will come down to redeem his people; to make you an everlasting name; to establish you upon his everlasting rock.... Even the king of glory shall come unto you; and shall redeem his people, and shall establish them in righteousness" (JST Psalm 24:8, 10).

Righteousness and Truth. Psalm 32:1, which reads, "Blessed is he whose transgression is forgiven, whose sin is covered," was changed in the JST to read, "Blessed are they whose transgressions are forgiven, and who have no sins to be covered." To Psalm 33:4 is added the statement that "the word of the Lord is given to the upright," while Psalm 36:5 adds that "the thoughts of a righteous man ascendeth up" to the heavens. Psalm 138:8, in which David is recorded as saying, "The Lord will perfect that which concerneth me," is improved to read, "The Lord will perfect me in knowledge, concerning his kingdom."

The Coming Forth of the Book of Mormon. Along with such textual corrections, the Joseph Smith Translation provides us with a revealed commentary on Psalm 85:11, which we are told is a prophecy of the coming forth of the Book of Mormon. The text is a future promise which states, "Truth shall spring out of the earth; and righteousness shall look down from heaven." The commentary on this verse comes to us in the context of a prophecy of Enoch, long lost to the Bible, but restored in the Joseph Smith Translation and presently canonized as a part of the book of Moses. In his prophetic description of events of the last days, Enoch, speaking in the first person for the Father, said:

> And righteousness will I send down out of heaven; and truth will I send forth out of the earth, to bear testimony of mine Only Begotten; his resurrection from the dead; yea, and also the resurrection of all men; and righteousness and truth will I cause to sweep the earth as with a flood, to gather out mine elect from the four quarters of the earth, unto a place which I shall prepare, an Holy City, that my people may gird up their loins, and be looking forth for the time of my

coming; for there shall be my tabernacle, and it shall be called Zion, a New Jerusalem (JST Genesis 7:70/Moses 7:62).

The Councils of Heaven

The knowledge of other doctrines restored to us through Joseph Smith also serve to unlock what would otherwise remain hidden to the reader of the book of Psalms. A fascinating illustration of this is the marvelous truth that Joseph Smith restored to us about the pre-earth life, our existence there as spirits, and the grand council in heaven where the plan of salvation was reviewed, the need for a Redeemer explained, and the Firstborn of our Father's sons chosen to fill that role. With Joseph Smith's help, these doctrines now lost to the world once again come to light in the Psalms, our Bible within a Bible, just as they do throughout the Bible itself. In fact, there are more references to heavenly councils in the book of Psalms than in any other book of scripture. Let me briefly illustrate this, using the Psalms once again as a case study to demonstrate how gospel truths have been lost or obscured by well-meaning but ignorant translators. Consider the following:

Psalm 82:1. It reads: "God standeth in the congregation of the mighty; he judgeth among the gods." The word "mighty" in this verse is a translation of the Hebrew word *ale* which very properly could have been translated "gods" or "heavenly beings." More perfect renderings of this verse are found in modern translations. For instance:

"God takes his stand in the courts of heaven to deliver judgment among the gods themselves." (New English Bible.)

"God stands in the divine assembly, among the gods he dispenses justice." (The Jerusalem Bible.)

"God presides in the divine council, in the midst of the gods adjudicates." (Anchor Bible Series.)[11]

Scholars, having now admitted that the passage is part of the heavenly council motif, conclude that the Lord is passing judgment on pagan gods. Latter-day Saints, however, immediately recognize it as a companion passage to Abraham 3 where the Lord shows Abraham a vision of the assembly of spirits destined to come to this earth. Some of this congregation of spirits were identified as the "noble and great," implying that a judgment had been made. Referring to the great ones, the Lord said, "These I will make my rulers," telling Abraham that he was one of those so chosen. (Abraham 3:22–23.) The Abraham account continues by telling how some of these spirits rebelled at the selection of the Son of Man as the chief messenger of God on earth and were cast out of this heavenly estate (Abraham 3:24–28).

The sixth verse of this Psalm reads: "Ye are gods; and all of you are children of the most High." One prominent secular scholar after nearly a hundred pages of analysis on this verse finally concluded that in it the Father is saying to his rebellious children, "I thought that ye were gods, but since you have proven yourself unworthy you will now be divested of your divine natures and forfeit the privilege of living in heaven."[12]

Psalm 89:5–8. The picture of the Lord in the midst of a heavenly council is common to many of the Psalms. Consider these verses in the King James Version and then their rendering in a modern translation:

"And the heavens shall praise thy wonders, O Lord: thy faithfulness also in the congregation of the saints.

"For who in the heaven can be compared unto the Lord? who among the sons of the mighty can be likened unto the Lord?

"God is greatly to be feared in the assembly of the saints, and to be had in reverence of all them that are about him."

Compare with:

"The heavens praise Thy wonderousness, O Yahweh, Likewise Thy Trustworthiness in the assembly of the gods.

"For who in the skies can be compared with Yahweh; who among the gods is like unto Yahweh?

"A god who inspires awe in the council of the gods, Who is great and fearful beyond all those who surround Him."[13]

Psalm 29:1–2 summons these same gods to do homage before the Lord, to bow down before him and praise his name, while Psalm 97:7 likewise bids all the gods to bow down before God. Psalm 103:20–21 is an invocation directed to the celestial assembly, Psalm 148:2 commands the angels of the Lord, all who constitute his house, to praise him. Psalm 97:9 records that God is supreme over all the gods, Psalm 96:4 says that God is to be feared over all the gods, and Psalm 95:3 states that God is a great king over all the gods.

SUMMARY AND CONCLUSIONS

From what Joseph Smith learned by revelation about the poetic writings and from the changes he made in them in his inspired translation, we can draw the following conclusions:

1. All scripture is not of equal worth. Indeed not everything claiming sanctuary in the holy writ is deserving of such protection. Joseph Smith paid relatively little attention to those books that do not contain the testimony of Christ, the doctrines of the kingdom, or prophetic utterances. This I suggest ought be taken as an example for us in both individual study and as we study together in our priesthood quorums, our auxiliary classes, and the religion classes taught here at the Brigham Young University and in the Seminary and Institute program. I for one have attended too many classes that lost sight of the beach in their zeal to collect empty shells.

2. If not directly from the Prophet Joseph Smith, then certainly from the abuse of the poetic writings which he sought to correct, we learn that you do not establish doctrine from poetry, from allegory, or might we add parables. They may be used to sustain good doctrine, but only after that doctrine has been plainly established in the form of unambiguous revelation. As Elder Boyd K. Packer so wisely taught us in a recent general conference, doctrines basic to the salvation of men are not relegated to obscure passages of scripture.[14]

3. As we learn from the messianic psalms and from the psalmic prophecies of the last days, there is no meaningful understanding of revelation without revelation. Many passages given contemporary explanations contain prophecy of future events. Much in the book of Psalms, like the rest of the Bible, is sealed to those who read without the light of revelation, be it the personal promptings of the Holy Ghost, commentary in the form of modern revelation, or the statements of living prophets.

4. David, along with many Old Testament prophets, described the apostasy and scattering of Israel and their latter-day gathering. He and others of the Psalmists knew the story of the Restoration in marvelous detail, even as they knew of events in the life of Christ in minute detail.

It was the apostle Paul who taught us that while the things of man can be understood by the spirit of man, the things of God are understood only by the Spirit of God (see 1 Corinthians 2:11). Thus we learn that it takes prophets to understand prophets, scripture to understand scripture, and the Spirit to understand the things of the Spirit. This was the principle that enabled Joseph Smith to read books sealed to the understanding of the supposedly learned (Isaiah 29:11-12). Describing what it meant for him and Oliver Cowdery to receive the Holy Ghost, Joseph Smith said: "Our minds being now enlightened, we began to have the scriptures laid open to our understandings, and the true meaning and intention of their more mysterious passages revealed unto us in a manner which we never could attain to previously, nor ever before had thought of" (JS-H 1:74).

When it came to the Bible, Joseph Smith spoke as one having authority, and rightly so, for save Jesus only, no man ever walked the face of the earth that had greater knowledge of the Bible than he had. A library containing every whit the world knows about the book would not rival his understanding. It is one thing to read the book and quite another to be instructed by its authors. Who among the world's scholars can boast of having stood face to face with Adam, Enoch, Noah, a messenger from Abraham's dispensation, Moses, John the son of Zacharias, Peter, James, and John? While religious leaders were claiming that the heavens were sealed to them, Joseph Smith was being personally tutored by ancient prophets who laid their hands upon his head and conferred upon him the power, keys, and authority they held.

Joseph Smith claimed the Holy Ghost as his textbook[15] and made his translation of the Bible from the original language—the language in which all the revelations were originally given—the language of revelation. Who but Joseph Smith could tell us that Seth was in the perfect likeness of his Father (see D&C 107:43), or could give a detailed description of Paul?[16] Joseph Smith knew the Bible, he knew its prophets, he knew its message, and he knew its central character, the Lord Jesus Christ, with whom he also stood face to face and by whom he was instructed. Joseph Smith was a living Bible, and he has done more to enhance the world's understanding of that great book than any other man who ever lived in it.

Joseph F. McConkie is associate professor of Ancient Scripture at BYU.

NOTES

1. Frederic W. Farrar, *History of Interpretation* (Grand Rapids, Mich.: Baker Book House, 1979), p. 33.

2. Roland Kenneth Harrison, *Introduction to the Old Testament* (Grand Rapids, Mich.: William B. Eerdmans Publishing Co., 1969), p. 1051.

3. Joseph Dan, holder of the Gershom Scholem Chair in Jewish mysticism at Hebrew University in Jerusalem, explained this in a lecture delivered at Brigham Young University, 3 October 1984.

4. Robert J. Matthews, *"A Plainer Translation": Joseph Smith's Translation of the Bible, A History and Commentary* (Provo, Utah: Brigham Young University Press, 1975), p. 87.

5. *The Interpreter's Bible,* 12 vols. (New York: Abingdon Press, 1956), 5:133.

6. *Messenger and Advocate* (Kirtland, Ohio, 1834–1837), 1:108–12.

7. Ibid., 1:111–12.

8. Ibid., 1:108.

9. Mitchell Dahood, *The Anchor Bible,* Psalms I, II, and III (Garden City, New York: Doubleday & Co., 1983), 3:79.

10. *Messenger and Advocate,* 1:109.

11. Dahood, 2:269.

12. I have paraphrased the argument of Julian Morgenstern, "The Mythological Background of Psalm 82," *Hebrew Union College Annual,* 14:114–17.

13. Ibid., 14:66–67.

14. Boyd K. Packer, "The Pattern of Our Parentage," *Ensign,* November 1984, p. 66.

15. *Teachings of the Prophet Joseph Smith,* comp. Joseph Fielding Smith (Salt Lake City: Deseret Book Co., 1961), p. 349.

16. Ibid., p. 180.

7

The Contribution of the JST to Understanding the Old Testament Prophets

Monte S. Nyman

When the Savior visited the Nephites in A.D. 34, he proclaimed that the law of Moses was fulfilled, but added, "I do not destroy the prophets, for as many as have not been fulfilled in me, verily I say unto you shall all be fulfilled" (3 Nephi 15:5–6). The Savior also taught the Nephites that when the prophecies of Isaiah were fulfilled, covenants with the house of Israel would be fulfilled (see 3 Nephi 20:11). Later he commanded that the words of Isaiah be searched (see 3 Nephi 23:1).

Undoubtedly, the Prophet Joseph Smith was aware of these teachings as he worked on his translation of the Bible. This awareness may account for more than one hundred changes the Prophet made in the book of Isaiah. Many of these changes can be attributed to the extensive quoting of the book of Isaiah in the Book of Mormon. However, many of the differences between the Book of Mormon text and the KJV are not carried over into the JST, and a few are further changed.

A study of these differences and changes leads to the conclusion that Joseph Smith did not finish his work on the book of

Isaiah. In fact, he left many areas untouched which obviously needed to be corrected. This was probably because he was not able to spend the time on the translation which he needed to spend. This conclusion is drawn from the fact that there are many significant changes made in the Book of Mormon text which are not carried over into the JST.

There are at least eighty-five significant differences between the KJV text and the Book of Mormon text of Isaiah. Many of these changes do not appear in the JST. Only those changes in the JST which are significantly different from the Book of Mormon text, or those which were obviously neglected by the Prophet, will be pointed out and discussed in this article.

THE BOOK OF ISAIAH

One verse in chapter 4 of Isaiah needs some clarification. Verse 1 of chapter 4 is placed at the end of chapter 3 in the JST. This verse change is attributed to the printing of the JST by the Reorganized Latter Day Saints and not to the Prophet Joseph Smith. An examination of the original JST manuscripts confirms that the Prophet did not initiate the change. While it cannot be ascertained why they made the change, the context of the verse refers to a gentile condition and not the beautiful and glorious branch of the Lord mentioned in verse 2 of chapter 4. It would seem, therefore, that the verse is more appropriately placed in chapter 3. In further support of the placement of the verse in chapter 3, we find that this is its location in the Hebrew Bible as well. It should also be noted that the chapter divisions are man-made and thus are based upon interpretation.

There are seven significant differences between the Book of Mormon and the KJV texts in chapter 9, only four of which are carried over into the JST. There is one significant difference in chapter 10 and one significant difference in chapter 12 between the KJV and the Book of Mormon text, neither of which are carried over into the JST. While all of these differences are significant, they are not as significant as the ones which were carried over.

There are nine significant differences between the KJV and the Book of Mormon texts of chapters 13 and 14. Three of these differences are not carried over into the JST. One of these (13:10) was changed in the 1981 edition of the Book of Mormon. The phrase, "The sun shall be darkened in *her* going forth" (found in the 1921 edition of the Book of Mormon), was changed to "*his* going forth," making it consistent with the KJV and JST. There seems to be no explanation for the use of one gender or the other.

The JST contains another change (Isaiah 13:2) which is not in the Book of Mormon text. The Book of Mormon and the KJV both say, "Lift ye up *a* banner upon the high mountain." The JST changes it to say, "Lift ye up *my* banner." This change seems necessary to ensure that the readers understand the banner to be of or from the Lord. While this is only implied in the other two texts, it is made certain in the JST.

Chapter 14 is the last of thirteen consecutive chapters quoted in 2 Nephi in the Book of Mormon. A comparison of these chapters with the JST indicates that the Book of Mormon was the primary source used by the Prophet to correct the biblical text, but he included only the majority of the differences at this time. Those changes which were less important were apparently left for a future time. That time never came because of other commitments and his tragic martyrdom.

The next thirteen chapters of Isaiah (15–27) are not quoted in the Book of Mormon. The Prophet made a few changes in verse 6 of chapter 16, but it is primarily a wording rearrangement. These chapters contain prophecies about the nations surrounding Israel and Judah. Perhaps the Prophet commenced work on these and determined that there were more important areas to work on. Whether he thought so is only speculation, but certainly the subsequent chapters of Isaiah are more important to our day.

The Prophet made some notes on chapters 26 and 27 of Isaiah in one of the manuscripts. All of the words which he copied down are italicized in the KJV. This suggests he was merely jotting words down for consideration. The italicized words in the KJV are words placed there by the translators to make the text more readable in English though there was no Hebrew equivalent in the original. In their honesty, they italicized these words to indicate the changes made. Joseph could have been aware of this fact, or at least may have been musing over them as possible areas of change, though no changes were made in the text.

The JST text of chapter 28 contains no changes from the KJV. However, here is an example of a change that could have been made:

KJV Isaiah 28:13

But the word of the Lord was unto them precept upon precept, precept upon precept; line upon line, line upon line; here a little, and there a little; that they might go, and fall backward, and be broken, and snared, and taken.

2 Nephi 28:30–31

For behold, thus saith the Lord God: I will give unto *the children of men* line upon line, precept upon precept, here a little and there a little; *and blessed are those who hearken unto my precepts, and lend an ear unto my counsel, for they shall learn wisdom; for unto him that receiveth I will give more; and from them that shall say, We have enough, from them shall be taken away even that which they have.*

Cursed is he that putteth his trust in man, or maketh flesh his arm, or shall hearken unto the precepts of men, save their precepts shall be given by the power of the Holy Ghost.

The last part of the KJV text quoted above does not make sense. It is obvious that something is missing (plain and precious parts). While Nephi does not identify whom he is quoting, it is obvious that he is quoting Isaiah, and the fuller text is compatible with the corrupted end of the KJV text. Undoubtedly, Joseph Smith would have made this change in due time.

All but the first two verses of chapter 29 of Isaiah are quoted in the Book of Mormon. There are also many additional verses and parts of verses from this chapter that were retained in the Book of Mormon text. Nineteen verses in the Book of Mormon, the original text taken from the plates of brass, had been reduced to only two short verses in the Masoretic text from which the KJV was translated. This was obviously the work of the great and abominable church. There are also ten other significant retentions in the other eighteen verses of the KJV which are quoted in the Book of Mormon. Most of these retentions are carried over in the JST, but a few of them are not. The first eight verses of JST chapter 29 are included in the longer excerpts of the JST found at the back of the new LDS edition of the Bible (1979). The Prophet's change in the second verse is best illustrated by comparison:

KJV Isaiah 29:1–2

Woe to Ariel, to Ariel, the city where David dwelt! add ye year to year; let them kill sacrifices.
Yet I will distress Ariel, and there shall be heaviness and sorrow: and it shall be unto *me as* Ariel.

JST Isaiah 29:1–2

Woe to Ariel, to Ariel, the city where David dwelt! add ye year to year; let them kill sacrifices.
Yet I will distress Ariel, and there shall be heaviness and sorrow; *for thus hath the Lord said unto me,* It shall be unto Ariel;

The added phrase in the JST, "For thus hath the Lord said unto me," does not affect the meaning, but the deletion of the two words *me as* out of the KJV does affect it. As written in the KJV, there was an obvious shift of subject; as changed, the subject is still Ariel or Jerusalem. This affects the interpretation of the next several verses. Nephi interpreted the verses as being fulfilled through the destruction of the Nephite nation, whose record would speak out of the ground to the Gentiles of the latter days through the Book of Mormon. It is unfortunate that Nephi did not quote verse 2 so that the wording from the plates of brass would be included. As corrected by the Prophet, the interpretation would be limited to Jerusalem. In the following verses, the pronouns in the JST are all changed to *her,* implying Jerusalem, and the word *Ariel,* which has been translated as Zion in the Book of Mormon text is left as Ariel in the JST.

There are several possible explanations of these differences. First, perhaps the Prophet did not complete his work and eventually would have made these changes. Second, Nephi was merely applying the scriptures to the known destiny of his people. Third, it is a dual prophecy, representing all of the house of Israel. The first possibility has been given general support throughout this paper; it is quite evident that there was much more Joseph Smith could have done, and would have done, if the time had been available to him. There is not much support for the second possibility other than Nephi's statement, "I did liken all scriptures unto us" (1 Nephi 19:23). There is much evidence against this idea. Nephi's quoting of Isaiah 29 included many verses which had been retained from the text of the plates of brass and definitely speaks of the coming forth of the Book of Mormon. All of this material has been carried over into the JST.

The third possibility probably has the most evidence in its favor. Jacob, the brother of Nephi, said that "Isaiah spake concerning *all* the house of Israel" (2 Nephi 6:5; emphasis added), and he quoted the same verses out of Isaiah chapter 49 to describe the Jews in Jerusalem (see 2 Nephi 6) that Nephi had quoted earlier to explain what would happen to the Nephites (see 1 Nephi 21–22). Certainly Jacob was aware of Nephi's interpretation. Jesus quoted the same verses in Isaiah 52 regarding the Nephites (see 3 Nephi 16:17–20) that he later quoted regarding the Jews (see 3 Nephi 20:32–34). Thus, verses 1 through 8 of chapter 29 concerns the Jews and the Nephites. Just as the Nephites were brought down to speak out of the dust, so were the Jews brought down by the Romans in A.D. 70.

The fact that there were many sacred records stored in Jerusalem is confirmed by the Jewish historian, Josephus, who wrote his record from them. Perhaps these records may still be in existence, protected by the Lord, and will someday be brought forth as was the Book of Mormon, and as will other records of the Nephites. If this is the correct interpretation, the transition verse in the JST is verse 8 instead of verse 2 where the Prophet changed it to read, "Yea, even so shall the multitude of all the nations be that fight against Mount Zion." Perhaps we have a combination of theories number one and number three: dual prophecy and the reality that the Prophet could not complete the text.

The next eighteen chapters of Isaiah are not quoted in the Book of Mormon, except for one verse (40:3). The Prophet made very few changes in these chapters, but most of the changes he made are very significant. In one verse, he substituted one word and added another, making it read "the houses of the city [instead of the multitude] shall be left *desolate*" (Isaiah 32:14). This description of the destruction of Israel is certainly more accurate than the KJV text. Chapter 34 has an interesting change in verse 7: the mythical *unicorn* is changed to a *re'em*, which is a wild ox in Hebrew. Apparently the Prophet was attempting to restore the literalness of the text. It is also significant that the Prophet separated the syllables of the word when he wrote it in the manuscript. This was before the Prophet had studied Hebrew; yet he restored it as it would have been pronounced in Hebrew. Here is an example of another type of change made in this chapter:

KJV Isaiah 34:16–17

Seek ye out of the book of the Lord, and read: no one of these shall fail, none shall want her mate: for my mouth it hath commanded, and his spirit it hath gathered them.

And he hath cast the lot for them, and his hand hath divided it unto them by line: they shall possess it for ever, from generation to generation shall they dwell therein.

JST Isaiah 34:16–17

Seek ye out of the book of the Lord, and read *the names written therein;* no one of these shall fail; none shall want *their* mate; for my mouth it hath commanded, and *my* Spirit it hath gathered them.

And *I* have cast the lot for them, and *I* have divided it unto them by line; they shall possess it for ever; from generation to generation they shall dwell therein.

This is a clearer rendering of those who have their callings and elections made sure. It also implies (correctly) through the change of the pronoun *her* to *their* that this is a joint experience of husband and wife. The other pronoun changes also verify this as the Lord's personal program. Chapter 35 also has a similar change to the last one made in chapter 34:

KJV Isaiah 35:8

And an highway shall be there, and a way, and it shall be called The way of holiness; the unclean shall not pass over it; but it shall be for those: the wayfaring men, though fools, shall not err therein.

JST Isaiah 35:8

And a highway shall be there; for a way *shall be cast up,* and it shall be called the way of holiness. The unclean shall not pass over *upon* it; but it shall be *cast up* for those *who are clean, and* the wayfaring men, though *they are accounted* fools, shall not err therein.

This additional information makes the text more consistent with Doctrine and Covenants 133:27–28 and Isaiah 11:16.

Chapters 36 through 39 of Isaiah are quotations of 2 Kings 18–20 about Isaiah and were not written by him. There are a few changes in the JST in these chapters. Verse 5 of chapter 36 is slightly different from the text which it was taken from (2 Kings 18:20). The awkward wording in the KJV is changed in the JST to be closer to the 2 Kings account. No meaning is altered. Chapter 37 has two changes. One of these verses, also changed in the 2 Kings account (v. 36), was discussed there. The other one was not changed in the 2 Kings account, which is further evidence that the Prophet did not complete his work on the historical books. The Isaiah account was changed as below:

KJV Isaiah 37:32

For out of Jerusalem shall go forth a remnant, and they that escape out of mount Zion: the zeal of the Lord of hosts shall do this.

JST Isaiah 37:32

For out of Jerusalem shall go forth a remnant; and they that escape out of *Jerusalem shall come up upon* mount Zion; the zeal of the Lord of hosts shall do this.

This was interpreted by Elder Orson Pratt to be a prophecy about the Mulekites coming to America, as recorded in the Book of Mormon. Certainly the JST verifies such an interpretation. Chapter 38 has three verses which the Prophet clarified to make it more readable:

KJV Isaiah 38:15–17

What shall I say? he hath both spoken unto me, and himself hath done it: I shall go softly all my years in the bitterness of my soul.

O Lord, by these things men live, and in all these things is the life of my spirit; so wilt thou recover me, and make me to live.

Behold, for peace I had great bitterness: but thou hast in love to my soul delivered it from the pit of corruption: for thou hast cast all my sins behind thy back.

JST Isaiah 38:15–17

What shall I say? he hath both spoken unto me, and himself hath *healed me.* I shall go softly all my years, *that I may not walk* in the bitterness of my soul.

O Lord, *thou who art the life of my spirit, in whom I live;* so wilt thou recover me, and make me to live; *and in all these things will I praise thee.*

Behold, I had great bitterness *instead of peace,* but thou hast in love to my soul, *saved me* from the pit of corruption, for thou hast cast all my sins behind thy back.

This testimony of Hezekiah concerning the Lord's healing of him is certainly more pronounced in the JST.

One of the great contributions of the JST to the understanding of Isaiah is in chapter 42. The majority of the verses changed are in the back of the new Church publication of the Bible. The significance of the changes is more apparent when compared to the KJV:

KJV Isaiah 42:19–25

Who is blind, but my servant? or deaf? as my messenger that I sent? who is blind as he that is perfect, and blind as the Lord's servant?

Seeing many things, but thou observest not; opening the ears, but he heareth not.

JST Isaiah 42:19–25

For I will send my servant unto you who are blind; yea, a messenger to open the eyes of the blind, and unstop the ears of the deaf;

And they shall be made perfect notwithstanding their blindness, if they will hearken unto the messenger, the Lord's servant.

Thou art a people, seeing many things, but thou observest not; opening the ears *to hear,* but *thou* hearest not.

The Lord is well pleased for his righteousness' sake; he will magnify the law, and make it honourable.	The Lord is *not* well pleased *with such a people, but* for his righteousness' sake he will magnify the law and make it honorable.
But this is a people robbed and spoiled; they are all of them snared in holes, and they are hid in prison houses: they are for a prey, and none delivereth; for a spoil, and none saith, Restore.	*Thou art* a people robbed and spoiled; *thine enemies,* all of them, *have* snared *thee* in holes, and they have hid *thee* in prison houses; they *have taken thee* for a prey, and none delivereth; for a spoil, and none saith, Restore.
Who among you will give ear to this? who will hearken and hear for the time to come? Who gave Jacob for a spoil, and Israel to the robbers? did not the Lord, he against whom we have sinned? for they would not walk in his ways, neither were they obedient unto his law.	Who among *them* will give ear *unto thee, or* hearken and hear *thee* for the time to come? *and* who gave Jacob for a spoil, and Israel to the robbers? did not the Lord, he against whom *they* have sinned? For they would not walk in his ways, neither were they obedient unto his law;
Therefore he hath poured upon him the fury of his anger, and the strength of battle: and it hath set him on fire round about, yet he knew not; and it burned him, yet he laid it not to heart.	therefore he hath poured upon *them* the fury of his anger, and the strength of battle; and *they* have set them on fire round about, yet *they* know not, and it burned *them,* yet *they* laid it not to heart.

These changes illustrate that it is not the servant who is blind, but those to whom the servant is sent. The servant's message will make these people perfect if they will hearken to it. The JST also identifies the people who will not hear as those people with whom the Lord is not pleased and, therefore, those to whom the servant is sent.

Beginning with chapter 48, the next seven chapters are quoted in the Book of Mormon, though they are not quoted consecutively as were the earlier chapters. It seems evident that the Prophet did not spend as much time on this section as he did on the earlier section. For example, in chapter 48, although every verse quoted in the Book of Mormon is different from the KJV

Monte S. Nyman

text, the Prophet made no changes in the JST. Similarly, there are no changes in the first twenty-two verses of chapter 49 and only one significant change in the whole chapter, that one being carried over from the Book of Mormon (see 2 Nephi 6:18)—even though there are many changes that are important.

The identification of the house of Israel as the Lord's servant in the Book of Mormon in this chapter is extremely important. Verse 1 has seven lines retained in the Book of Mormon describing Israel as being scattered abroad. Verses 12 and 15 also retain the identification of the house of Israel. The servant is identified in verse 8 and the location of Israel is declared to be in the "isles of the sea." Such important information would take top priority in the devil's plan to take away plain and precious parts from the Bible.

There is one change in the JST in chapter 50 which is not attributable to the Book of Mormon. In verse 5, the KJV and the Book of Mormon read, "The Lord God hath opened mine ear." The JST changes it to read, "The Lord hath *appointed* mine ear." With the other retentions in the Book of Mormon, it can be interpreted to be the servant Israel whom the Lord has "appointed." The JST change does not alter the meaning, but amplifies it. The servant's ear was opened but he was also appointed. Apparently, the Prophet was inspired to assure this concept.

There is one change in chapter 52 which is not in the Book of Mormon or the KJV. The last verse states, "So shall he sprinkle many nations." The JST changes the word *sprinkle* in the first phrase to *gather*. The explanation given by the Savior in the Book of Mormon is preceded by the declaration that he (the Lord) will gather his people in from their long dispersion (see 3 Nephi 21:1). Following a further amplification of this gathering, the Savior quotes the second phrase of the last verse. This implies that he has been interpreting the first phrase of the verse. The word *sprinkle* is certainly related to the word *gather* in that both imply a scattered condition. The context, as interpreted by the Savior himself, is that the Lord's servant will bring forth a marvelous work and a wonder (the Book of Mormon). This is to be the instrument used to gather the house of Israel; to do so, the Book of Mormon must be sprinkled among the nations where Israel has been scattered. Again, Joseph Smith may have changed the word to amplify the desired outcome rather the means of attaining that outcome.

The last two complete chapters of Isaiah quoted in the Book of Mormon are typical of the other chapters in this section. Some of the differences in the Book of Mormon text are carried over into the JST and some are not. For example, in 53:9, the word *violence* in the KJV is retained as *evil* in the Book of Mormon. This Book of Mormon difference is consistent with New Testament passages (see Hebrews 4:15). The first two verses in chapter 55 are also quoted in the Book of Mormon, the last time the book of Isaiah is quoted. There is a significant change in the second verse which is not carried over in the JST, another evidence that Joseph did not complete his work in this area of his translation.

In the last twelve chapters of Isaiah, which are not quoted in the Book of Mormon, there are seven significant changes. The first is in Isaiah 60:22 where the KJV reads, "I the Lord will hasten it in *his* time." The JST changes *his* to *my* time, which is in keeping with the context of the statement. In chapter 62, the meanings of two words *Hephzibah* and *Beulah* in the marriage of the land are changed to *Delightful* and *Union* (see 62:4–5). This interpretation is given in the subsequent clause of the KJV. In 63:17, the JST makes it clear that the people were responsible for the hardening of their hearts, rather than the Lord, as stated in the KJV. This traces back to a concept corrected in Genesis and Exodus. In 64:5–6, a text is rearranged to clarify the real meaning:

KJV Isaiah 64:5–6	*JST Isaiah 64:5–6*
Thou meetest him that rejoiceth and worketh righteousness, those that remember thee in thy ways: behold, thou art wroth; for we have sinned: in those is continuance, and we shall be saved.	Thou meetest him that worketh righteousness, and rejoiceth him that remembereth thee in thy ways: in righteousness there is continuance, and such shall be saved.
But we are all as an unclean thing, and all our righteous-	But we have sinned; we are all as an unclean thing, and all our

nesses are as filthy rags; and we all do fade as a leaf; and our iniquities, like the wind, have taken us away.

righteousnesses are as filthy rags; and we all do fade as a leaf; and our iniquities, like the wind, have taken us away.

The Doctrine and Covenants also rearranges other verses in chapter 64. This was not done in the JST, which is further evidence that Joseph Smith did not complete his work. The first two verses of the next chapter were also changed:

KJV Isaiah 65:1–2

I am sought of them that asked not for me; I am found of them that sought me not: I said, Behold me, behold me, unto a nation that was not called by my name.
I have spread out my hands all the day unto a rebellious people, which walketh in a way that was not good, after their own thoughts;

JST Isaiah 65:1–2

I am *found* of them *who seek after me, I give unto all them* that ask of me; I *am not found* of them that sought me not, *or that inquireth not after me.*

I said unto my servant, Behold me, look upon me: I will send you unto a nation that is not called after my name, for I have spread out my hands all the day to a people who walketh not in my ways, and their words are evil and not good, *and they walk after* their own thoughts.

The concept of the need for someone to seek the Lord—whether Jew or Gentile—is clearer in the JST than the KJV. In addition, the italicized word *things* in Isaiah 65:4 of the KJV is changed to *beasts* in the JST, a change that is consistent with the context. The last JST change made in the book of Isaiah is in 65:20.

KJV Isaiah 65:20

There shall be no more thence an infant of days, nor an old man that hath not filled his days: for the child shall die an hundred years old; but the sinner being an hundred years old shall be accursed.

JST Isaiah 65:20

In those days there shall be no more thence an infant of days, nor an old man that hath not filled his days; for the child shall *not die, but shall live to be* an hundred years old; but the sinner, *living to be* an hundred years old, shall be accursed.

These clarifying conditions of the Millennium are implied in the KJV but made certain in the JST.

The Prophet Joseph Smith certainly worked a great deal upon the Old Testament book of Isaiah. It should be emphasized, however, that his work was far from completed. There are many significant changes contained in his work but many more which could have been made.

THE BOOK OF JEREMIAH

There are eight chapters in the book of Jeremiah where significant changes were made by the Prophet Joseph Smith. Four of these eight chapters had only one verse changed in them. Most of the changes in all eight chapters centered around two topics: the false concept of the Lord repenting, and the commanding of prophets to rise up early and warn the people. It seems probable that the Prophet had his attention drawn to the clarification of the rising up of the prophets as he was searching out the verses concerning the Lord repenting.

For an object lesson regarding the house of Israel, the Lord directed Jeremiah to the potter's house. Just as marred clay in the potter's hand was put back into the large batch of clay to be reworked, so would the house of Israel be reworked by the Lord, enabling them to become a chosen vessel. In describing the Lord's actions, the KJV twice states that the Lord "will repent of the evil that [he] thought to do unto them." The JST substitutes the word *withhold* for *repent of* in both verses (see 18:8, 10). This is another example of a variant meaning of the Hebrew word. The Lord has no need of repentance because he does no evil, but he can and does change his judgments according to people's reactions to the conditions of his prophecies.

While making this change, the Prophet's attention was apparently drawn to verse 14, which taught that even the heathen's reasoning was better than theirs, because the heathen utilized the ways of nature, while Judah was not doing what was natural for her to do. The rearrangement by the Prophet makes this verse much more understandable.

KJV Jeremiah 18:14

Will a man leave the snow of Lebanon which cometh from the rock of the field? or shall the cold flowing waters that come from another place be forsaken?

JST Jeremiah 18:14

Will *you not* leave the snow *of the fields* of Lebanon; shall *not* the cold flowing waters that come from another place *from the rock,* be forsaken?

Chapter 26 of Jeremiah has three verses in the KJV which state that the Lord will repent. Verses 3 through 6 give a conditional prophecy that if they will turn from their evil ways the Lord "may repent me of the evil," but if they do not hearken to his prophets, he will make this city like Shiloh (a central city of northern Israel which was destroyed). The JST changes verse 3 to read that if "they will hearken, and turn every man from his evil way, and repent, I will turn away the evil which I purpose to do unto them." The JST also changes verse 5 from ". . . the prophets, whom I sent unto you, both rising up early, and sending them" to "*commanding them* to rise up early, and sending them." The KJV implies that the Lord was the one who rose up early, but the JST clarifies that the Lord commanded the prophets to rise.

The JST also adds this phrase to the end of verse 6: *"For ye have not hearkened unto my servants the prophets,"* thus verifying that the Lord does not destroy a nation before they are warned by the prophets (see 2 Nephi 25:9). This clarification by the Prophet Joseph probably led him to the other areas of the book of Jeremiah where the record spoke of rising up early. In each instance, the Prophet changed the text to read that the Lord commanded the prophets to rise, rather than simply stating that he himself rose early. The Lord's spirit is immortal, and obviously is not in need of sleep as are mortal beings. These changes were made in 29:19; 35:14–15; and 44:4. Verse 14 of chapter 35 is slightly different from the other verses, in that the Lord says "commanding you to" rather than "commanding them."

Verse 13 of chapter 26 also changes the KJV "and the Lord will repent him of the evil" to "and repent and the Lord will turn away the evil," thus again placing the responsibility upon the people. Verses 18 through 20 are also changed to correct the false concept of the Lord repenting. These verses are the words of the elders who defended against putting Jeremiah to death:

KJV Jeremiah 26:18–20	JST Jeremiah 26:18–20
Micah the Morasthite prophesied in the days of Hezekiah king of Judah, and spake to all the people of Judah, saying, Thus saith the Lord of hosts; Zion shall be plowed like a field, and Jerusalem shall become heaps, and the mountain of the house as the high places of a forest.	Micah the Morasthite prophesied in the days of Hezekiah king of Judah, and spake to all the people of Judah, saying, Thus saith the Lord of hosts; Zion shall be ploughed like a field, and Jerusalem shall become heaps, and the mountain of the house *of the Lord* as the high places of a forest.
Did Hezekiah king of Judah and all Judah put him at all to death? did he not fear the Lord, and besought the Lord, and the Lord repented him of the evil which he had pronounced against them? Thus might we procure great evil against our souls.	Did Hezekiah, king of Judah, and all Judah put him at all to death? Did he not fear the Lord and beseech the Lord and repent? and the Lord turned away the evil which he had pronounced against them? Thus *by putting Jeremiah to death* we might procure great evil against our souls.
And there was also a man that prophesied in the name of the Lord, Urijah the son of Shemaiah of Kirjath-jearim, who prophesied against this city and against this land according to all the words of Jeremiah:	But there was a man among the priests, rose up and said, that, Urijah the son of Shemaiah of Kirjath-jearim, prophesied in the name of the Lord, who also prophesied against this city, and against this land, according to all the words of Jeremiah.

The changes not only correct the erroneous idea of God repenting, but also make the text more understandable and historically consistent with the subsequent verses. Verse 10 of chapter 42 has the same kind of change, substituting the KJV "for I repent me of the evil" to "and *I will turn away* the evil."

There are two places in Jeremiah where the Prophet clarified or emphasized the meaning through altering and sometimes rearranging the wording, the first in 2:24. The Prophet moved the word *not* from the next to the last phrase to the last phrase. The

Lord is comparing Judah to a wild ass who has learned the way of the wilderness and is free to follow the desires of her heart. He then asks, "In her occasion who can turn her away?" The question seems to be, "Who can take away her freedom?" The KJV marginal note reads, "Or, reverse it?" The JST renders the answer, "All they that seek her will weary themselves; in her month they shall *not* find her." If she follows her natural instincts for freedom, she will not be caught.

Other commentators, following the corrupted text, suggest that *in her occasion* and *in her month* refer to the male animals seeking her out in the time of her periodic breeding seasons, during which time she will be caught. The JST fits the context of the following verses better. The Lord admonishes the wild ass (Judah) to "withhold thy foot from being unshod, and thy throat from thirst." In other words, she is invited to maintain her freedom by avoiding those who are seeking to capture her as she satisfies her thirst at the waterhole.

The other change of wording comes in chapter 30 of Jeremiah:

KJV Jeremiah 30:12–15

For thus saith the Lord, Thy bruise is incurable, and thy wound is grievous.

There is none to plead thy cause, that thou mayest be bound up: thou hast no healing medicines.

All thy lovers have forgotten thee; they seek thee not; for I have wounded thee with the wound of an enemy, with the chastisement of a cruel one, for the multitude of thine iniquity; because thy sins were increased.

Why criest thou for thine affliction? thy sorrow is incurable for the multitude of thine iniquity: because thy sins were increased, I have done these things unto thee.

JST Jeremiah 30:12–15

For thus saith the Lord, thy bruise is *not* incurable, *although* thy wounds *are* grievous.

Is there none to plead thy cause, that thou mayest be bound up? *Hast thou* no healing medicines?

Have all thy lovers forgotten thee, do they *not* seek thee? For I have wounded thee with the wound of an enemy, with the chastisement of a cruel one, for the multitude of thine iniquities; because thy sins are increased.

Why criest thou for thine affliction? *Is thy* sorrow incurable? It was for the multitude of thine iniquities, and because thy sins are increased I have done these things unto thee.

The JST reverses the meaning of these verses, showing that Israel's condition is curable and she is now ready (in the latter days) to be restored to her promised blessings. The fact that the scriptural statements in the KJV are changed to questions in the JST further points to this meaning. The first word of verse 16 is changed from *therefore* to *but,* which also fits the context better.

It seems that the Prophet did not spend a great deal of time on the book of Jeremiah. He made some significant changes and undoubtedly would have made many more if the time had been available to him. For instance, in Matthew 27:9, we have reference to Jeremiah's prophecy about Judas Iscariot's betrayal of Christ for thirty pieces of silver. While Zechariah actually made such a prophecy, it is very possible that Jeremiah had earlier recorded the same prophecy.

In Jeremiah 8:8, the KJV marginal note suggests an alternate reading that "the false pens of the scribes worketh for falsehood." Other translations also support this alternate reading. There is little evidence that Joseph Smith corrected many of these types of errors. The confused chronological order of the various chapters of Jeremiah suggests that there are several arrangements which he could have corrected. Someday, when the plates of brass are returned or the translation of the Bible commenced by Joseph Smith is completed, as has been promised, we'll know the answer to this question.

THE BOOKS OF EZEKIEL AND DANIEL

It seems apparent that the Prophet did not spend much time on the books of Ezekiel and Daniel. Only five verses are changed significantly in Ezekiel, three of them in chapter 23. Only one word is changed in the book of Daniel. All of the changes in these two books are of a historical nature, making the account consistent with the established practices or actions of the Lord, or internally consistent with itself.

In Ezekiel 14:9, the KJV reads, "And if the prophet be deceived when he hath spoken a thing, I the Lord have deceived that prophet, and I will stretch out my hand upon him, and will destroy him from the midst of my people Israel." Joseph Smith corrected this verse to say, "And if the prophet be deceived when he hath spoken a thing, I the Lord have *not* deceived that prophet; *therefore* I will stretch out my hand. . . ." The Lord does not deceive his prophets.

In chapter 23 of Ezekiel, the Lord uses an allegory to teach that Samaria and Jerusalem, the capital cities of the two nations of Israel, had alienated themselves from the Lord by committing whoredoms or worshipping other gods. The KJV represents this alienation as being in their minds and from their symbolic lovers (other nations). Joseph Smith made changes in verses 17, 22, and 28 showing that the nations of Israel were alienated in their minds from *the Lord by* these symbolic lovers. These changes make the verses consistent with the rest of the allegory.

Chapter 48 describes the gates of the city seen in vision by Ezekiel. In the KJV verse 35 gives the name of the city, saying, "And the name of the city from that day shall be, The Lord is there." The JST says, "And the name of the city from that day shall be *called, Holy; for* the Lord *shall be* there." The sentence in the KJV makes little sense, but the JST makes it consistent with Isaiah 60:1–2, 14 and Revelation 21:2–3.

Chapter 5 of Daniel gives the account of a message from God being written upon the wall of the palace of the king of Babylon. Verses 25–28 give the message that was written and the interpretation of each word. The last word of the message, *Upharsin* is rendered *Peres* in the interpretive verse. Joseph changed the word in the interpretive verse to be the same as the word in the message, thus restoring consistency.

THE TWELVE PROPHETS

Of the twelve books of the so-called minor prophets (Hosea through Malachi), only five have any changes made in them. These are mostly in Zechariah (five) and in Amos (seven). Hosea has one change, Jonah two, and Joel three. Again, it seems that the Prophet did not have time to do much work on this section. Seven of the eighteen changed verses deal with the false concept of the Lord repenting. Apparently the Prophet went through the entire Old Testament endeavoring to correct this false idea.

The first of the seven changes regarding the Lord repenting occurs in Hosea 11:8. The KJV reads, "Mine heart is turned within me, my repentings are kindled together." The Prophet changed this verse to read, "Mine heart is turned *toward thee, and my mercies are extended to gather thee.*" While Joseph's attention was undoubtedly drawn to this verse by the false concept of the Lord repenting, his correction also teaches another great concept—the gathering of Ephraim or Israel in the latter days. The gathering is implied in the beginning of the verse, and so the change makes for consistency within the verse as well as within the book of Hosea (see Hosea 1:10–11; 2:23; 3:4–5). It is also consistent with the teachings of other prophets (see Isaiah 6:13; Jeremiah 3:14; Ezekiel 6:8–10; Amos 9:8–9; Micah 2:12). This is the only verse changed in Hosea.

The book of Joel has two verses changed regarding the Lord repenting.

KJV Joel 2:13–14

And rend your heart, and not your garments, and turn unto the Lord your God: for he is gracious and merciful, slow to anger, and of great kindness, and repenteth him of the evil.

Who knoweth if he will return and repent, and leave a blessing behind him; even a meat offering and a drink offering unto the Lord your God?

JST Joel 2:13–14

And rend your heart, and not your garments, *and repent,* and turn unto the Lord your God: for he is gracious and merciful, slow to anger, and of great kindness, and *he will turn away* the evil *from you.*

Therefore repent, and who knoweth *but* he will return and leave a blessing behind him; that you may offer a meat offering, and a drink offering, unto the Lord your God?

These verses encourage or invite the people to repent and escape the destruction of the Second Coming. The verses following in Joel speak of the gathering of the righteous to Jerusalem and Zion, thus further validating the change made by the Prophet.

There is only one other change made in the book of Joel. The context is the description of a nation which will come upon the Lord's land "whose teeth are the teeth of a lion" (1:6). The JST shows this to be a symbolic description by adding "whose teeth are *as* the teeth of a lion." Quite obviously a symbolic representation, this is typical of many changes which Joseph apparently made to insure that the reader would be able to understand the difference between the literal and the symbolic.

The book of Amos has more changes in it (seven) than any of the twelve prophets, and these changes seem to center around the same problem, the Lord's repenting.

KJV Amos 7:3, 6	JST Amos 7:3, 6
The Lord repented for this: It shall not be, saith the Lord.	And the Lord *said, concerning Jacob, Jacob shall repent* for this, *therefore I will not utterly destroy him,* saith the Lord.
The Lord repented for this: This also shall not be, saith the Lord God.	*And the Lord said, concerning Jacob, Jacob shall repent of his wickedness; therefore I will not utterly destroy him,* saith the Lord God.

These verses tell of Amos seeing a series of three visions from the Lord. In the first two, Amos pleads for his people, the descendants of father Jacob. Besides correcting the idea that the Lord repents, the changes make another important point. The KJV would lead one to believe that the Lord changed his mind or his actions at the time of Amos' ministry. This is not historically accurate—Israel was captured and destroyed shortly thereafter, as the rest of chapter 7 foretells. The JST shows that Jacob will later repent, and therefore, the Lord will not utterly destroy them, but will leave a remnant so this future repentance can take place. This is a constant theme throughout the text of the Old Testament prophets.

Other changes in chapter 3 of Amos are also related to the false concept of the Lord repenting. The KJV reads, "Shall there be evil in a city, and the Lord hath not done it?" (Amos 3:6). This is inconsistent with the teachings of the Book of Mormon, "All things which are good cometh of God; and all which is evil cometh of the devil" (Moroni 7:12). This same concept is taught in the New Testament (see James 1:17; 3 John 1:11). As worded in the JST, this problem is removed, "Shall there be evil in a city, and the Lord hath not *known* it?" The omniscience of God prevents the hiding of evil from him.

The next verse, Amos 3:7, shows what the Lord does about his knowledge of evil. There are two words changed in the JST which at that time fit better in the context. The KJV says, "Surely the Lord God will do nothing, but he revealeth his secret unto his servants the prophets." The JST says, "Surely the Lord God will do nothing, *until* he revealeth *the* secret unto his servants the prophets." This, of course, is a famous missionary scripture in the Church. Understood in this context, it is even more important. The word *until* is consistent with 2 Nephi 25:9, which teaches that the Lord will not destroy a nation until he warns them by the prophets. Amos, along with others such as Isaiah and Micah, is warning Israel prior to her destruction. The words *the secret* instead of *his secret* make it consistent with the previous verse wherein it is attempted to keep the evil in the city hidden.

Had the Prophet had the time, he would have undoubtedly made a similar change concerning evil in Isaiah 45:7 where it states that the Lord *creates evil*. The Lord does not create evil, but will bring destruction upon a people ripened in iniquity (see Genesis 15:16; 1 Nephi 17:35), which is the context of the Isaiah verse and is supported by other translations such as the RSV, "I make weal (prosperous) and create woe (calamity)." This is strong evidence that the Prophet did not complete the work.

There are three other changes in the book of Amos, all of them in chapter 4. These are not as significant as other changes in the book, but make the text more understandable.

KJV Amos 4:3

And ye shall go out at the breaches, every cow at that which is before her; and ye shall cast them into the palace, saith the Lord.

JST Amos 4:3

And ye shall go out at the breaches, every *one* before *his enemy;* and ye shall be cast *out of your* palaces, saith the Lord.

These verses are usually interpreted as a rebuke against the women of Samaria, particularly those whose husbands are in leadership positions. The italicized words in the KJV imply the uncertainty of the text. The use of the masculine pronoun by the Prophet is a little troublesome. Perhaps the rebuke is not limited to the women but the cow is a symbolic representation of the leaders. Perhaps verse 3, in speaking of the coming conquest, expands the group to include all of the people. Verse 5 changes another phrase to a more sensible reading. The KJV reading "for this liketh you" is changed in the JST to "thus do ye." Verse 6 changes the first word from *and* to *therefore,* thus showing more clearly that the following judgment spoken of in the verse is a result of wickedness. Many more clarifications probably could have been made by the Prophet had he thoroughly studied the book of Amos.

The two verses changed in the book of Jonah both concern the false concept of the Lord repenting:

KJV Jonah 3:9–10	JST Jonah 3:9–10
Who can tell if God will turn and repent, and turn away from his fierce anger, that we perish not?	Who can tell, if *we* will *repent, and turn unto God, but he will* turn away from us his fierce anger, that we perish not?
And God saw their works, that they turned from their evil way; and God repented of the evil, that he had said that he would do unto them; and he did it not.	And God saw their works that they turned from their evil way *and repented;* and God *turned away* the evil that he had said he would *bring* upon them.

These verses describe how the people of Nineveh heeded Jonah's message and repented. These changes are based upon a misunderstanding of the Hebrew word, as are many earlier changes of this nature.

The remaining changes in the twelve prophets are in the book of Zechariah. A total of five verses are changed in three chapters. Four of these changes clarify a meaning either symbolically or literally. The *eyes* of the Lord (4:10) in the KJV is changed to *servant* in the JST. It is a clarification of the vision shown to Zechariah. In another vision shown to him (6:5), the *four spirits* of the KJV are identified as *four servants* in the JST. In chapter 8, both verses 7 and 13 state that the Lord will *save* his people in the last days. The Prophet Joseph changed the word to *gather* which is more consistent with the context. In the explanation of the vision spoken of above (4:14), the KJV tells of two anointed ones standing *by* the Lord, while the JST represents them as standing *before* the Lord. That is the end of the vision and no further comment is given. The change seems to be a clarification of the supremacy of the Lord, however, this line of reasoning is only supposition.

There are seven books of the twelve prophets which had no changes made in them, but there probably would have been many more alterations had the Prophet worked further on this section. This conclusion is drawn from the Savior's quotation of Malachi, chapters 3 and 4, to the Nephites in the meridian of time. There are several differences in the two texts, but only one is significant. The KJV speaks of the *Sun* of righteousness and the Book of Mormon text speaks of the *son* of Righteousness (see 3 Nephi 25:2). A discussion of this difference will be left to a more appropriate time when the Book of Mormon retentions are being considered.

Further evidence of Joseph not spending large amounts of time on this text is given in his account of the angel Moroni appearing to him in September 1823 and quoting these same two chapters. Chapter 4, verse 1 has two significant changes in it, and verses 5 and 6 as quoted were drastically different. The first change is a wording change to clarify the Second Coming. The last verses changed may have been a paraphrase by the angel (see D&C 2) to make certain that the Prophet Joseph Smith understood them. This conclusion is drawn from the fact that they are quoted exactly the same in the Book of Mormon and the KJV. Furthermore, in writing an epistle to the Saints, Joseph also quoted these verses exactly as they are found in the Malachi text and then added: "I might have rendered a plainer translation than this, but it is sufficiently plain to suit my purposes as it stands" (D&C 128:18). It seems logical that Malachi's original words were translated correctly, but with the passage of time, the meanings of words change; therefore, the angel Moroni clarified the meaning to Joseph.

The purpose of changes in all of the twelve prophets seems to have been primarily to correct the idea portrayed in the KJV that God repents. As Joseph discovered these false statements, his reading of surrounding passages—to determine the context of the verses and thus enable him to make a proper correction—also pointed up other errors. This can be concluded because the changes are clustered in certain sections. Most changes would fit this explanation. The exceptions may have been from questions raised by others or from the Prophet's own study. Nevertheless, it seems obvious that the Prophet did not complete his study and we can assume that some changes which should have been made have not been made.

On the other hand, one must not overlook the importance of the changes which *were* made. Through the efforts of Joseph Smith, the Church and the world, if they will heed his words, can come to a greater knowledge and understanding of the Old Testament prophets. The footnoting in the new publication of the Bible by The Church of Jesus Christ of Latter-day Saints has done a great service for its members by making available many of these significant changes.

The challenge given to us repeatedly by the Savior and the prophets throughout time is to search the scriptures. The meaning of the word *search* is to look in every possible place. One of the most important places to look for an understanding of the Old Testament prophets is the Joseph Smith Translation of the Bible.

Monte S. Nyman is associate dean of
Religious Education and professor of
Ancient Scripture at BYU.

8

The JST and the Synoptic Gospels: Literary Style

Robert L. Millet

What scholars for years have called the "Synoptic Problem" entails the study of relationships between the synoptic Gospels—Matthew, Mark, and Luke. These three have a similar perspective and point of view with regard to the manner in which the ministry of Jesus is presented. In this article, we will consider two aspects of the Joseph Smith Translation of the synoptic Gospels which I feel suggest a restoration of content, and which therefore have interesting implications for the Latter-day Saint intent on further pursuing synoptic relationships. These are: (1) the accentuation of distinct literary styles of each of the Gospels; and (2) addition and insertion of new backgrounds and contexts in the Gospels.

GOSPEL PERSPECTIVES

Each of the Gospel writers sought to bear witness of the Savior in his own way. The Gospels were never intended to be biographical in scope or even to serve as classical "lives" of

Christ. It may be, for example, that no more than thirty days or so of the life of Jesus is specifically presented in the canonical Gospels. What we have available to us are testimonies of the Lord's Divine Sonship, abbreviated narratives of how it was that the Mortal Messiah "abolished death, and . . . brought life and immortality to light through the gospel" (2 Timothy 1:10).

Even though the synoptic Gospels all have a similar perspective, each has a peculiar style and particular points of emphasis, usually as a result of its intended audience. Matthew apparently wrote to a Jewish audience and sought to prove from the Old Testament that Jesus of Nazareth was the Anointed and Appointed One, the Promise of the ages. Mark and Luke seem to have written to a gentile audience; Mark's work is a fast-moving narrative, Luke's a sermon and parable-filled account.[1]

Matthew

Matthew's work is appropriately known as the "Gospel of the Church." It is, indeed, the only New Testament Gospel to use the term *church* (Greek *ekklesia*) in making reference to the organized community of believers. Peter's confession at Caesarea Philippi ("Thou art the Christ, the Son of the living God") is acknowledged and commended by the Master as of divine origin. The Lord continues: "And I say also unto thee, That thou art Peter, and upon this rock *I will build my church;* and the gates of hell shall not prevail against it. And I will give unto thee the keys of the kingdom of heaven" (Matthew 16:13–19; emphasis added). The significant contribution of Matthew's Gospel in this regard (i.e., the matter of the Church) is grasped by simply comparing the synoptics in parallel. Mark's account (8:29–30) contains 23 words, Luke's account (9:20–21) contains 22 words, while Matthew's description consists of 128 words.

Further instructions as to how to regulate the Church are given in what we have as Matthew 18. Subjects discussed include the need for conversion (vv. 1–5); the principle of removing harmful elements from the members' lives and thus from the Church (vv. 7–9); member activation (vv. 12–14); resolving differences between individual Saints (vv. 15–17); and the need for genuine forgiveness (vv. 21–35). The instructions regarding the resolution of differences between members (cf. similar counsel in D&C 42:84–92) conclude with this matter of policy: "And if he [the accused] shall neglect to hear them [witnesses], *tell it unto the church:* but if he neglect to hear the church, let him be unto thee as an heathen man and a publican" (Matthew 18:17; emphasis added).

The JST of Matthew is a stronger witness than the King James Version (KJV) that one of Matthew's areas of stress is the place of the Church in administering the gospel to the Saints. The JST places a much greater stress upon the fact that the Church (through the holy priesthood) administered the gospel and, through the establishment of standards and commandments, sought to structure the lives of the members in strait and narrow ways. The need for *commandments* within the Christian community became an important insight and contribution of Joseph Smith through his inspired translation of Matthew. Concluding his masterful Sermon on the Mount, the Savior therefore set the ultimate standard for the believer, and couched it in a new terminology: "Ye are therefore *commanded* to be perfect, even as your Father who is in heaven is perfect" (JST Matthew 5:50).

To his disciples during the Sermon on the Mount, Jesus added this bit of counsel:

KJV Matthew 6:26	*JST Matthew 6:29–30*
Behold the fowls of the air: for they sow not, neither do they reap, nor gather into barns; yet your heavenly Father feedeth them. Are ye not much better than they?	Behold the fowls of the air, for they sow not, neither do they reap, nor gather into barns; yet your heavenly Father feedeth them. Are ye not much better than they? *How much more will he not feed you?* *Wherefore take no thought for these things, but keep my commandments wherewith I have commanded you.*

The occasion of the healing of the two blind men provides another opportunity for us to see the emergence of this theme in the JST:

KJV Matthew 9:29–30

Then touched he their eyes, saying, According to your faith be it unto you.

And their eyes were opened: and Jesus straitly charged them, saying, See that no man know it.

JST Matthew 9:35–36

Then touched he their eyes, saying, According to your faith, be it unto you.

And their eyes were opened: and straitly he charged them, saying, *Keep my commandments, and see ye tell no man in this place, that no man know it.*

It was not enough for the healed men to keep the miracle a secret; they must *keep the commandments* to be a part of the community of believers.

The cost of discipleship is enunciated in an important discourse to his disciples, just after Peter's confession. The Lord here defines what it means for one to "take up his cross." Note: "Then said Jesus unto his disciples, If any man will come after me, let him deny himself, and take up his cross and follow me. *And now for a man to take up his cross, is to deny himself all ungodliness, and every worldly lust, and keep my commandments. Break not my commandments for to save your lives:* for whosoever will save his life *in this world,* shall lose it *in the world to come.* And whosoever will lose his life *in this world,* for my sake, shall find it *in the world to come. Therefore, forsake the world, and save your souls:* for what is a man profited, if he shall gain the whole world, and lose his own soul?" (JST Matthew 16:25–29.

Finally, it was not only the function of the Church to administer the gospel through the ordinances (see JST Matthew 5:1–4; 18:10–11), but also see to it that those within the Church lived lives consistent with the high standards set by its founder. As we mentioned earlier, chapter 18 of Matthew deals with the conduct of Church members, and provides direction on dealing with problems that might arise. In the JST, we get a clearer picture of what the Savior intended when he spoke of rooting out evil influences within and between persons in the Church. "And if thine eye offend thee, pluck it out and cast it from thee; it is better for thee to enter into life with one eye, rather than having two eyes to be cast into hell fire. *And a man's hand is his friend, and his foot, also; and a man's eye, are they of his own household."* (JST Matthew 18:6-9; cf. JST Mark 9:40-47.)

A second major area of stress in the Gospel of Matthew is Jesus' denunciation of Judaism. A more detailed treatment of the relationship between Jesus and the Jews of the first century will be given in a subsequent article in this volume,[2] but we will note a few examples here. Jesus chided the Jews of his day with becoming enamored with the externals, with means rather than ends—he attacked their empty formalism and hypocrisy. This theme is far more prominent in Matthew than in the other Gospels.

Because the leaders of the Jews misunderstood and misread the "signs of the times," they failed to recognize him through whom the Law had been given anciently. Therefore, at best their preaching was empty, certainly when compared with the Master who "taught them as *one having authority from God, and not as having authority from the Scribes"* (JST Matthew 7:37; emphasis added). Again, many of the specific charges of the Savior against the Jewish leaders will be considered later in this book. For the time being, note the impact of the JST on what is already a scathing denunciation—chapter 23 of the Gospel of Matthew.

KJV Matthew 23:1-3, 15, 24, 31-32, 36-37

Then spake Jesus to the multitude, and to his disciples,

Saying, The scribes and the Pharisees sit in Moses' seat:

All therefore whatsoever they bid you observe, that observe and do; but do not ye after their works: for they say, and do not.

Woe unto you, scribes and Pharisees, hypocrites! for ye compass sea and land to make one proselyte, and when he is made, ye make him twofold

JST, Matthew 23:1-2, 12, 21, 28-29, 33-37

Then spake Jesus to the multitude, and to his disciples, saying, The Scribes and the Pharisees sit in Moses' seat.

All, therefore, whatsoever they bid you observe, *they will make you observe and do; for they are ministers of the law, and they make themselves your judges.* But do not ye after their works; for they say, and do not.

Woe unto you, Scribes and Pharisees, hypocrites! For ye compass sea and land to make one proselyte; and when he is made, ye make him two-fold

more the child of hell than yourselves.	more the child of hell than *he was before, like unto yourselves.*
Ye blind guides, which strain at a gnat, and swallow a camel.	Ye blind guides, who strain at a gnat, and swallow a camel; *who make yourselves appear unto men that ye would not commit the least sin, and yet ye yourselves, transgress the whole law.*
Wherefore ye be witnesses unto yourselves, that ye are the children of them which killed the prophets.	Wherefore, ye are witnesses unto yourselves *of your own wickedness,* and ye are the children of them who killed the prophets;
Fill ye up then the measure of your fathers.	*And will fill up the measure then of your fathers; for ye, yourselves, kill the prophets like unto your fathers.*
Verily I say unto you, All these things shall come upon this generation.	Verily I say unto you, All these things shall come upon this generation. *Ye bear testimony against your fathers, when ye, yourselves, are partakers of the same wickedness. Behold your fathers did it through ignorance, but ye do not; wherefore, their sins shall be upon your heads. Then Jesus began to weep over Jerusalem, saying,*
O Jerusalem, Jerusalem, thou that killest the prophets, and stonest them which are sent unto thee, how often would I have gathered thy children together, even as a hen gathereth her chickens under her wings, and ye would not!	O Jerusalem! Jerusalem! *Ye who will kill the prophets, and will stone* them who are sent unto you; how often would I have gathered your children together, even as a hen gathers her chickens under her wings, and ye would not.

A third area of emphasis in Matthew is Jesus as the fulfillment of God's promise to Israel. Matthew's Gospel was written by a man intent on building a bridge between the old covenant and the new, or between what we have come to call the two

Testaments. His was the witness, like Jacob, that "none of the prophets have written, nor prophesied, save they have spoken concerning this Christ" (Jacob 7:11).

As recorded in the JST, Jesus spoke clearly and directly to Simon and Andrew when he called them to their discipleship. "And he said unto them, *I am he of whom it is written by the prophets;* follow me, and I will make you fishers of men" (JST Matthew 4:18; emphasis added). The Christ of which the Prophets had written was now among the people, and the JST of Matthew is an even stronger witness that Jesus of Nazareth was that Living Fulfillment.

During the infancy narrative, we note a reference which attests to the place of Jesus as Messiah. The wise men come from the east seeking to behold and participate in a marvelous event at hand. They ask, "Where is the child that is born, the *Messiah* of the Jews?" (JST Matthew 3:2; emphasis added). It is not the King, but the *Messiah* of the Jews whom they seek. Further, with regard to the childhood of Christ, we are given a remarkable insight by Joseph Smith:

KJV Matthew 2:22–3:1

But when he heard that Archelaus did reign in Judea in the room of his father Herod, he was afraid to go thither: notwithstanding, being warned of God in a dream, he turned aside into the parts of Galilee:

And he came and dwelt in a city called Nazareth: that it might be fulfilled which was spoken by the prophets, He shall be called a Nazarene.

JST Matthew 3:22–27

But when he heard that Archelaus did reign in Judea in the stead of his father Herod, he was afraid to go thither; but, notwithstanding, being warned of God in a *vision,* he went into *the eastern part of Galilee:*

And he came and dwelt in a city called Nazareth, that it might be fulfilled which was spoken by the prophets, He shall be called a Nazarene.

And it came to pass that Jesus grew up with his brethren, and waxed strong, and waited upon the Lord for the time of his ministry to come.

And he served under his father, and spake not as other men, neither could he be taught;

	for he needed not that any man should teach him.
	And after many years, the hour of his ministry drew nigh.
Chapter 3	
In those days came John the Baptist, preaching in the wilderness of Judea,	And in those days came John the Baptist, preaching in the wilderness of Judea,

These verses not only supply an excellent transition between Christ's infancy and the beginning of John's ministry (note the lack of transition in the KJV from 2:23 to 3:1), but in addition point up the fact that our Lord received instructions from the heavens as well as from mortal teachers. His Divine Sonship is strongly affirmed in the JST.

We referred earlier to Matthew 23 as perhaps the greatest collection of denunciations by the Lord. At the close of that chapter, the JST adds a few words which further attest to Christ's divine position. "Behold, your house is left unto you desolate! For I say unto you, that ye shall not see me henceforth, *and know that I am he of whom it is written by the prophets,* until ye shall say, Blessed is he who cometh in the name of the Lord, *in the clouds of heaven, and all the holy angels with him. Then understood his disciples that he should come again on the earth, after that he was glorified and crowned on the right hand of God.*" (JST Matthew 23:38–41.)

Mark

The Gospel of Mark is a fast-flowing, active account which moves rapidly from John the Baptist to the passion narrative. It is also an account of dramatic *personal reactions.*[3] In this Gospel, greater stress is placed upon persons being offended at Jesus; the sadness, fear, amazement, and ignorance of the disciples; and the righteous rebuke of the Twelve by the Lord for their present nearsightedness. It is interesting to note, therefore, the accentuation in the JST of such matters as the *fear* of the disciples (see JST Mark 9:31), their *astonishment* (see JST Mark 9:6), and additional mention of persons *taking offense* at the Savior (see JST Mark 11:34; 12:44; 14:31).

In chapter 10 of Mark the disciples are concerned as to who can be saved. Peter reminds the Lord that the Twelve have left all to follow him, and is assured by Christ that all losses will be recompensed a hundredfold in the world to come. The King James text then records the following statement by Jesus: "But many that are first shall be last; and the last first" (Mark 10:28–31). Note the same discussion in the JST: "But there are *many who make themselves first,* that shall be last, and the last first. *This he said, rebuking Peter.*" (JST Mark 10:30–31.)

The following from the Prophet's translation of chapter 14 of Mark is worthy of a closer look. Given that Mark chose in his Gospel account to stress the weakness and ignorance of the Twelve, what do we conclude about the following from the JST?

And they came to a place which was named Gethsemane, *which was a garden;* and the disciples began to be sore amazed, and to be very heavy, *and to complain in their hearts, wondering if this be the Messiah.*

And Jesus knowing their hearts, said to his disciples, Sit ye here, while I shall pray.

And he taketh with him, Peter, James, and John, *and rebuked them,* and said unto them, My soul is exceeding sorrowful, even unto death; tarry ye here and watch. (JST Mark 14:36–38.)

Luke

The Gospel of Luke is the first of a two-part work (Luke-Acts) written by Luke, the missionary companion of Paul. Luke is writing specifically to a gentile friend, Theophilus (see Acts 1:1; JST Luke 3:19–20), but generally to a broad gentile audience. The work is put forward to emphasize the universal scope of the message of Christ, and provides a background for a discussion of the systematic spread of the gospel from Jerusalem to all Judea, to Samaria, and finally to the ends of the earth (see Acts 1:8).

Joseph Smith's translation of Luke provides an even stronger gentile flavor to the account. In chapter 3 of Luke, for example, the Prophet adds five verses (175 words), which insertion not only provides a meaningful transition between verses 4 and 5 in the Authorized Version (and thus a doctrinal bridge between the first and second comings of the Christ), but also lays a foundation for the concept that the spread of the gospel will even encompass those outside of the house of Israel.

KJV Luke 3:2–6

the word of God came unto John the son of Zacharias in the wilderness.

And he came into all the country about Jordan, preaching the baptism of repentance for the remission of sins;
As it is written in the book of the words of Esaias the prophet, saying, The voice of one crying in the wilderness, Prepare ye the way of the Lord, make his paths straight.

JST Luke 3:2–11

Now in this same year, the word of God came unto John, the son of Zacharias, in the wilderness.

And he came into all the country about Jordan, preaching the baptism of repentance for the remission of sins.
As it is written in the book of the prophet Esaias; *and these are the words,* saying, The voice of one crying in the wilderness, Prepare ye the way of the Lord, and make his paths straight.

For behold, and lo, he shall come, as it is written in the book of the prophets, to take away the sins of the world, and to bring salvation unto the heathen nations, to gather together those who are lost, who are of the sheepfold of Israel;

Yea, even the dispersed and afflicted; and also to prepare the way, and make possible the preaching of the gospel unto the Gentiles;

And to be a light unto all who sit in darkness, unto the uttermost parts of the earth; to bring to pass the resurrection from the dead, and to ascend up on high, to dwell on the right hand of the Father,

Until the fulness of time, and the law and the testimony shall be sealed, and the keys of the kingdom shall be delivered up again unto the Father;

Every valley shall be filled, and every mountain and hill shall be brought low; and the crooked shall be made straight, and the rough ways shall be made smooth; And all flesh shall see the salvation of God.	*To administer justice unto all; to come down in judgment upon all, and to convince all the ungodly of their ungodly deeds, which they have committed; and all this in the day that he shall come;* *For it is a day of power;* yea, every valley shall be filled, and every mountain and hill shall be brought low; the crooked shall be made straight, and the rough ways made smooth; And all flesh shall see the salvation of God.

We find in the JST of Luke additional cultural explanations—insights which might be given to Gentiles perhaps less familiar with living patterns of the Jews. For example, in the same chapter 3 of Luke, we find John the Baptist counseling the multitude to share their surplus with those less fortunate. To the publicans he directs: "Exact no more [of those from whom you take taxes] than that which is appointed you." (Luke 3:13.) The following is added in the JST: *"For it is well known unto you, Theophilus, that after the manner of the Jews, and according to the custom of their law in receiving money into the treasury, that out of the abundance which was received, was appointed unto the poor, every man his portion; And after this manner did the publicans also, wherefore John said unto them, Exact no more than that which is appointed you."* (JST Luke 3:19–20.)

Another example of this type of addition (cultural clarifications) in the JST is found in chapter 17 of Luke. Here the Lord is enumerating some of the signs incident to his coming in glory. He speaks of the fact that on that great and dreadful day

> Two shall be in the field; the one shall be taken, and the other left.
> And they answered and said unto him, Where, Lord, *shall they be taken.*
> And he said unto them, Wheresoever the body is *gathered;* or, in other words, whithersoever the saints are gath-

ered, thither will the eagles be gathered together; *or, thither will the remainder be gathered together.*

This he spake, signifying the gathering of his saints; and of angels descending and gathering the remainder unto them; the one from the bed, the other from the grinding, and the other from the field, whithersoever he listeth. (JST Luke 17:35–38.)

A final item to consider is the fact that expressions occur in the JST of Luke which are generally recognized as Pauline sayings. In chapter 3 of the JST, John the Baptist speaks of the "fulness of time" (JST Luke 3:8), an expression found in Paul's letter to the Ephesians (see 1:10). In chapter 12 of Luke, Jesus explains to the Twelve that "the laborer is worthy of his hire; for the law saith, That a man shall not muzzle the ox that treadeth out the corn." (JST Luke 12:33.) In this case, Jesus is citing an Old Testament passage (see Deuteronomy 25:4), and drawing contemporary application. Paul refers to the same matter in 1 Corinthians 9:9 and 1 Timothy 5:18. The same is true with the phrase "thief in the night," referring to the suddenness of our Lord's second coming in glory. It occurs in the JST of Luke (12:44) and also in 1 Thessalonians 5:2 (cf. 2 Peter 3:10), but not in Matthew, Mark, or John. We know that Luke and Paul were intimately associated, and certainly the two men would have influenced the thought and writings of each other. The Joseph Smith Translation strengthens the tie between Luke and Paul.

THE JST AND THE SYNOPTIC GOSPELS: BACKGROUNDS AND SETTINGS

The second main area which I feel suggests a restoration of content in the JST has to do with the addition or reconstitution of settings and backgrounds in the Gospels. The form critic has long been concerned with "getting behind the sources" to discuss the earliest *Sitz im Leben* or "setting in life" for sayings or sermons or events in the life of Christ. Serious-minded Latter-day Saints cannot, therefore, ignore the fact that the Joseph Smith Translation of the Gospels frequently introduces new or unusual settings for many of what have become proverbial sayings of the

Savior. This occurs occasionally in Matthew and Mark, and quite often in Luke. We will now consider three examples of this phenomenon.

In chapter 9 of Matthew, Jesus has just explained why his disciples do not fast after the pattern of the Pharisees, or even like the Baptist's followers. "The days will come," the Lord prophesies, "when the bridegroom shall be taken from them, and then shall they fast" (Matthew 9:15). The next verse in the KJV begins the discussion of the new cloth and the new wine. Note the insertion in the JST:

> But the days will come, when the bridegroom shall be taken from them, and then shall they fast.
> *Then said the Pharisees unto him, Why will ye not receive us with our baptism, seeing we keep the whole law?*
> *But Jesus said unto them, Ye keep not the law. If ye had kept the law, ye would have received me, for I am he who gave the law.*
> *I receive not you with your baptism, because it profiteth you nothing.*
> *For when that which is new is come, the old is ready to be put away.*
> For no man putteth a piece of new cloth on an old garment. (JST Matthew 9:17–22.)

The JST provides an additional doctrinal setting for the discussion of cloth and wine: Jesus has rejected the baptism of the Pharisees and stressed that all old covenants are superseded by the new and everlasting covenant. (Cf. D&C 22.)

In chapter 14 of Luke, Christ has been discoursing on the cost of Christian discipleship. From the KJV we read: "So likewise, whosoever he be of you that forsaketh not all that he hath, he cannot be my disciple. Salt is good: but if the salt have lost his savour, wherewith shall it be seasoned?" (Luke 14:33–34.) The Master's intent is apparent: a disciple who is not willing to forsake all for the cause of righteousness is like salt that no longer spices, heals, or preserves. The JST, however, provides an expanded meaning:

> So likewise, whosoever of you forsaketh not all that he hath he cannot be my disciple.

> *Then certain of them came to him, saying, Good Master, we have Moses and the prophets, and whosoever shall live by them, shall he not have life?*
>
> *And Jesus answered, saying, Ye know not Moses, neither the prophets; for if ye had known them, ye would have believed on me; for to this intent they were written. For I am sent that ye might have life. Therefore I will liken it unto salt* which is good;
>
> But if the salt has lost its savor, wherewith shall it be seasoned? (JST Luke 14:34–37.)

In this expanded context, good salt is compared to the man that accepts modern revelation and living oracles, and who discerns the hidden meaning and fulfillment of scripture.

Finally, one of the most fascinating alterations in the King James text occurs in chapter 16 of Luke. In this chapter there is an abrupt movement in subject matter from verses 17 to 19: Jesus explains that he is the fulfillment of the Law and the Prophets; he establishes strict standards for marriage and divorce; he then delivers the parable of the rich man and Lazarus. Note the flow of conversation in the Prophet's inspired revision:

> And it is easier for heaven and earth to pass, than for one tittle of the law to fail.
>
> *And why teach ye the law, and deny that which is written; and condemn him whom the Father hath sent to fulfill the law, that ye might all be redeemed?*
>
> *O fools! for you have said in your hearts, There is no God. And you pervert the right way; and the kingdom of heaven suffereth violence of you; and you persecute the meek; and in your violence you seek to destroy the kingdom; and ye take the children of the kingdom by force. Woe unto you, ye adulterers!*
>
> *And they reviled him again, being angry for the saying, that they were adulterers.*
>
> *But he continued, saying,* Whosoever putteth away his wife, and marrieth another, committeth adultery; and whosoever marrieth her who is put away from her husband, committeth adultery. *Verily I say unto you, I will liken you unto the rich man.*
>
> For there was a certain rich man, who was clothed in purple, and fine linen, and fared sumptuously every day. (JST Luke 16:19–24.)

Such changes represent far more than grammatical improvement, harmonization, or even helpful commentary. If, as someone has suggested, text without context leads to pretext, then surely Joseph Smith is rendering a remarkable service—seeking to enhance our understanding of passages through supplying lost settings or backgrounds.

CONCLUSION

We live in a marvelous age, the times of restitution. We are a part of an era in which God has seen fit to restore plain and precious truths to his people through his appointed servants. As noted earlier, the Lord said to Sidney Rigdon that the work of Bible translation would eventuate in the unfolding of the scriptures, even as they are in the bosom of the Lord Himself (see D&C 35:20). It is my testimony that Joseph Smith the Prophet was doing far more than toying with the scriptures, even more than offering helpful commentary upon King James passages. His translation of the synoptic Gospels points toward the reality of a restoration of ancient happenings and ancient sayings. That Joseph Smith made changes in the text consistent with the peculiar styles and themes of the Gospel writers suggests that the Prophet was sensitive to the *intent,* as well as the *content* of the original writers. That he added or altered contexts or settings suggests his awareness of words or doings not evident in our oldest manuscripts. Like his ancient prophetic counterpart, Joseph Smith was able to view things "not visible to the natural eye," things not available even to those with an eye toward the most ancient extant texts. Knowing what we know of the eternal value of Joseph Smith's work with the Bible, we, like those among whom Enoch ministered in an earlier day, ought to declare forthrightly: Truly "a seer hath the Lord raised up unto his people" (JST Genesis 6:38; Moses 6:36).

Robert L. Millet is assistant professor of
Ancient Scripture at BYU.

NOTES

1. A detailed treatment of each of the Gospels and their messages is contained in Robert L. Millet, "As Delivered from the Beginning: The Formation of the Canonical Gospels," A Symposium on Apocryphal Literature, BYU Religious Studies Center, October 1983, Provo, Utah.

2. See Robert L. Millet, "Looking Beyond the Mark: Insights from the JST into First-Century Judaism," found herein.

3. See Merrill C. Tenney, *New Testament Survey* (Grand Rapids, Mich.: Eerdman's Publishing Co., 1961), p. 164.

9

The Sermon on the Mount in the JST and the Book of Mormon

Robert A. Cloward

Speaking to Joseph Smith the Lord said, "This generation shall have my word through you" (D&C 5:10). This is particularly true for the Sermon on the Mount. Through the Prophet Joseph Smith, this generation can discover the true meaning and intent of the Sermon to a much greater extent than before. We have not been given a perfect record of Jesus' words, but "all things are written by the Father" (3 Nephi 27:26), and that which we have has been granted unto us to try our faith (see 3 Nephi 26:9).

Through the power of God we have the Joseph Smith Translation of the Bible, which reveals many keys to a correct understanding of the Sermon on the Mount. In addition, we have the Book of Mormon, which contains not only a repetition of the Sermon in Bountiful, but much more explanation by the Savior of its principles. It is the intent of this paper to show how the JST and the Book of Mormon enlarge our understanding of the Sermon and make it more applicable in our day. By way of introduction, I will list the major contributions of these two revealed sources, which will later be discussed in detail.

MAJOR CONTRIBUTIONS OF THE JST TO UNDERSTANDING THE SERMON

Some of the major contributions of the JST are:
1. The JST includes transition statements which tie the Sermon into a whole, dispelling the notion that the biblical writers artificially concatenated a collection of sayings given on various occasions.
2. The JST helps define the audience of the Sermon.
3. The JST makes the Sermon more clearly applicable to our day, showing how it contains instructions for missionaries and ministers in the kingdom.
4. The JST reveals to whom the beatitudes apply.
5. The JST restores an introduction to the beatitudes which stresses the fundamental theme of coming unto Christ through the first principles and ordinances of the gospel.
6. The JST clears up misconceptions about appropriate attitudes and response toward persecution.
7. The JST identifies the salt of the old and new covenants.
8. The JST shows how Jesus as the Giver of the law of Moses honored that law and taught that it pointed the way to perfection.
9. The JST, when considered with the Book of Mormon, illustrates the transition from the old law to the new.
10. The JST reveals specific reasons why the scribes and Pharisees were rejected by the Lord.
11. The JST restores conversations and feelings of the Savior and his disciples—even the hesitancy of some of the disciples to face the requirements of their missionary call.
12. The JST identifies the words Jesus gave to his disciples for specific missionary encounters.
13. The JST teaches how the mysteries of the kingdom may be obtained.

MAJOR CONTRIBUTIONS OF THE BOOK OF MORMON TO UNDERSTANDING THE SERMON

Besides sharing many of the major contributions cited above for the JST, the Book of Mormon adds more of its own:

1. The Book of Mormon contains Jesus' statement that he intentionally presented the same "sayings" in both Galilee and Bountiful.
2. The Book of Mormon indicates that Jesus' words were to be written soon after they were given, dispelling the notion that biblical writers created many of the Sermon's expressions from clouded recollection or sketchy notes or from their own independent literary art.
3. The Book of Mormon gives immediate context to the three chapters of the Sermon by including fifteen additional chapters of related teachings from Jesus' Nephite ministry.
4. The Book of Mormon states that not a hundredth part of the things Jesus taught were included, and promises that a fuller account of his teachings will be revealed if we believe in that which we have.
5. The Book of Mormon shows that the Sermon was intended as part of a scriptural tool for the gathering of Israel in the last days.
6. The Book of Mormon clearly indicates changes in intended audience for different parts of the Sermon, identifying which instructions apply only to full-time ministers.
7. The Book of Mormon relates a specific fulfillment of the treading down of salt which loses its savor.
8. The Book of Mormon puts the Lord's Prayer into a context of instruction on many kinds of prayers, clarifying the intent for which it was given.

ACCOUNTS AND VERSIONS

We have record of two remarkably similar presentations of Jesus' Sermon. Of the Galilee Sermon, we have the accounts of Matthew and Luke. For each of these, I will consider two versions, the King James Version and the Joseph Smith Translation. JST Matthew 5:3 through 7:35 is the more perfect version of Matthew's account. Nearly three-fourths of the verses of KJV Matthew have been changed in some way by Joseph Smith, and *many* verses which nowhere occur in KJV have been added.

We have a more perfect version of Luke's account in JST

Luke 6:20–49. Nearly half of the KJV Luke verses have been changed in some way; one new verse has been added and one deleted. Inspired changes also occur in the wording and settings of later JST Luke passages which recall words similar to those of the Sermon (see JST Luke 8:16; 11:2–4, 10–14, 34–37; 12:24–37, 67–68; 13:23–24; 14:35–38; 16:13, 16–23 and KJV parallel passages from Luke). The Prophet did not overtly harmonize the Matthew and Luke accounts, and comparison of all versions is enlightening.

At the time of the Bountiful Sermon, Nephi was singled out by the Lord as responsible for the records (see 3 Nephi 23:7), but the account we have is a later abridgment by Mormon, who was commanded to include only a fraction of what had been written (see 3 Nephi 26:6–12). We do not know for certain whether Mormon abridged the written account of the Bountiful Sermon. The Lord specifically stated that the Bountiful Sermon included the same teachings he had given during his mortal ministry (see 3 Nephi 15:1). This implies that the Galilee Sermon, contrary to the views of a host of higher critics, was given much as we have it in the biblical accounts.

AUDIENCE AND SETTING

Crucial to understanding the Sermon is knowing to whom Jesus was speaking. Such statements as "Blessed are the poor in spirit" or "Take therefore no thought for the morrow" can be puzzling if we are unsure to whom they refer.

In KJV Matthew, the audience is introduced as follows: "And seeing the multitudes, he went up into a mountain: and when he was set, his disciples came unto him: And he opened his mouth, and taught them, saying," (KJV Matthew 5:1–2). Taken in connection with KJV Matthew 8:1, this verse seems to imply that Jesus left the multitudes, taught the Galilee Sermon privately to "his disciples," and encountered the multitudes again after the Sermon. JST Matthew corrects this impression by distinguishing between the disciples and others who were listening:

KJV Matthew 7:28-29	JST Matthew 7:36-37

And it came to pass, when Jesus had ended these sayings, the people were astonished at his doctrine:
  For he taught them as one having authority, and not as the scribes.
	And it came to pass when Jesus had ended these sayings *with his disciples,* the people were astonished at his doctrine;
	  For he taught them as one having authority *from God,* and not as *having authority from* the Scribes.

Without the JST addition, one wonders if the astonished people in KJV Matthew 7:28 are the same as the disciples in KJV Matthew 5:1. By changing the antecedent of "them" from "the people" to "his disciples," the JST makes clear that the Sermon was directed to the disciples, and it was the people who were merely listening who compared his teaching with the scribes and were astonished at his doctrine.

In Matthew, however, the word *disciples* is ambiguous. The *Twelve* are called disciples (see Matthew 10:1; 11:1), but the word may also refer to any group of followers such as the disciples of John the Baptist (see KJV Matthew 9:14; 11:2).

Luke's account more plainly identifies the disciples to whom Jesus spoke. Before the Sermon, as it is recorded in Luke 6, the Lord spent a night alone in prayer, after which he called his disciples unto him and chose twelve, naming them apostles (see Luke 6:13-16). Luke makes clear that the Twelve are only part of Jesus' disciples, although, like Matthew, he still distinguishes the disciples from the multitude (KJV Luke 6:17). After healing all the multitude, Jesus "lifted up his eyes on his disciples," and the Sermon is addressed to them (see Luke 6:17-20). At the end of the Sermon, Luke comments that Jesus had spoken "in the audience of the people" (Luke 7:1), probably referring to listeners from the multitude.

Taken together, and with the help of the JST, Matthew and Luke identify those present at the Galilee Sermon: (1) The disciples; i.e., his newly ordained Twelve Apostles and other faithful followers; and, in addition, (2) other people from among the multitudes who have gathered to hear him. Although many people come to hear Jesus, the Sermon is intended for the disciples.

Mark's account also indicates that the Sermon was intended primarily for the Twelve, who were being called to full-time ministry (KJV Mark 3:14).

In 3 Nephi, the setting and intended audience are much more readily apparent. After giving the Twelve power to baptize and teaching them his "doctrine," Jesus commands them to go forth and declare his words to the people and to the ends of the earth (see 3 Nephi 11:41). The Sermon, which directly follows, is introduced this way: "And it came to pass that when Jesus had spoken these words unto Nephi, and to those who had been called, . . . behold, he stretched forth his hand *unto the multitude,* and cried *unto them,* saying:" (3 Nephi 12:1; emphasis added). Certain parts of the sermon, therefore, were intended for the newly ordained Twelve, and certain parts for the multitude of people who were present.

The religious setting in Bountiful is very different from that of Galilee. Nephi earlier identified the survivors of the destruction at the time of Christ's crucifixion as "the more righteous part of the people" who had "received the prophets and stoned them not" and "had not shed the blood of the saints" (3 Nephi 10:12). By contrast, Jesus' audience in Galilee included curious onlookers, even Gentiles.

Several variations in the two Sermons are based on differences in cultural setting. There are also variations in the Sermons which result from the time of delivery. Because the atonement of Christ and his resurrection from the dead occurred between the two, the law of Moses was in effect during the Galilee Sermon but superseded by the time of the Bountiful Sermon. Much will be said about this in the commentary which follows.

DISCIPLES AND BEATITUDES

KJV Matthew gives nine beatitudes, but the corresponding beatitudes in both JST Matthew and 3 Nephi are preceded by an extensive introduction as follows:

KJV Matthew	JST Matthew 5:3–4	3 Nephi 12:1–2
(no corresponding material between 5:2 and 5:3)		Blessed are ye if ye shall give heed unto the words of these twelve whom I have chosen from among you to minister unto you, and to be your servants; and unto them I have given power that they may baptize you with water; and after that ye are baptized with water, behold, I will baptize you with fire and with the Holy Ghost; therefore blessed are ye if ye shall believe in me and be baptized, after that ye have seen me and know that I am.
	Blessed are they who shall believe on me;	
	and again, more blessed are they who shall believe on your words, when ye shall testify that ye have seen me and that I am.	And again, more blessed are they who shall believe in your words because that ye shall testify that ye have seen me, and that ye know that I am.
	Yea, blessed are they who shall believe on your words, and come down into the depth of humility, and be baptized in my name; for they shall be visited with fire and the Holy Ghost, and shall receive a remission of their sins.	Yea, blessed are they who shall believe in your words, and come down into the depths of humility and be baptized, for they shall be visited with fire and with the Holy Ghost, and shall receive a remission of their sins.

Understanding concepts introduced here is paramount for understanding the Sermon:

1. Only in the JST and the Book of Mormon do we learn that the beginning of the Sermon is an unmistakable *call to missionary labors*. In Galilee, Jesus calls the disciples, and especially the Twelve, to testify of him. In Bountiful, he calls the whole multitude! The call to service is an invitation to blessedness, extended by him whose power it is to bless everlastingly.

2. The familiar beatitudes which follow the call identify those who may also attain blessedness through the invitation of the Lord's missionary witnesses.

3. Blessedness for the poor in spirit, those that mourn, the meek, those who hunger and thirst after righteousness, the merciful, the pure in heart, the peacemakers, and those who are persecuted for the Lord's name's sake begins when they *come unto Christ*. The phrase "who come unto me" is specifically added to the first of these in JST Matthew and 3 Nephi (see JST Matthew 5:5; 3 Nephi 12:3).

4. In Galilee, multitudes came and "sought to touch him" (Luke 19), and in Bountiful all present felt his wounds. Now he teaches them that it is not enough to come and feel. They can only receive the promised blessings if they come unto him *through the first principles and ordinances of the gospel*. For example, to enter the kingdom of heaven, the poor in spirit must come unto Christ and be born of water and of the spirit (see John 3:5). Those who hunger and thirst after righteousness will be "filled *with the Holy Ghost*" (JST Matthew 5:8; 3 Nephi 12:6), but this blessing results from their coming unto Christ and receiving the ordinances of salvation.

A closer look at the pronouns in the beatitudes shows a shift in the last of the nine. All of the previous beatitudes are directed to third plural "they." Compare especially the eighth: "Blessed are all *they* that are persecuted for my name's sake; for *theirs* is the kingdom of heaven" (JST Matthew 5:12); and the ninth: "And blessed are *ye* when men shall revile *you,* and persecute *you,* and shall say all manner of evil against *you* falsely, for my sake" (JST Matthew 5:13). The pronouns in the ninth beatitude are second plural. Christ is teaching that persecution is not only the lot of those who desire to come unto him, it is also a reality for his witnesses. This link between the last two beatitudes is only clear in the JST and in 3 Nephi, where the relationship between the missionaries ("ye") and those they teach ("they") is explained by the added introductions.

The four beatitudes in KJV Luke 6:20–23, unlike KJV Matthew, are all second plural "ye," leading many to stumble into the false conclusion that *the disciples* are the poor, they who hunger, and they who weep. The JST corrects the first three Luke beatitudes to third person and leaves just the fourth (which corresponds to the ninth in JST Matthew) in second person.[1] Thus, in both JST Matthew and JST Luke the beatitudes intended for missionaries and the ones intended for those they teach are consistently differentiated.

Now note the blessing promised to the persecuted in Matthew. For the converts who endure persecution for the Lord's name's sake (taking that name upon themselves through baptism), the promise of the eighth beatitude is "theirs is the kingdom of heaven." To the missionary witnesses, who are reviled and persecuted and spoken evil of falsely for the Lord's sake (as part of the sacrifice required in his service), compare the versions of the promise of the ninth beatitude:

KJV Matthew 5:12	*JST Matthew 5:14*	*3 Nephi 12:12*
Rejoice, and be exceeding glad: for great is your reward in heaven: for so persecuted they the prophets which were before you.	*For ye shall have great joy,* and be exceeding glad; for great *shall be* your reward in heaven; for so persecuted they the prophets which were before you.	*For ye shall have great joy* and be *exceedingly* glad, for great *shall be* your reward in heaven; for so persecuted they the prophets *who* were before you.

KJV Matthew could mislead us into presuming that we should be glad if we are being persecuted. Jesus did not teach that. Neither did he teach that the promise of great joy and exceeding gladness comes only because we endure present persecution. The blessing of the ninth beatitude is only understood when we see it in JST

Matthew and 3 Nephi as the last of a cycle of blessings which began with a missionary call to bring others to Christ. The reward comes when we with those who have responded to our message enjoy the blessings of heaven together (see D&C 18:15-16).

SALT AND LIGHT

In a short transition section between the beatitudes and the teachings on old law and new, Jesus introduces the twin symbols of covenant discipleship—salt and light. Now that the audience and the missionary orientation of the Sermon are understood, we can accurately identify those to whom they refer. During his Perean ministry, he identified the previous salt and light in an exchange unique to JST Luke:

KJV Luke 14:34-35	JST Luke 14:35-38
	Then certain of them came to him, saying, Good Master, we have Moses and the prophets, and whosoever shall live by them, shall he not have life?
	And Jesus answered, saying, Ye know not Moses, neither the prophets; for if ye had known them, ye would have believed on me; for to this intent they were written. For I am sent that ye might have life. Therefore I will liken it unto
Salt is good: but if the salt have lost his savour, wherewith shall it be seasoned?	salt *which* is good; But if the salt *has* lost *its* savor, wherewith shall it be seasoned?
It is neither fit for the land, nor yet for the dunghill; but men cast it out. He that hath ears to hear, let him hear.	It is neither fit for the land, nor yet for the dung hill; men cast it out. He *who* hath ears to hear, let him hear. *These things he said, signifying that which was written, verily must all be fulfilled.*

The JST makes clear that Moses and the prophets had been good salt. The law and the witness given through them were intended to bring people to a knowledge of Christ. But to those who rejected their witness and even suggested that they stand in place of Christ, they became adulterated salt, salt to be cast out, salt to be trodden under foot of men.

The law and the prophets, distorted and misunderstood by the Jewish teachers of Jesus' day, had ceased to savor. The light of the Mosaic law and of generations of sacrificial fires was about to be superseded by the transcendent light of the great and last sacrifice. New apostles and new disciples were to replace the salt of the former covenant, for, as Jesus taught, "except your righteousness shall exceed that of the Scribes and Pharisees, ye shall in no case enter into the kingdom of heaven" (JST Matthew 5:22).

Jesus therefore commissions new salt. JST Matthew and 3 Nephi express the Savior's words in the form of a commission, leaving no doubt as to its source. In place of "Ye are the salt" (KJV Matthew 5:13) and "Ye are the light" (KJV Matthew 5:14), we read "*I give unto you to be* the salt" and "*I give unto you to be* the light" (JST Matthew 5:15, 16; 3 Nephi 12:13, 14).

In more recent revelation, the Lord has defined the twin symbols. In the Doctrine and Covenants he identifies priesthood holders of our day as "a light unto the Gentiles" and "a savior unto my people Israel" (D&C 86:11). Another Doctrine and Covenants teaching is that "When men are called unto mine everlasting gospel, and covenant with an everlasting covenant, they are accounted as the salt of the earth and the savor of men" (D&C 101:39).

With light, Jesus teaches the responsibility of covenant discipleship. The Galilean disciples and the Bountiful multitude must let their light shine. In the extensive teachings of the resurrected Christ following the Bountiful Sermon, abundant references to light demonstrate how this is to be done. Jesus there refers to himself as the law and the light (see 3 Nephi 15:5, 9; 18:16) and to the Twelve as a light unto their people (see 3 Nephi 15:11–12). He urges the whole multitude to hold up their light that it may shine unto the world, and he explains, "Behold I am the light which ye shall hold up—*that which ye have seen me do*" (3 Nephi 18:24; emphasis added). By doing the works of Christ, they let his light shine through them, and others seeing their good works glorify their Father who is in heaven (see 3 Nephi 12:16).

With salt, Jesus teaches the jeopardy of covenant discipleship. However, this can hardly be understood without the JST and the Book of Mormon:

KJV Matthew 5:13	JST Matthew 5:15	3 Nephi 12:13
Ye are the salt of the earth: but if the salt have lost his savour, wherewith shall it be salted? it is thenceforth good for nothing, but to be cast out, and to be trodden under foot of men.	*Verily, verily, I say unto you, I give unto you to be* the salt of the earth; but if the salt *shall lose* its savor, wherewith shall *the earth* be salted? *the salt shall* thenceforth *be* good for nothing, but to be cast out, and to be trodden under foot of men.	*Verily, verily, I say unto you, I give unto you to be* the salt of the earth; but if the salt *shall lose* its savor wherewith shall *the earth* be salted? *The salt shall be* thenceforth good for nothing, but to be cast out and to be trodden under foot of men.

The perplexing verse in KJV Matthew becomes a lucid rhetorical question in JST Matthew and in 3 Nephi, teaching that if the salt (the disciples) lose their savor (cease to administer the covenant and its saving ordinances) to the earth (all mankind), then there is no way for the earth (all mankind) to be salted (to receive the covenant and its ordinances). The result: *The salt* is cast out and trodden under foot of men.

Note that these verses in JST Matthew and 3 Nephi consistently use the future tense "shall." This is not a description by the Lord of the current status of the salt of the scribes and Pharisees, like the JST Luke 14:35–38 passage cited earlier. Here, Jesus plainly states the jeopardy which accompanies the commission of the salt of the new covenant. If the listening apostles and disciples (or those who stand in their places when their work is finished) fail to savor the earth, their fate will be the same as that of the misguided leaders of the Jews.

At least two scriptural examples demonstrate how literal this jeopardy can be. In 1833, the Saints who had moved to Jackson County, Missouri, to establish the center place of Zion were judged of the Lord and were driven out of the county by their persecutors. The Lord explained: "For they were set to be a light unto the world, and to be the saviors of men; And inasmuch as they are not the saviors of men, they are as salt that has lost its savor, and is thenceforth good for nothing but to be cast out and trodden under foot of men" (D&C 103:9–10).

Jesus' teachings in Bountiful include a second example. He teaches that if the Gentiles in the New World reject the fulness of the gospel and become wicked and hypocritical in the last days, "they shall be as salt that hath lost its savor" and shall be cast out and trodden under the foot of the house of Israel (see 3 Nephi 16:6–15, especially v. 15).

THE OLD LAW AND THE NEW

Jesus now moves on to a discussion of law. With a clear understanding of his brief introduction on old law and new, we will be prepared to properly interpret the more extensive following section with his expansions on the law. In the introduction, the time differences between the biblical and Book of Mormon accounts provide the key. The four verses in Matthew, particularly in the JST, have an entirely different cast from the four in 3 Nephi. Taken together, they weave a total pattern of the work of Jesus Christ through *both* the law of Moses and the law of the gospel. Compare, for example, Jesus' teachings on the fulfillment of the Mosaic law:

KJV Matthew 5:17–18	JST Matthew 5:19–20	3 Nephi 12:17–18
Think not that I am come to destroy the law, or the prophets: I am not come to destroy, but to fulfil.	Think not that I am come to destroy the law, or the prophets; I am not come to destroy, but to fulfil.	Think not that I am come to destroy the law or the prophets. I am not come to destroy but to fulfil;

| For verily I say unto you, Till heaven and earth pass, one jot or one tittle shall in no wise pass from the law, till all be fulfilled. | For verily I say unto you, heaven and earth *must* pass *away, but* one jot or one tittle shall in no wise pass from the law, *until* all be fulfilled. | For verily I say unto you, one jot *nor* one tittle *hath not passed away* from the law, *but in me it hath* all *been* fulfilled. |

The JST dispels the problematic time reference of the two "till" statements in KJV Matthew 5:18.[2] The idea that the Mosaic law remained in effect for Christians was the error of the Judaizers who sought to impose this law on gentile converts to Christianity (see Acts 15; Galatians 1–5). In JST Matthew 5:19, Jesus establishes during his mortal ministry that the law will remain intact until it is all fulfilled. In 3 Nephi 12:18, he reports to the Nephites after his resurrection that the law did remain intact, and (with his atonement and resurrection) it had all been fulfilled.

The JST is indispensable for restoring the intent of the next two verses in Matthew:

KJV Matthew 5:19–20

Whosoever therefore shall break one of these least commandments, and shall teach men so, he shall be called the least in the kingdom of heaven: but whosoever shall do and teach them, the same shall be called great in the kingdom of heaven.

For I say unto you, That except your righteousness shall exceed the righteousness of the scribes and Pharisees, ye shall in no case enter into the kingdom of heaven.

JST Matthew 5:21–22

Whosoever, therefore, shall break one of these least commandments, and shall teach men so *to do,* he shall *in no wise be saved* in the kingdom of heaven; but whosoever shall do and teach *these commandments of the law until it be fulfilled,* the same shall be called great, *and shall be saved* in the kingdom of heaven.

For I say unto you, except your righteousness shall exceed *that* of the Scribes and Pharisees, ye shall in no case enter into the kingdom of heaven.

In the JST Matthew version, Jesus declares that commandment breakers and those who teach others to break commandments are not saved. At the same time, he ennobles the law of Moses and shows that as long as this law was in force, those who obeyed its commandments would be saved.[3]

The clash in Galilee was not between the old law and the new, both given by Jesus Christ. The clash was between the misinterpretation of the old law by the scribes and Pharisees and their misperception of the new law as a perversion of the old. Had they been obedient to the old law, it would have pointed them toward perfection, they would have been called great, and they would have been saved in the kingdom of heaven. They also would have recognized the Giver of the law when he came personally among them.

In Bountiful, there were no scribes and Pharisees, and the Mosaic law had been fulfilled. The corresponding verses therefore carry an entirely different message:

> And behold, *I have given you the law and the commandments of my Father,* that ye shall believe in me, and that ye shall repent of your sins, and come unto me with a broken heart and a contrite spirit. Behold, *ye have the commandments before you, and the law is fulfilled.*
> Therefore come unto me and be ye saved; for verily I say unto you, that except ye shall *keep my commandments, which I have commanded you at this time,* ye shall in no case enter into the kingdom of heaven. (3 Nephi 12:19–20; emphasis added.)

"Commandments" in JST Matthew 5:21 refers to the commandments of the law of Moses. "Commandments" in 3 Nephi 12:19–20 refers to belief in Christ, repentance from sin, coming unto him with a broken heart and a contrite spirit, and, as mentioned earlier in the Sermon, baptism and the visitation of the Holy Ghost.

The JST and the Book of Mormon affirm that the law of Moses was given as a saving law. Those who did not obey its commandments forfeited their salvation, as well as those who, like the scribes and Pharisees, perverted the law and carved from it jots and tittles until it no longer pointed people to Christ. In Galilee, Jesus commended the spirit of obedience which should have attended the keeping and teaching of the law of Moses, but was wholly lacking in the scribes and Pharisees. Perfect obedience to the commandments of the old law was required of the disciples whom he was training for the ministry. Such a spirit would lead directly to the proper observance of the commandments of the new law when the old law had been fulfilled. In Bountiful, Jesus introduced the higher commandments, and then showed how a correct application of the spirit of the old law would lead obedient disciples to perfection under the new law.

LAWS UNTO PERFECTION

Jesus now begins the "sayings" to which he will refer in the parable which concludes his Sermon. "Whosoever heareth *these sayings of mine,* and doeth them, I will liken him unto a wise man, which built his house upon a rock" (KJV Matthew 7:24). The Lord does not destroy the old law. His sayings renew, refine, lift, and build upon it, for all godly law leads line upon line to perfection. (Cf. 2 Nephi 28:27–30.)

In this section of the Sermon, Jesus cites six laws which are familiar to his listeners, beginning an expansion on each with the phrase "But I say unto you." For three of his examples—Thou shalt not kill, Thou shalt not commit adultery, and Love thy neighbor as thyself—the Lord's expansion *renews* the existing commandment. He also adds illustrations to show the spirit that ought to attend obedience to the existing law and is required under the new covenant. For his other examples—the laws condoning divorce for insufficient cause, gospel oaths, retaliation for personal injury, and the telestial principle of hating one's enemies—the Lord's expansion *replaces* the existing lower standard, which had been adapted to human weaknesses, with a higher standard. For each of his six examples, Jesus teaches a more perfect law.

The JST and the Book of Mormon provide many keys to the meaning and intent of Jesus' sayings which are not available in the KJV. For example, JST Matthew differs from KJV Matthew in Jesus' introductions of his six examples. All six citations of the law in KJV Matthew use the word *said* (see KJV Matthew 5:21, 27, 31, 33, 38, 43). In 3 Nephi, all six use "written" (see 3 Nephi 12:21, 27, 31, 33, 38, 43). JST Matthew uses "said" three times and "written" three times (see JST Matthew 5:23, 29, 35, 37, 40, 45). It is unlikely that these differences are based on which citations were from written sources and which were not. All six reflect passages from the Old Testament as it has come to us. The differences more likely reflect the orientation of the people to the law. Oral law was a burning issue among the Jews, with Pharisees and Sadducees locked into heated debate over whether the oral was valid in addition to the written. Righteous Nephites, on the other hand, were not multiplying oral interpretation upon oral interpretation. They were keeping the law of Moses as they had it recorded in written form, but they already understood the higher standards and were looking forward to the coming of Christ (see 2 Nephi 25:23–30).

Both JST Matthew and 3 Nephi delete the phrase "without a cause" from Jesus' saying on anger against a brother (see JST Matthew 5:24; 3 Nephi 12:22). This phrase, which provides a rationalization for anger, does not reflect the higher-law context of this section of the Sermon.[4]

Jesus' example of reconciliation with one's brother before making an offering is beautifully linked by JST Matthew and 3 Nephi to the undergirding Sermon theme of coming unto Christ:

KJV Matthew 5:23–24	JST Matthew 5:25–26	3 Nephi 12:23–24
Therefore if thou bring thy gift to the altar, and there rememberest that thy brother hath ought against thee;	Therefore, *if ye shall come unto me, or* if thou bring thy gift to the altar, and there rememberest that thy brother hath aught against thee,	Therefore, *if ye shall come unto me, or shall desire to come unto me,* and rememberest that thy brother hath aught against thee—
Leave there thy gift before the altar, and go thy way; first be reconciled to thy brother, and then come and offer thy gift.	Leave *thou* thy gift before the altar, and go thy way *unto thy brother, and* first be reconciled to thy brother, and then come and offer thy gift.	Go thy way *unto thy brother, and* first be reconciled to thy brother, and then come *unto me with full purpose of heart,* and *I will receive you.*

All who come unto Christ or desire to come unto him should first be reconciled to any who have ill feelings against them. Under the law of Moses, one way to approach the Lord was to bring a gift to the temple altar of sacrifice. In his Galilee Sermon Jesus teaches a more perfect way to keep the law of Moses. By the time of the Bountiful Sermon, altar gifts had been superseded. From out of the New World darkness which accompanied the destruction at the time of his great and last sacrifice, the voice of the Lord declared the need for a sacrifice of a broken heart and a contrite spirit (3 Nephi 9:19–20). The Bountiful Sermon teaches that coming unto Christ with the offering of a broken heart and a contrite spirit under the new covenant also requires that the offerer first be reconciled to his brother.

The Lord further emphasizes the theme of the obedience of the heart in connection with his saying against lust:

KJV Matthew 5:27–28	JST Matthew 5:29–31	3 Nephi 12:27–30
Thou shalt not commit adultery:	thou shalt not commit adultery.	thou shalt not commit adultery;
But I say unto you, That whosoever looketh on a woman to lust after her hath committed adultery with her already in his heart.	But I say unto you, that whosoever looketh on a woman to lust after her, hath committed adultery with her already in his heart.	But I say unto you, that whosoever looketh on a woman, to lust after her, hath committed adultery already in his heart.
	Behold, I give unto you a commandment, that ye suffer none of these things to enter into your heart,	*Behold, I give unto you a commandment, that ye suffer none of these things to enter into your heart;*
	for it is better that ye should deny yourselves of these things, wherein ye will take up your cross, than that ye should be cast into hell.	*For it is better that ye should deny yourselves of these things, wherein ye will take up your cross, than that ye should be cast into hell.*

The additional verses in JST Matthew and 3 Nephi intensify the Lord's commandment that we protect *our hearts* from adultery. He requires that his followers deny themselves of sins of the heart. In a context recorded later in JST Matthew, Jesus explains the phrase "take up your cross":

KJV Matthew 16:24

Then said Jesus unto his disciples, If any man will come after me, let him deny himself, and take up his cross, and follow me.

JST Matthew 16:25-26

Then said Jesus unto his disciples, If any man will come after me, let him deny himself, and take up his cross and follow me.
And now for a man to take up his cross, is to deny himself all ungodliness, and every worldly lust, and keep my commandments.

Only with the added verses in the JST and in the Book of Mormon can we see the fulness of the Savior's saying on adultery. In the Sermon, Jesus is renewing the law against adultery, adding that this law can point us to perfection if we also protect our hearts from adultery and deny ourselves all ungodliness and every worldly lust.

In the Galilee Sermon, Jesus continues this theme. He recommends plucking out an offending eye or cutting off an offending hand. In JST Matthew we find his explanation that these expressions are figurative: "And now this I speak, a parable concerning your sins; wherefore, cast them from you, that ye may not be hewn down and cast into the fire" (JST Matthew 5:34; cf. JST Mark 9:40-48).

JST Matthew includes an interesting teaching on meekness in persecution:

KJV Matthew 5:40-41

And if any man will sue thee at the law, and take away thy coat, let him have thy cloke also.

JST Matthew 5:42-43

And if any man will sue thee at the law, and take away thy coat, let him have *it; and if he sue thee again, let him have* thy cloak also.

And whosoever shall compel thee to go a mile, go with him twain.

And whosoever shall compel thee to go a mile, *go with him a mile; and whosoever shall compel thee to go with him twain, thou shalt* go with him twain.

As JST Matthew 5:14 averts the mistaken impression that we should be glad if we are persecuted, JST Matthew 5:42–43 averts the mistaken impression that we should make unnecessary concessions in the face of persecution. We do not turn the other cheek because we want to be smitten again. We turn the other cheek instead of striking back. JST Luke further emphasizes this point:

KJV Luke 6:29–30

And unto him that smiteth thee on the one cheek offer also the other; and him that taketh away thy cloke forbid not to take thy coat also.

JST Luke 6:29–30

And unto him *who* smiteth thee on the cheek, offer also the other; *or, in other words, it is better to offer the other, than to revile again.* And him *who* taketh away thy cloak, forbid not to take thy coat also.

For it is better that thou suffer thine enemy to take these things, than to contend with him. Verily I say unto you, Your heavenly Father who seeth in secret, shall bring that wicked one into judgment.

In Luke's account of the Sermon, this section follows directly after the beatitudes and the woes, still in the context of response to persecution. Jesus admonishes his disciples to seek godly attitudes—loving, lending to, blessing, doing good to, and praying for their enemies—that they may be the children of the Highest (see Luke 6:27–35).

We now reach the climax of Jesus' teachings on law. In one terse statement, he sums up the whole intent of both the old law and the new.

KJV Matthew 5:48	JST Matthew 5:50
Be ye therefore perfect, even as your Father which is in heaven is perfect.	*Ye are therefore commanded to* be perfect, even as your Father *who* is in heaven is perfect.

The clearer JST phrasing of the commandment to be perfect follows directly from JST Matthew 5:21–22. This is a time of transition from the old law to the new. As the apostle Paul explains, "The law [of Moses] was our schoolmaster until Christ" (JST Galatians 3:24).

Through the Book of Mormon, we better understand the perfection Jesus requires. In the Bountiful sermon, Jesus teaches, "Therefore I would that ye should be perfect *even as I, or your Father who is in heaven* is perfect" (3 Nephi 12:48; emphasis added). Later he teaches the Twelve, "What manner of men ought ye to be? Verily I say unto you, even as I am." (3 Nephi 27:27; see also KJV Matthew 28:18–20; D&C 93:16–28.)

OUTWARD AND INWARD WORSHIP

Jesus' Sermon next turns to (1) almsgiving, (2) prayer, (3) fasting, and (4) attention to wealth. His missionary disciples must learn how the inward focus of the new law replaces the outward performances and ordinances (see 2 Nephi 25:30; Mosiah 13:30; Alma 30:3) of the old law.

In this section the JST elucidates the Matthew account in several places. For example, a narrative phrase in JST Matthew 6:1 reestablishes the intended audience for the Galilee Sermon:

KJV Matthew 6:1	JST Matthew 6:1	3 Nephi 13:1
Take heed that ye do not your alms before men, to be seen of them: otherwise ye have no reward of your Father which is in heaven.	*And it came to pass that, as Jesus taught his disciples, he said unto them,* Take heed that ye do not your alms before men, to be seen of them; other-	*Verily, verily, I say that I would that ye should do alms unto the poor; but* take heed that ye do not your alms before men to be seen of them; otherwise ye have no

| wise ye have no reward of your Father *who* is in heaven. | reward of your Father *who* is in heaven. |

The JST includes an additional phrase of Jesus' teaching on doing alms in secret:

KJV Matthew 6:3

But when thou doest alms, let not thy left hand know what thy right hand doeth:

JST Matthew 6:3

But when thou doest alms, let *it be unto thee as* thy left hand *not knowing* what thy right hand doeth;

Here, as in JST Matthew 5:34, Jesus specifies that he is speaking figuratively. In both cases, the addition is not included in the Bountiful Sermon.

Differences between the rendition of the Lord's Prayer in the JST and the Book of Mormon establish that this prayer was never meant to be repeated verbatim as a substitute for the prayer of the heart (see JST Matthew 6:9–16; 3 Nephi 13:9–15). Luke reports a third occasion when Jesus taught another similar but not identical prayer (see JST Luke 11:1–4). It is ironic that the Lord's Prayer in any form is memorized to be repeated endlessly by certain Christians, when Jesus has just taught, "But when ye pray, use not vain repetitions, as the hypocrites do" (JST Matthew 6:7).

Later in his Nephite ministry, Jesus teaches the Twelve and the multitude abundantly on proper prayer—individual prayer (3 Nephi 17:3; 18:15, 18–20), prayer in meetings (3 Nephi 18:16, 22–25, 30), prayer on the sacrament (3 Nephi 18:3–11), family prayer (3 Nephi 18:21), baptismal prayer (3 Nephi 11:23–25, 27), and confirmation prayer (Moroni 2:2–3). More importantly, he shares with them prayer experiences so sublime that they cannot be recorded (see 3 Nephi 17:9–25; 19:16–36). The Book of Mormon therefore helps us apply the Lord's Prayer in the light of its Sermon context; that is, Jesus uses it to teach simple principles of unhypocritical worship.

On the whole, the section on prayer in 3 Nephi agrees with KJV Matthew, while JST Matthew differs from both. Coinciding Bible and Book of Mormon passages, not available for most of the JST, offer an aid to help us determine the nature of the Prophet's work with the Bible. In some cases, changes found *only* in the JST may include inspired clarifications, added by the Prophet for the benefit of our dispensation.

For example, the substitution in JST Matthew 6:13 of "trespasses" for "debts" parallel to JST Matthew 6:16, suggests to us a proper understanding of what we should ask the Father to forgive (cf. Luke 11:4, "our sins"). Similarly, the substitution in JST Matthew 6:7 of "hypocrites" for "heathen," parallel to JST Matthew 6:2, 5, 17, makes the injunction against vain repetitions more uniformly part of the warnings against hypocrisy in worship. The substitution in JST Matthew 6:14 of "suffer us not to be led into temptation" for "lead us not into temptation" (cf. also JST Luke 11:4) dispels for our day the notion that we would need to ask the Father not to impose temptation on us. In the JST, the couplet "suffer us not to be led into temptation, but deliver us from evil" is a synthetic parallelism, reemphasizing our need to plead that the Father protect us from temptations into which the adversary may lead us, or into which we may lead ourselves.[5]

JST Matthew also includes the definition of an expression in Jesus' teaching on attention to wealth:

KJV Matthew 6:22	JST Matthew 6:22	3 Nephi 13:22
The light of the body is the eye: if therefore thine eye be single, thy whole body shall be full of light.	The light of the body is the eye; if therefore thine eye be single *to the glory of God,* thy whole body shall be full of light.	The light of the body is the eye; if, therefore, thine eye be single, thy whole body shall be full of light.

The added phrase in the JST Matthew 6:22 completes the parallel teachings on hearts and eyes: True disciples must have

	their hearts	set	on the treasures	of heaven
and	their eyes	single	to the glory	of God.

Modern translators have given misleading renditions of Matthew 6:22 based only on their knowledge of Greek, (e.g., Anchor Bible "and if your eye is healthy . . ."; N.E.B. "If your eyes are sound . . ."; N.A.S.B. "if therefore your eye is clear . . ."). Joseph Smith's translation is based on his knowledge of the requirements of discipleship in this dispensation (cf. D&C 4, especially v. 5).

NEEDS OF FULL-TIME MINISTERS

At this point there is an important transition in 3 Nephi, and JST Matthew includes three verses not found in KJV. They are quoted here for comparison, beginning with the final verse of the preceding section.

KJV Matthew 6:24–25	JST Matthew 6:24–28	3 Nephi 13:24–25
No man can serve two masters: for either he will hate the one, and love the other; or else he will hold to the one, and despise the other. Ye cannot serve God and mammon.	No man can serve two masters, for either he will hate the one, and love the other; or else he will hold to the one and despise the other. Ye cannot serve God and Mammon. *And, again, I say unto you, go ye into the world, and care not for the world; for the world will hate you, and will persecute you, and will turn you out of their synagogues.* *Nevertheless, ye shall go forth from house to house, teaching the people; and I will go before you.*	No man can serve two masters; for either he will hate the one and love the other, or else he will hold to the one and despise the other. Ye cannot serve God and Mammon. *And now it came to pass that when Jesus had spoken these words he looked upon the twelve*

	And your heavenly Father will provide for you, whatsoever things ye need for food, what ye shall eat; and for raiment, what ye shall wear or put on.	*whom he had chosen, and said unto them: Remember the words which I have spoken. For behold, ye are they whom I have chosen to minister unto this people.*
Therefore I say unto you, Take no thought for your life, what ye shall eat, or what ye shall drink; nor yet for your body, what ye shall put on. Is not the life more than meat, and the body than raiment?	Therefore I say unto you, take no thought for your life, what ye shall eat, or what ye shall drink; nor yet for your *bodies,* what ye shall put on. Is not the life more than meat, and the body than raiment?	Therefore I say unto you, take no thought for your life, what ye shall eat, or what ye shall drink; nor yet for your body, what ye shall put on. Is not the life more than meat, and the body than raiment?

Note that the words of the Sermon in 3 Nephi are interrupted by a narrative insertion specifying that the instructions which follow pertain only to the Twelve. Such insertions consistently distinguish in 3 Nephi between Jesus' instructions to the Twelve and his instructions to the multitude.

In Galilee, *all* of his instructions are directed to his disciples, especially the newly called Twelve. Although others from among the multitude hear his words, he does not speak directly to them. Nevertheless, at the points in the Galilee sermon which correspond to audience-focus insertions in 3 Nephi, JST Matthew insertions make clear that in Galilee, Jesus did not change audiences (see JST Matthew 6:25; 7:1, 3–6).

In both the Bountiful and the Galilee sermons, when Jesus says, "Take no thought for your life, what ye shall eat, or what ye shall drink; nor yet for your bodies, what ye shall put on," he is speaking only to those entering *full-time ministry.* In Bountiful, only the Twelve are so counseled. To those of the Bountiful multitude who would *not* be involved in full-time ministry, "Ye cannot serve God and Mammon" meant "earn your living, but maintain proper priorities." To the Nephite Twelve and to those in Galilee who would go "into the world" and "from house to house, teaching the people," these same words meant, "seek ye first the kingdom of God, and his righteousness; and all these things shall be added unto you" (KJV Matthew 6:33; 3 Nephi 13:33). Commenting on the command to "seek ye first . . ." Elder Bruce R. McConkie wrote:

> It is common to quote this command as one directing men to seek, through righteousness, the things of the celestial world. Counsel so to do is never inappropriate. But, actually, as seen from the Inspired Version accounts of Matthew and Luke, Jesus is directing his ministers "to build up the kingdom of God" (JST Matthew 6:38), and to seek "to bring forth the kingdom of God" (JST Luke 12:34), meaning the Church of Jesus Christ, which is the kingdom of God on earth. They were being sent forth, as are the missionaries in this day, to preach the gospel so that converts might come into the Church or kingdom, thereby building it up in strength and power.[6]

Several additional changes in this section (as well as in the following chapter) restore parts of conversations and give us a glimpse of the inner feelings of the disciples in Galilee. In JST Matthew 6:25, Jesus tells them as they go out to preach, "care not for the world." In the remaining fourteen verses of JST Matthew 6, he uses the verb "to take thought for" (i.e., to worry about, to be anxious over) six times (five in KJV). In spite of his reassurances, JST Matthew reveals that at least some of Jesus' disciples *were* concerned. They murmur and say they cannot obey him. Hearing their murmuring, he responds:

KJV Matthew 6:32	JST Matthew 6:36-37
	Why is it that ye murmur among yourselves, saying, We cannot obey thy word because
(For after all these things do the Gentiles seek:)	*ye have not all these things, and seek to excuse yourselves, saying that,* after all these things do the Gentiles seek.
for your heavenly Father knoweth that ye have need of all these things.	*Behold, I say unto you, that* your heavenly Father knoweth that ye have need of all these things.

The parenthesized statement in KJV is part of the disciples' complaint and does not appear in the Bountiful Sermon. They say that they cannot obey Jesus' word because he and other disciples have rationalized their poverty by labeling worldly things Gentile. Jesus reassures them that their Heavenly Father knows their temporal needs, and adds: "Wherefore, seek not the things of this world but seek ye first to build up the kingdom of God, and to establish his righteousness, and all these things shall be added unto you. Take, therefore, no thought for the morrow; for the morrow shall take thought for the things of itself. Sufficient unto the day shall be the evil thereof."[7] (JST Matthew 6:38–39.) The intent of this counsel and of this whole section of the Sermon is only clear because the JST and the Book of Mormon inform us that Jesus was giving instructions for full-time ministers.

"SAY UNTO THEM"

Jesus continues his Sermon with additional items of instruction. His intended audience in Galilee is still "his disciples," whereas in Bountiful he shifts his focus from the Twelve back to the multitude for the remainder of the Sermon (see JST Matthew 7:1, 14, 16; 3 Nephi 14:1). The Savior's words in this section are rich with imagery and parable—a masterpiece of apperceptive teaching.

In JST Matthew, independent from all the other versions, we are given the intimate opportunity to visit the Savior in Galilee as he converses with his disciples and further prepares them for their missions by telling them what to say. This is a masterpiece of a different nature—a revelation given to us through the Prophet Joseph Smith.

For many situations, even life-threatening ones, Jesus counsels the Twelve, "But when they deliver you up, take no thought how or what ye shall speak. For it is not ye that speak, but the Spirit of your Father which speaketh in you" (KJV Matthew 10:19–20; cf. JST Luke 12:9–14). But he knows their needs, and gives them succinct messages to use in specific upcoming missionary situations. These are introduced with five instances of the phrase "say unto them" and two other instances of similar expressions in the first section of JST Matthew 7, none of which are found in KJV Matthew.

He begins by telling them how to teach the people about judging:

KJV Matthew 7:1–4	JST Matthew 7:1–5
	Now these are the words which Jesus taught his disciples that they should say unto the people.
Judge not, that ye be not judged.	Judge not *unrighteously,* that ye be not judged; *but judge righteous judgment.*
For with what judgment ye judge, ye shall be judged: and with what measure ye mete, it shall be measured to you again.	For with what judgment ye *shall* judge, ye shall be judged; and with what measure ye mete, it shall be measured to you again.
And why beholdest thou the mote that is in thy brother's eye, but considerest not the beam that is in thine own eye?	And *Again, ye shall say unto them,* Why *is it that* thou beholdest the mote that is in thy brother's eye, but considerest not the beam that is in thine own eye?
Or how wilt thou say to thy brother, Let me pull out the mote out of thine eye; and, behold, a beam is in thine own eye?	Or how wilt thou say to thy brother, Let me pull out the mote out of thine eye; and *canst not* behold a beam in thine own eye?

"The people," to whom the disciples will speak these words, are commanded to judge righteous judgment. At this early point in their ministry, the Twelve are to teach "the lost sheep of the house of Israel," and not the Gentiles or the Samaritans (see KJV Matthew 10:5–6). Therefore, this message is for the Jews, whose models of judgment are their religious leaders and local synagogue councils. Just prior to the time of the Sermon in the accounts in Matthew, Mark, and Luke, Jesus had been teaching in the synagogues of Galilee, and was there confronted by those who judged him guilty of breaking the law by healing on the Sabbath day (see JST Matthew 4:22; Mark 3:1–7; Luke 6:6–11).

Referring to such models of unrighteous judgment, Jesus tells his disciples in the Sermon to teach the people about motes and beams.

In the following verses, the image of motes and beams is given explicit application as Jesus directs his disciples' attention to religious leaders among the listening multitude. He first describes their unrighteous judgment, and then tells the disciples how to speak of motes and beams to them:

KJV Matthew 7:5	JST Matthew 7:6–8
	And Jesus said unto his disciples, Beholdest thou the Scribes, and the Pharisees, and the Priests, and the Levites? They teach in their synagogues, but do not observe the law, nor the commandments; and all have gone out of the way, and are under sin.
	Go thou and say unto them, Why teach ye men the law and the commandments, when ye yourselves are the children of corruption?
Thou hypocrite, first cast out the beam out of thine own eye; and then shalt thou see clearly to cast out the mote out of thy brother's eye.	*Say unto them, Ye hypocrites, first cast out the beam out of thine own eye; and then shalt thou see clearly to cast out the mote out of thy brother's eye.*

Earlier in the Sermon, Jesus taught his disciples to avoid hypocritical religion. Here, he instructs them how to confront the models of such unrighteousness and how to teach the people to righteously judge it.[8]

The subsequent message is for all the world. Jesus identifies for his disciples the foundation of their teaching:

KJV Matthew 7	JST Matthew 7:9
(No corresponding material, between 7:5 and 7:6)	*Go ye into the world, saying unto all, Repent, for the kingdom of heaven has come nigh unto you.*

John the Baptist taught the message of repentance and the coming of the kingdom (see KJV Matthew 3:2). Jesus' message was the same (see KJV Matthew 4:17). Now the Lord tells his disciples to take this message into the world.

Some things they are *not* to teach, as JST Matthew continues:

KJV Matthew 7:6	JST Matthew 7:10–11
	And the mysteries of the kingdom ye shall keep within yourselves; for it is not meet to
Give not that which is holy unto the dogs, neither cast ye your pearls before swine, lest they trample them under their feet,	give that which is holy unto the dogs; neither cast ye your pearls *unto* swine, lest they trample them under their feet.
	For the world cannot receive that which ye, yourselves, are not able to bear; wherefore ye shall not give your pearls unto
and turn again and rend you.	*them, lest they* turn again and rend you.

Giving holy things to dogs and pearls to swine is the Lord's figurative language for giving the mysteries of the kingdom to those who are not prepared to receive them.

After explaining to the Nephite Twelve the essence of the gospel and the commandment to repent which was to "all ye ends of the earth" (3 Nephi 27:20), Jesus commanded them to write the things which they had seen and heard, "save it be those which are forbidden" (3 Nephi 27:23). Like the Nephite Twelve, the disciples in Galilee had been taught things which they were to keep to themselves—not that the mysteries are not available to all, but each must receive them when he is prepared.

The additions in JST Matthew 7:10–11 tie Jesus' figurative use of pearls in the Sermon to his later parable on the pearl of great price (see JST Matthew 13:47). In that parable, the merchantman was "*seeking* goodly pearls." No one cast them to him. When by his own effort and desire he found the pearl of great price, he sold all that he had and bought it.[9]

The next "say unto them" phrase in JST Matthew tells how one can obtain the mysteries of the kingdom:

KJV Matthew 7:7-8	JST Matthew 7:12-13
Ask, and it shall be given you; seek, and ye shall find; knock, and it shall be opened unto you:	*Say unto them, Ask of God;* ask, and it shall be given you; seek, and ye shall find; knock, and it shall be opened unto you.
For every one that asketh receiveth; and he that seeketh findeth; and to him that knocketh it shall be opened.	For every one that asketh, receiveth; and he that seeketh, findeth; and unto him that knocketh, it shall be opened.

The added sentence in JST Matthew 7:12 illustrates a recurring type of contribution of the JST—the tying of successive parts in the KJV into a whole. In this case, two seemingly unrelated items of instruction—not giving that which is holy to dogs, and asking, seeking, knocking—are brought together. *The disciples* are not to indiscriminately share holy things, and *their hearers,* if they want these things, should be invited to ask them of God.

To this teaching, JST Matthew restores the interjection of the disciples, who anticipate that their hearers will tell them God will not heed their request:

KJV Matthew 7	JST Matthew 7:14-15
(No corresponding material, between 7:8 and 7:9)	*And then said his disciples unto him, they will say unto us, We ourselves are righteous, and need not that any man should teach us. God, we know, heard Moses and some of the prophets; but us he will not hear.*
	And they will say, We have the law for our salvation, and that is sufficient for us.

Those who would so respond to the invitation to ask prove themselves to be among the dogs and swine unprepared for holy things. Their self-description, as the disciples anticipate it, identifies them as the same self-righteous, unteachable, law-bound, God-forsaken Jewish leaders to whom Jesus has referred throughout the Galilee Sermon. To them also the disciples are to give the terse foundation message intended for all the world: "Repent, for the kingdom of heaven has come nigh unto you" (JST Matthew 7:9). This time, however, Jesus gives the two parts of the message in somewhat different terms. The teaching on the nearness of the kingdom comes first, in the form of a poignant lesson about how the Father responds to his children that ask:

KJV Matthew 7:9–11	JST Matthew 7:16–21
	Then Jesus answered, and said unto his disciples, thus shall ye say unto them,
	What man among you, having a son, and he shall be standing out, and shall say, Father, open thy house that I may come in and sup with thee, will not say, Come in, my son; for mine is thine, and thine is mine?
Or what man is there of you, whom if his son ask bread, will he give him a stone?	Or what man is there *among* you, *who,* if his son ask bread, will give him a stone?
Or if he ask a fish, will he give him a serpent?	Or if he ask a fish, will he give him a serpent?
If ye then, being evil, know how to give good gifts unto your children, how much more shall your Father which is in heaven give good things to them that ask him?	If ye then, being evil, know how to give good gifts unto your children, how much more shall your Father *who* is in heaven give good things to them that ask him?
Therefore all things whatsoever ye would that men should do to you, do ye even so to them: for this is the law and the prophets.	Therefore, all things whatsoever ye would that men should do to you, do ye even so to them; for this is the law and the prophets.

The kingdom is nigh unto all, and the Perfect Father responds to the needs of his children when they ask. Jesus elsewhere teaches that the gifts which the Father gives come "through the Holy Spirit, to them who ask him" (JST Luke 11:14). James adds that he "giveth to all men liberally, and upbraideth not." "But," says James, "let him ask in faith, nothing wavering." (James 1:5–6.)

Only with the additional verses in JST Matthew do we learn that the Golden Rule, as given in the Galilee Sermon (JST Matthew 7:21), is part of the words the disciples are to say to the Jewish leaders, who have claimed, "We have the law for our salvation, and that is sufficient for us" (JST Matthew 7:15). Earlier, Jesus climaxed the section on laws unto perfection by commanding his disciples to be perfect even as their Father who is in Heaven is perfect (see JST Matthew 5:50). Seen in its complete context, the Golden Rule is a second climax which follows directly from the first. The disciples are to declare to the Jewish leaders that it is the essence of the law and the prophets to recognize and follow the example of the Perfect Father.

If the Jewish leaders will ask, they can obtain even the mysteries of the kingdom. But they are not willing to ask. Jesus therefore tells the disciples to present the other part of the foundation message; the JST adds that they must *repent* and enter in at the strait gate. The Sermon audiences in both Bountiful and Galilee are familiar with the main entry gates to walled cities, where the masses daily course in and out on the main road. Repentance, Jesus teaches, is not such a gate. It is a narrow, almost hidden, gate found only by those who are willing to leave the beaten path in order to find eternal life.

Guided by the extensive additions revealed in the JST, we see how the items of instruction at this point near the end of the Sermon become for the disciples in Galilee a guide for their missionary message. They are told its simple foundation. They are instructed what to teach to all the world and what to invite their listeners to seek on their own. They are told how to warn the people against their detractors and how to speak to the detractors themselves.

HEARING AND DOING

Jesus now concludes the Sermon with three admonitions on hearing and doing. This final section, although much the same in all five versions, is enriched by an overall understanding of the importance of *doing* the Lord's will which pervades the JST and the Book of Mormon.

First, the disciples in Galilee and the multitude in Bountiful are warned against false prophets who come to them like wolves in sheep's clothing. The intent of this expression is clear when we recognize Jesus' repeated references to his messengers as sheep, and even as "sheep in the midst of wolves" (KJV Matthew 10:16). They must be "wise servants, and as harmless as doves" (JST Matthew 10:14). When evil deceivers come, pretending discipleship, they may be judged by their fruits; that is, by what they *do* (see KJV Matthew 7:16–20; KJV Luke 6:43–45; 3 Nephi 14:16–20).

Second, Jesus warns that the day is coming when he will be the Judge of all.

KJV Matthew 7:21	*JST Matthew 7:30–31*
Not every one that saith unto me, Lord, Lord, shall enter into the kingdom of heaven; but he that doeth the will of my Father which is in heaven.	*Verily I say unto you, it is* not every one that saith unto me, Lord, Lord, *that* shall enter into the kingdom of heaven; but he that doeth the will of my Father *who* is in heaven. *For the day soon cometh, that men shall come before me to judgment, to be judged according to their works.*

Jesus' stress on doing his Father's will, strengthened by the verse unique to JST Matthew, recalls his declaration at the very beginning of his words to the Twelve in Bountiful: "I have suffered the will of the Father in all things from the beginning" (3 Nephi 11:11). Now he requires that those who would have the gate of the kingdom of heaven opened when they knock also must do his Father's will. Comparing the version in Luke, we note that the will of the Father is equated with the words of the Son: "And why call ye me, Lord, Lord, and do not the things which I *say*?" (KJV Luke 6:46; emphasis added). Those who merely hear, or hear and pretend to do, will not enter the kingdom. "Therefore, when once the Lord of the kingdom is risen up, and hath shut the door of the kingdom, then ye shall stand without, and knock at the door, saying, Lord, Lord, open unto us. But the Lord shall answer and say unto you, I will not receive you, for ye know not from whence ye are." (JST Luke 13:25.)

Excuses for not doing the will of the Father and the Son will be offered aplenty: "Many will say to me in that day: Lord, Lord, have we not prophesied in thy name, and in thy name have cast out devils, and in thy name done many wonderful works?" (3 Nephi 14:22; cf. KJV Matthew 7:22 and JST Matthew 7:32). "We have eaten and drunk in thy presence, and thou hast taught in our streets" (Luke 13:26). Note the Savior's answers in the Sermon:

KJV Matthew 7:23	JST Matthew 7:33	3 Nephi 14:23
And then will I profess unto them, I never knew you: depart from me, ye that work iniquity.	And then will I say, Ye never knew me; depart from me ye that work iniquity.	And then will I profess unto them: I never knew you; depart from me, ye that work iniquity.

Elder Bruce R. McConkie has written:

> Two answers of equivalent meaning are recorded to his question; both are answers that will be given to those saints who have not endured to the end, who have not kept the commandments, and who have not pressed forward with a steadfastness in Christ after baptism....
>
> "I never knew you, and you never knew me! Your discipleship was limited; you were not perfect members of my kingdom. Your heart was not so centered in me as to cause you to endure to the end; and so for a time and a season you were faithful; you even worked miracles in my name; but in the end it shall be as though I never knew you."[10]

The Savior finishes with a third admonition—a parable of hearing and doing, and as Luke reports, of coming unto Christ. The concept of coming to him ties together the beatitudes at the beginning of the Sermon in JST Matthew and in 3 Nephi. Now it becomes part of the final parable, which is here quoted from JST Luke:

Whosoever *cometh to me,* and *heareth my sayings* and *doeth them,* I will show you to whom he is like.

He is like a man who built a house, and digged deep, and laid the foundation on a rock, and when the flood arose, the stream beat vehemently upon that house, and could not shake it; for it was founded upon a rock.

But he who *heareth* and *doeth not,* is like a man that without a foundation built a house upon the earth; against which the stream did beat vehemently, and immediately it fell; and the ruin of that house was great. (JST Luke 6:47–49; emphasis added.)

SUMMARY

It would be difficult to overstate the significance of Jesus' Sermon on the Mount. With this Sermon, the Savior instructed the first priesthood quorum organized in the meridian of time. They were commanded to bear to all the world the invitation to come unto Christ, to receive the ordinances of salvation, and to seek perfection. With this Sermon, the Savior taught how the religious law which had guided the house of Israel for more than a millennium was to be fulfilled and superseded.

The resurrected Lord deliberately repeated the Sermon to a second Quorum of Twelve and to a multitude of righteous witnesses in Bountiful, where the anticipation of his coming had spanned the six hundred years since the arrival of their ancestors in the New World. To these witnesses, the Sermon was also a call to missionary service and a command to establish the higher law, which would unfold two centuries of peace and righteousness among them.

If properly understood, the Sermon has renewed relevance for our dispensation. New apostles and missionary witnesses are again taking the invitation to come unto Christ to a world filled with sin and hypocrisy. We have been commanded to gather Israel from its long dispersion and to establish the covenant among them.

During his ministry among the Nephites, the Savior gave them a sign that the final gathering of Israel would begin "when *these things* which I declare unto you . . . shall be made known unto the Gentiles . . ." (3 Nephi 21:2; emphasis added; cf. 3

Nephi 29:1ff). The Bountiful Sermon contains the foundation principles of "these things." The Savior specifically commanded that the Sermon and the teachings which accompanied it be written, as a scriptural tool to be given to the Gentiles for the gathering of Israel in the last days (see 3 Nephi 16:4–7; 23:4).

Through the revelations of God to the Prophet Joseph Smith, the sign has appeared. The teachings of which Jesus spoke are now available to all in the Book of Mormon. In addition, God has prepared biblical scriptures to work together with the Book of Mormon in this dispensation. The Joseph Smith Translation unlocks the meaning and intent of the Sermon as it was first given in Galilee, making the two givings of the Sermon one in the Lord's hand.

We too must accept the Lord's challenge to be doers of the word. If we study and apply the teachings of the Sermon, as they are revealed to this dispensation, we too may inherit the promise that "whoso remembereth these sayings of mine and doeth them, him will I raise up at the last day" (3 Nephi 15:1).

Robert A. Cloward is director of the LDS Institute of Religion, University of Tennessee.

NOTES

1. The Greek expression in the first three beatitudes in Luke is literally "blessed (are) the poor," "blessed (are) those hungering now," "blessed (are) those weeping now"—similar to the beatitudes of Matthew. The second plural "be ye," or "are ye" in Luke is italicized in current editions of the KJV and is inferred from the second plural *second half* of each beatitude, "for *yours* is the kingdom of God," etc. The fourth beatitude in Luke has a different form, literally "blessed are you when . . ." and the KJV contains no italics. The JST Luke changes to third plural occur only in the beatitudes with italics in KJV.

2. Compare the similar idiom on the passing of heaven and earth in KJV Matthew 24:35; KJV Mark 13:31; KJV Luke 21:33, all of which agree with the sense of JST Matthew 5:20.

3. Some have falsely reasoned from KJV Matthew 5:19–20 that Jesus was observant of the Jewish law and was only a reformer speaking out against the hypocrisy of the scribes and Pharisees. The Christian view of the replaced law, they claim, was introduced later by others, notably Paul. The JST clearly lays aside this misinterpretation.

4. Many modern versions also leave out the phrase "without a cause," in KJV Matthew 5:22, saying it was added by copyists and does not occur in the earliest extant manuscripts. However, the same argument is used for excising the phrase "For thine is the kingdom, and the power, and the glory for ever. Amen" from the Lord's Prayer in KJV Matthew 6:13. The JST not only includes that phrase in JST Matthew 6:15, but strengthens it ("forever *and ever*") and essentially restores it to KJV Luke 11:4 ("for thine is the kingdom and power. Amen.") Those who are inclined to disparage or vindicate the JST by comparing individual changes with modern biblical criticism concentrate on trees and miss the forest.

5. Robert J. Matthews places this change in a general category with many other changes which show the direction of the JST away from the concept that God is responsible for the good or evil men do. See Robert J. Matthews, *"A Plainer Translation": Joseph Smith's Translation of the Bible, A History and Commentary* (Provo, Utah: Brigham Young University Press, 1975), p. 314.

6. Bruce R. McConkie, *Doctrinal New Testament Commentary,* 3 vols. (Salt Lake City: Bookcraft, 1966–73), 1:244.

7. In a later context in JST Luke, Jesus implies a more down-to-earth source of sustenance for disciples who are "of doubtful mind" about food and clothing during their ministry (see JST Luke 12:33).

8. For a discussion of Jesus' own confrontations with Jewish leaders, see Robert L. Millet, "Looking Beyond the Mark: Insights from the JST into First-Century Judaism," in this volume.

9. On the need for each to seek individually, see also the parable of the ten virgins (JST Matthew 25:1–12), in which the five wise virgins told the five foolish virgins they would need to buy their own oil.

10. Bruce R. McConkie, *The Mortal Messiah,* 4 books (Salt Lake City: Deseret Book Co., 1979–81), 2:172–73.

10

Looking Beyond the Mark: Insights from the JST into First-Century Judaism

Robert L. Millet

In speaking of Joseph Smith the Prophet, President Wilford Woodruff observed:

> His mind was opened by the visions of the Almighty, and the Lord taught him many things by vision and revelation that were never taught publicly in his days; for the people could not bear the flood of intelligence which God poured into his mind.[1]

Latter-day Saints, however, should be filled with gratitude for what God *did* see fit to make known to the restored Church through that "choice seer," the man who in modern times beheld "things which were not visible to the natural eye" (Moses 6:36).

Through his work of inspired revision of the King James Bible (JST), the Prophet Joseph restored to the world many plain and precious truths concerning Jesus Christ—his parables, miracles, his personality and power. In addition, invaluable insights concerning his ministry among the Jews are now available. This paper will deal specifically with the state of Judaism at the time of Jesus, as such things are elucidated in the JST.

INTRODUCTION

Seven hundred years before Jesus walked the roads of his beloved Palestinian homelands, Isaiah the prophet spoke of the coming Messiah as one who would mature "as a tender plant, and as a root out of a dry ground" (Isaiah 53:2). Indeed, he would grow up "as a choice and favored plant whose strength and achievement did not come because of the arid social culture in which he dwelt; it was not poured into him by the erudition of Rabbinic teachers; but it came from the divine source from whence he sprang."[2] This root-stock or "stem of Jesse" would grow to godhood in a sterile and barren religious soil, in the midst of great learning but gross darkness. The social and religious backdrop of the life of Christ—the setting of first-century Judaism in Palestine—provides the supreme element of contrast in the unfolding drama of the mortal ministry of the Son of God: the Anointed One was the Light which shone; a benighted generation bound by traditions and customs was the darkness which refused to comprehend the light.

After ages of bondage, the Jews of the first century had riveted themselves upon the hope of deliverance. Anticipation was great and expectations were legion, for "the Jews taught that the kingdom of God should immediately appear" (JST Luke 19:11). And yet, "the Jews were looking for a redeemer quite different from the Christ. It was a temporal salvation that they desired. It was an earthly kingdom for which they longed. It was not faith, repentance, and baptism for which they sought, but national vindication, the destruction of gentile oppressors, and the establishment of a kingdom of peace and justice."[3] With such limited vision and perspective, it is not difficult to see how a people could "discern the face of the sky" but not "discern the signs of the times" (Matthew 16:3). Jesus the Christ was the ultimate sign, the fulfillment of the Mosaic ordinances and utterances, and, ironically, the great *end* to all of Judaism's myriad *means*. Nevertheless, a stiffnecked generation refused to focus upon the Mark, and chose instead to look for a Messiah of their own making.

JESUS, THE JEWS, AND THE LAW

In the purest sense, Jesus was an observant Jew. He loved and honored the law of Moses, and sought to keep the statutes and ordinances associated therewith. His divine perspective allowed him to view the law in the spirit in which it was given, as a "schoolmaster" (literally "pedagogue," "tutor," or "attendant") for a wayward people in need of structure and direction. "Christ Himself," taught Joseph Smith, "fulfilled all righteousness in becoming obedient to the law which he had given to Moses on the mount, and thereby magnified it and made it honorable, instead of destroying it."[4] Until the time of the infinite atonement was past, the Master taught that the law was to be observed and kept. "Heaven and earth must pass away," he emphatically declared, "but one jot or one tittle shall in no wise pass from the law, until all be fulfilled. Whosoever, therefore, shall break one of these least commandments, and shall teach men so to do, he shall in no wise be saved in the kingdom of heaven; but whosoever shall do and teach these commandments of the law until it be fulfilled, the same shall be called great, and shall be saved in the kingdom of heaven." (JST Matthew 5:20–21.)

It is not difficult to fathom how a people could become so enamored with the extremities and extensions of the pure instruction of heaven that they might begin eventually to ignore and overlook the core teachings, the "weightier matters of the law." Those who become easily bored by the basics and who constantly seek to engage in the peripheral and esoteric may come to trade plainness for blindness (see Jacob 4:14). Such was obviously the state of things at the time of Christ. Had the Pharisees been more intense in their study of the pure law (rather than the commentaries upon it) and more eager to apply its teachings (rather than seeking for further things which they could not understand), they might have distilled the central message of the Torah and thereby recognized Jesus of Nazareth as the giver of the law and the promised Messiah. Such was not, however, to be the case. Even though Judaism represented the closest approximation to the ancient gospel ("Salvation is of the Jews," Jesus explained to the Samaritan woman—John 4:22), the failure of individuals and congregations to accept and receive the living oracles sealed their doom. One of the most interesting insertions of the Prophet Joseph Smith into the King James Bible is found in chapter 9 of Matthew's Gospel. Note the relationship between rejecting (or ignoring) the law and rejecting the Christ:

KJV Matthew 9:15–16

And Jesus said unto them, Can the children of the bridechamber mourn, as long as the bridegroom is with them? but the days will come when the bridegroom shall be taken from them, and then shall they fast.

No man putteth a piece of new cloth unto an old garment, for that which is put in to fill it up taketh from the garment, and the rent is made worse.

JST Matthew 9:16–22

And Jesus said unto them, Can the children of the bridechamber mourn, as long as the bridegroom is with them?
But the days will come, when the bridegroom shall be taken from them, and then shall they fast.
Then said the Pharisees unto him, why will ye not receive us with our baptism, seeing we keep the whole law?[5]
But Jesus said unto them, Ye keep not the law. If ye had kept the law, ye would have received me, for I am he who gave the law.
I receive not you with your baptism, because it profiteth you nothing.
For when that which is new is come, the old is ready to be put away.
For no man putteth a piece of new cloth *on* an old garment; for that which is put in to fill it up, taketh from the garment, and the rent is made worse.

Not only does the preceding addition provide a marvelous topical transition and establish the social and doctrinal setting for the discussion of new cloth and new bottles (Jesus has rejected the baptism of the Pharisees—cf. D&C 22); it also underscores the fact that those who accept and follow divine direction come to recognize and accept the Divine Director; those who set the law at naught and seek to become a law unto themselves are condemned by the law and rejected by the Lawgiver. Another passage from Luke teaches this same principle.

KJV Luke 14:33–35	JST Luke 14:34–38
So likewise, whosoever he be of you that forsaketh not all that he hath, he cannot be my disciple.	So likewise, whosoever of you forsaketh not all that he hath he cannot be my disciple. *Then certain of them came to him, saying, Good Master, we have Moses and the prophets, and whosoever shall live by them, shall he not have life? And Jesus answered, saying, Ye know not Moses, neither the prophets; for if ye had known them, ye would have believed on me; for to this intent they were written. For I am sent that ye might have life. Therefore I will*
Salt is good: but if the salt have lost his savour, wherewith shall it be seasoned?	*liken it unto salt which is good;* But if the salt has lost its savor, wherewith shall it be seasoned?
It is neither fit for the land, nor yet for the dunghill; but men cast it out. He that hath ears to hear, let him hear.	It is neither fit for the land, nor yet for the dung hill; men cast it out. He *who* hath ears to hear, let him hear. *These things he said, signifying that which was written, verily must all be fulfilled.*

Jesus' criticism of the leaders of the Jews was largely for their perverted priorities, for confusing tokens with covenants, ritual with religion. Further, he condemned their adherence to the "traditions of the elders" as "teaching the doctrines and the commandments of men" (JST Mark 7:6–7; JST Matthew 15:8). In the eyes of the Lord, to present oneself as a master and expert of the law and then to miss the undergirding intent and antitype of the law was the height of hypocrisy. In a sense, it was to be guilty of a profanation and violation of the entire Mosaic code. "Ye blind guides," Jesus said in a scathing denunciation, "who strain at a gnat, and swallow a camel; who make yourselves appear unto men that ye would not commit the least sin, and yet ye yourselves, transgress the whole law" (JST Matthew 23:21). In addition, the Lord chastened the leaders of the Jews for being so caught up in the observance of the traditions of the elders (see Matthew 15:1–9; Mark 7:1–9) that they had ceased to observe the very law around which those vain traditions had been established. In an insightful passage from the Sermon on the Mount, Christ explained to his disciples:

KJV Matthew 7:3–5	JST Matthew 7:4–8
And why beholdest thou the mote that is in thy brother's eye, but considerest not the beam that is in thine own eye?	*And again, ye shall say unto them,* Why *is it that thou* beholdest the mote that is in thy brother's eye, but considerest not the beam that is in thine own eye?
Or how wilt thou say to thy brother, Let me pull out the mote out of thine eye; and, behold, a beam is in thine own eye?	Or how wilt thou say to thy brother, Let me pull out the mote out of thine eye; and *canst not* behold a beam in thine own eye?
	And Jesus said unto his disciples, Beholdest thou the Scribes, and the Pharisees, and the Priests, and the Levites? They teach in their synagogues, but do not observe the law, nor the commandments; and all have gone out of the way, and are under sin.
	Go thou and say unto them, Why teach ye men the law and the commandments, when ye yourselves are the children of corruption?
Thou hypocrite, first cast out the beam out of thine own eye; and then shalt thou see clearly	*Say unto them,* Ye hypocrites, first cast out the beam out of thine own eye; and then shalt

| to cast out the mote out of thy brother's eye. | thou see clearly to cast out the mote out of thy brother's eye. |

A similar passage from Mark points toward misplaced zeal and priorities among Jewish leaders. Jesus is chiding the Jews for failure to keep the regulations of the law regarding care of one's parents (see Exodus 20:12). Note the account in the JST:

KJV Mark 7:9–10

And he said unto them, Full well ye reject the commandments of God, that ye may keep your own tradition.

For Moses said, Honour thy father and thy mother; and, Whoso curseth father or mother, let him die the death:

JST Mark 7:9–12

And he said unto them, *Yea, altogether* ye reject the commandment of God, that ye may keep your own tradition.

Full well is it written of you, by the prophets whom ye have rejected.

They testified these things of a truth, and their blood shall be upon you.

Ye have kept not the ordinances of God; for Moses said, Honor thy father and thy mother; and whoso curseth father or mother, let him die the death *of the transgressor, as it is written in your law; but ye keep not the law.*

SPIRITUAL STUMBLINGS OF THE JEWS

Jesus stood as a marked contrast to the rabbis of his day. He taught the people "as one having authority from God, and not as having authority from the Scribes" (JST Matthew 7:37). The ability to teach with spiritual authority is a gift granted to those who pay the price of fasting, prayer, and scripture study (see Alma 17:2–3). Jesus had paid such a price and much more, while his Jewish counterparts had attended more to what the learned had said *about* the law than what had actually been said *in* the law. "Ye do err therefore," Christ said to the Sadducees, "because ye know not, and understand not the Scriptures, neither the power of God" (JST Mark 12:28). Here even the Sadducees—who rejected the oral interpretations so dear to the heart of the Pharisees—are scolded for their lack of scriptural insight. Had the leaders of the Jews prayerfully studied and taught from the scriptures of the day, there would have been a power and an authority behind the words they spoke. Had they accepted Jesus as the Christ and entered in at the strait gate, they would have enjoyed the ratifying influence of the Holy Ghost in their declarations. Elder Bruce R. McConkie has written:

> Many great doctrinal revelations come to those who preach from the scriptures. When they are in tune with the Infinite, the Lord lets them know, first, the full and complete meaning of the scriptures they are expounding, and then he ofttimes expands their views so that new truths flood in upon them, and they learn added things that those who do not follow such a course can never know.[6]

Needless to say, first-century Judaism may be characterized as a generation who, for the most part, did *not* follow such a course. Consequently, the teachers of the day lacked the confirming spiritual power that was so evident in the works and words of Jesus.

Jesus chided the Pharisees and scribes for remaining content with a sterile form of worship, a hollow shell of a system wanting in the life that is breathed into religious practice through current revelation. Truly, as Nephi had taught almost six hundred years before, "from them that shall say, We have enough, from them shall be taken away even that which they have" (2 Nephi 28:30). Traditions are evident among some rabbis concerning a noticeable absence in ancient Judaism of the spirit of prophecy and revelation.[7] Some date the loss of the Holy Spirit or the divine Shekhinah from the destruction of the first temple, others with the deaths of the Old Testament prophets.[8] One ancient Jewish writer observed: "When the last of the Prophets, Haggai, Zechariah, and Malachi died, the Holy Spirit departed from Israel."[9] Another account: "At first, before Israel sinned against morality, the Shekhinah abode with each individual; as it is said, 'For the Lord thy God walketh in the midst of thy camp' (Deuteronomy

23:15). When they sinned, the Shekhinah departed from them."[10] E. R. Goodenough spoke of later Judaism and made the distinction between what he called the "horizontal" and "vertical" paths to holiness. In describing the horizontal path, Goodenough explained:

> Man walked through this life along the road God had put before him, a road which was itself the light and law of God, and God above rewarded him for doing so. Man was concerned with proper observances to show respect to God, and with proper attitudes and acts toward his fellow men, but apart from honoring God, he looked to God only for the divine rod and staff to guide him when he was weak. . . . This seems to me the *Wesen* of halachic or rabbinic or talmudic or Pharisaic Judaism. . . .[11]

Further, Goodenough observed:

> Alongside rabbinic Judaism in Palestine in the century or so before the fall of Jerusalem there sprang up a rash of other sects. The Essenes we know by name, but we have only external and inadequate reports of their views. Then we have documents, like the strange apocalypses of Enoch and Baruch, Noah, Adam, and the rest, whose interest seems to be in a hero who had trod not a horizontal path but a vertical one up to the throne of God, and had returned to tell men of another world.[12]

In summary, Goodenough proposed that there was eventually within Judaism "the tension between the two basic types of religious experience . . . , the religion of the vertical path by which man climbs to God and even to a share in divine nature, as over against the legal religion where man walks a horizontal path through this world according to God's instructions."[13] In the end, according to Goodenough, Rabbinic or Pharisaic Judaism won out, and the vertical path to God within Judaism was suppressed and gradually forgotten.[14] The fact that many in the first century had reached the point of personal apostasy to the degree that they no longer accepted modern prophets or even personal revelation is evident in the following from the Sermon on the Mount:

KJV Matthew 7:7–10

Ask, and it shall be given you; seek, and ye shall find; knock, and it shall be opened unto you:

For every one that asketh receiveth; and he that seeketh findeth; and to him that knocketh it shall be opened.

Or what man is there of you, whom if his son ask bread, will he give him a stone?

Or if he ask a fish, will he give him a serpent?

JST Matthew 7:12–19

Say unto them, Ask of God, ask, and it shall be given you; seek, and ye shall find; knock, and it shall be opened unto you.

For every one that asketh, receiveth; and he that seeketh, findeth; and unto him that knocketh, it shall be opened.

And then said his disciples unto him, they will say unto us, We ourselves are righteous, and need not that any man should teach us. God, we know, heard Moses and some of the prophets; but us he will not hear.

And they will say, We have the law for our salvation, and that is sufficient for us.

Then Jesus answered, and said unto his disciples, thus shall ye say unto them,

What man among you, having a son, and he shall be standing out, and shall say, Father, open thy house that I may come in and sup with thee, will not say, Come in, my son; for mine is thine, and thine is mine?

Or what man is there *among* you, who, if his son ask bread, will give him a stone?

Or if he ask a fish, will he give him a serpent?

Perhaps more than any other place in the Gospels, the above passage from the Prophet's inspired revision demonstrates the static and inert condition of the days of Jesus. Much like the people in our day who eschew the Book of Mormon as an unnecessary addition to the total and complete and inerrant Bible, the Jews of the first century had stumbled into a pathetic state of blindness perfectly characterized by the statement: "God, we know, heard Moses and some of the prophets; *but us he will not hear.*" How typical of those who are "past feeling" to so respond.

"Have ye inquired of the Lord?" Nephi asked his rebellious brothers concerning their lack of understanding regarding the destiny of the house of Israel. "We have not," they responded, "for *the Lord maketh no such thing known unto us.*" (1 Nephi 15:8-9; emphasis added.) In Christ's day the spirit of true inquiry was all but gone. Absent was the awareness of the need for the spirit of prophecy and revelation. Elder Orson Pratt explained:

> The Jews had apostatized before Jesus came among them to that degree, that there were sects and parties among them, just as we find in the Christian world since; and *these Jewish sects were destitute of the spirit of prophecy which their ancient fathers had;* they were destitute of the ministration of angels, and scarcely one feature existed which was among their fathers in the days of their righteousness. It was because of this that the Jews were broken off, and the Gentiles were grafted in, and were made partakers of the riches, blessings and glories formerly enjoyed by the ancient Jews.[15]

As an illustration of the elevation of the wise interpreter of the law over the simple man with prophetic mantle and inspiration, note the following short observation of one Jewish mind: "Although the gift of prophecy was taken away from the prophets, it remained with the wise; hence it may be inferred that the wise are greater than the prophets."[16] One rather humorous but poignant rabbinic anecdote is given in the Babylonian Talmud. It seems that a debate had ensued between a Rabbi Eliezer and a number of his colleagues. The account is as follows:

> On that day R. Eliezer brought forward every imaginable argument, but they did not accept them. Said he to them: "If the *halachah* agrees with me, let this carob-tree prove it!" Thereupon the carob-tree was torn a hundred cubits out of its place—others affirm four hundred cubits. "No proof can be brought from a carob-tree," they retorted. Again he said to them: "If the *halachah* agrees with me, let the stream of water prove it!" Whereupon the stream of water flowed backwards. "No proof can be brought from a stream of water," they rejoined. Again he urged: "If the *halachah* agrees with me, let the walls of the building be inclined to fall." But R. Joshua

rebuked them, saying: "When scholars are engaged in a *halachic* dispute, what have ye to interfere?" Hence they did not fall, in honour of R. Joshua, nor did they resume the upright, in honour of R. Eliezer; and they are still standing thus inclined. Again he said to them: "If the *halachah* agrees with me, let it be proved from Heaven!" Whereupon a Heavenly Voice cried out: "Why do ye dispute with R. Eliezer, seeing that in all matters the *halachah* agrees with him!" But R. Joshua arose and exclaimed: "It is not in heaven." What did he mean by this? — Said R. Jeremiah: "That the Torah had already been given at Mount Sinai; we pay no attention to a Heavenly Voice, because Thou hast long since written in the Torah at Mount Sinai. . . ."[17]

An absentee God and an unresponsive Deity exerts little influence upon the hearts and minds of his children. Those who subscribe to a belief in such a Being are only a stone's throw removed from an outright denial of their God's existence. "It is easier for heaven and earth to pass," the Lord declared, "than for one tittle of the law to fail." And then in a discerning and stinging manner, Christ continued to address the leaders of the Jews: "*Why teach ye the law, and deny that which is written;* and condemn him whom the Father hath sent to fulfil the law, that ye might all be redeemed? *O fools! for you have said in your hearts, There is no God.* And you pervert the right way; and the kingdom of heaven suffereth violence of you; and you persecute the meek; and in your violence you seek to destroy the kingdom." (JST Luke 16:19–21; emphasis added.)

The Jews of the meridian dispensation made their destruction sure when they determined upon a course which denied the place and efficacy of continuing revelation. "Woe unto you, lawyers!" the Savior said. "For *ye have taken away the key of knowledge, the fulness of the scriptures;* ye enter not in yourselves into the kingdom; and those who were entering in, ye hindered." (JST Luke 11:53; emphasis added.) Elder McConkie has written concerning this verse:

> The devil wages war against the scriptures. He hates them, perverts their plain meanings, and destroys them when he can. He entices those who heed his temptings to delete and discard, to change and corrupt, to alter and amend, thus taking away

the key which will aid in making men "wise unto salvation" (2 Timothy 3:15–17).

Accordingly, Jesus is here heaping wo upon those who have contaminated and destroyed scriptures which would have guided and enlightened the Jews.[18]

In a much broader sense, to take away "the fulness of the scriptures" is to deny and hinder the spirit of revelation, inasmuch as *scripture* represents that which is uttered by the power of the Holy Ghost (see D&C 68:3–4). There stood One among the Jews who, with his associates (as legal administrators), offered to the world of the first century living scripture, living fruit from the living tree of life. Those who were earnest in their hearts partook of the fruit and lived. Those who chose to "walk in darkness at noon day" rejected the fruit and denied themselves access to God's new covenant with Israel, and, equally important, fellowship with the Mediator of that covenant.

Robert L. Millet is assistant professor of Ancient Scripture at BYU.

NOTES

1. *Journal of Discourses,* 26 vols. (London: Latter-day Saints' Book Depot, 1855–86), 5:83–84.

2. Bruce R. McConkie, *The Promised Messiah: The First Coming of Christ* (Salt Lake City: Deseret Book Company, 1978), p. 478.

3. Joseph F. McConkie, "Messianic Expectations Among the Jews," *A Symposium on the New Testament* (Salt Lake City: The Church of Jesus Christ of Latter-day Saints, Church Educational System, 1980), p. 128.

4. Joseph Smith, *History of The Church of Jesus Christ of Latter-day Saints,* 7 vols. (Salt Lake City: The Church of Jesus Christ of Latter-day Saints, 1972), 5:261.

5. "Now the process by which a man was made a proselyte [convert to Judaism] was threefold: it consisted of circumcision,

immersion in water (i.e., baptism), and the presentation of an offering in the Temple. Of these rites baptism assumed a growing importance." (W. D. Davies, *Paul and Rabbinic Judaism* [Philadelphia: Fortress Press, 1980], p. 121.) See also Joachim Jeremias, *Jerusalem in the Time of Jesus* (Philadelphia: Fortress Press, 1969), p. 320; Louis Ginzberg, *The Legends of the Jews,* 7 vols. (Philadelphia: Jewish Publication Society, 1937), 3:88; F. F. Bruce, *The Book of the Acts* (Grand Rapids, Mich.: Wm. B. Eerdmans Publishing Co., 1979), p. 64; W. F. Flemington, "Baptism," in *Interpreter's Dictionary of the Bible,* 5 vols. (Nashville, Tenn.: Abingdon Press, 1962–76), 1:348–49.

6. Bruce R. McConkie, *The Promised Messiah,* pp. 515–16.

7. I am indebted to Catherine Thomas for calling a number of these statements to my attention. Some of the statements are cited in Catherine Thomas's "Cessation and Restoration of Divine Revelation in Israel," unpublished manuscript.

8. See Ginzberg, *Legends,* 6:441–42.

9. Yomah 9b and Sotah 48b, as cited in Thomas, "Cessation and Restoration of Divine Revelation in Israel," p. 4.

10. Sotah 3b, as cited in ibid.

11. E. R. Goodenough, *Jewish Symbols in the Greco-Roman Period,* 13 vols. (New York: Bollingen Foundation, 1953), 1:18.

12. Ibid., pp. 18–19.

13. Ibid., pp. 19–20.

14. See Goodenough's discussion in ibid., pp. 3–32.

15. Orson Pratt in *Journal of Discourses,* 16:345 (emphasis added).

16. Cited in Ginzberg, *Legends,* 6:442.

17. TB BABA BAZIA 59B; see also Milton Steinberg, *Basic Judaism* (New York: Harcourt, Brace & World, 1947), pp. 68–69.

18. Bruce R. McConkie, *Doctrinal New Testament Commentary,* 3 vols. (Salt Lake City: Bookcraft, 1966–73), 1:624–25.

11

The JST and the New Testament Epistles

Clyde J. Williams

On 7 March 1831 the Prophet Joseph Smith received the following instruction: "And now, behold, I say unto you, it shall not be given unto you to know any further concerning this chapter, until the New Testament be translated, and in it all these things shall be made known; Wherefore I give unto you that ye may now translate it, that ye may be prepared for the things to come" (D&C 45:60–61).

From this passage we learn at least two key concepts concerning Joseph Smith and his translation of the New Testament: at this time Joseph was instructed to begin the translation of the New Testament,[1] and he was told that many things would be made known to him as a direct result of this endeavor. This illustrates the important point that the Lord's prophet needed a scripture study program, and through this process of translation the Lord would reveal many important truths. From questions and discussions held while the translation progressed, Joseph was led to inquire about and receive some of the most significant doctrine to be revealed in this dispensation.

In Kirtland, Ohio, the Prophet Joseph recorded: "I completed the translation and review of the New Testament, on the 2nd of February, 1833, and sealed it up, no more to be opened till it arrived in Zion."[2] This would seem to indicate that the major portion of the Prophet's work on the New Testament occurred over a two-year period from March 1831 to February 1833. During this time the Prophet made significant changes in the New Testament.

In considering the impact of the Joseph Smith Translation upon the New Testament Epistles, the following questions will be treated: How many changes did Joseph make in each Epistle? Are any of the JST changes supported by the Greek New Testament? Do modern translations support any of the JST changes? How is the character of Paul clarified by the JST? What significant doctrines have been clarified in the New Testament Epistles? Underlying all that is presented in this paper is the desire to show the divinely prophetic nature of Joseph Smith's work in this branch of his calling.[3]

WHERE ARE THE CHANGES?

The accompanying chart provides a perspective on the changes the Prophet made in the New Testament Epistles. The degree of significance of each change is not reflected in the chart. One can, however, get an idea of the books which received the largest number and percentage of changes. Notice that, overall, 438 verses (16 percent of the verses in the New Testament Epistles) were changed in some degree by the Prophet Joseph.

Epistle	Number of Verses	Number of Verses Changed	Percent of Verses Changed
Romans	433	119	27
1 Corinthians	437	70	16
2 Corinthians	257	25	10
Galatians	149	13	9
Ephesians	155	15	10
Philippians	104	14	13

Epistle	Number of Verses	Number of Verses Changed	Percent of Verses Changed
Colossians	95	9	9
1 Thessalonians	89	7	8
2 Thessalonians	47	7	15
1 Timothy	113	15	13
2 Timothy	83	8	10
Titus	46	2	4
Philemon	25	1	4
Hebrews	303	50	17
James	108	20	19
1 Peter	105	24	23
2 Peter	61	20	33
1 John	105	17	16
2 John	13	0	0
3 John	14	0	0
Jude	25	2	8
Total	2,767	438	16
	2,767		(Average)

THE JOSEPH SMITH TRANSLATION AND GREEK

My sole purpose in discussing the changes made by Joseph Smith which are supported by the Greek New Testament is to show a further witness of Joseph Smith's divine calling. It should be remembered that as far as we know Joseph did not study Greek in his lifetime. Furthermore, we realize how little formal schooling he acquired during his life. Though the vast majority of JST changes are not reflected in our oldest extant New Testament texts, a few of the changes are. For Joseph to make several changes supported by the Greek would seem to indicate the influence of the Lord.

This writer is not skilled in the Greek language. However, by using a Greek Bible dictionary, a word study, and an interlinear

Greek-English New Testament, much was found to support changes made by the Prophet in the New Testament Epistles.

In the King James Version we are told "faith is the *substance* of things hoped for, the evidence of things not seen" (Hebrews 11:1; emphasis added). In the JST, the word *substance* is replaced by the word *assurance* which "gives the true idea" of the Greek word *hupostasis*.[5]

In another chapter in Hebrews, the JST changes the word *testament* to *covenant* (Hebrews 9:15, 18, 20) which is the appropriate translation of the Greek word *diatheke*.[6] In several instances in 1 Peter, the Saints are told in the KJV to have honest, chaste, and good *conversation* (see 1 Peter 2:12; 3:1, 2, 16). The JST corrects the word *conversation* to *conduct,* which more accurately corresponds to the Greek.[7]

In the KJV, Titus 2:11 reads: "For the grace of God that bringeth salvation hath appeared to all men." In the JST we find this variation, which is supported by the Greek text: "For the grace of God which bringeth salvation *to all men* hath appeared."[8] Salvation has been made available to all men through the gospel of Jesus Christ. Other examples could be cited, but space will not permit.

THE JST AND OTHER TRANSLATIONS

One of the criticisms still leveled at the Prophet Joseph Smith by his enemies concerns his statement, "We believe the Bible to be the word of God as far as it is translated correctly" (A of F 8), and the statement in the Book of Mormon "that there are many plain and precious things taken away from the book [the Bible]" (1 Nephi 13:28). It should come as no surprise that well over a hundred thousand changes were made from the KJV to the Revised Standard Version in an effort to correct, interpret, and render the holy writ more accurate. This effort was not the first nor the last, as numerous other translations of varying worth have appeared. In and of themselves they seem to vindicate the Prophet's concerns with the accuracy of portions of the Bible.

Comparing the JST with other translations has nothing to do with whether the Prophet was right or wrong in his translation.

His effort stands alone and independent from all the secular translations. His translation was based on the Holy Spirit as his guide and not secular learning. However, it would seem significant to find several verses changed by the Prophet in the 1830s that were later changed to the same meaning or wording by scholarly translators.

The following are a few examples from among many which could be cited where the JST rendition is corroborated by one or more of the following modern translations: The New International Version (NIV), the Revised Standard Version (RSV), the Jerusalem Bible (JB), and the New English Bible (NEB). Unless otherwise indicated, all scripture references are from the King James Version.

In the KJV, Paul is quoted as saying, "I know nothing *by* myself" (1 Corinthians 4:4; emphasis added). The JST improves the wording by replacing the word *by* with *against*. The RSV makes the same word change, and the NIV and JB carry the same meaning. In Romans 13:2 the JST changes the word *damnation* to *punishment*. The RSV and NEB conform in this wording change. Perhaps one of the most interesting comparisons is found in James 2:4. The JST renders this verse, "Are ye not then *in yourselves* partial judges, and become evil in your thoughts?" (emphasis added). This is contrasted with the KJV which reads "Are ye not then partial in yourselves, and are become judges of evil thoughts?" (James 2:4). The JST is supported by the RSV and NIV which speak of "judges with evil thoughts."

Other changes made by Joseph are agreed with by modern translations. Once again the main point to be made here is that Joseph Smith as an unlearned young man made corrections by the direction of the Spirit. Some of these same changes would later be made by those in the scholarly world.

THE CHARACTER OF PAUL

Because of several confusing passages in his Epistles, the apostle Paul is perhaps one of the most misunderstood writers in scriptural history. In Romans one gets the impression that Paul is carnal and sinful (see Romans 7:14–15), and that he blames sin and not himself for his errors (see Romans 7:17, 20). Paul is cited as saying he has the will to do right but that he does not know how to perform that which is right (see Romans 7:18). The good he desires to do, he does not do and the evil he desires to avoid he does (see Romans 7:19). "These are strange statements, coming from a man like Paul so many years after he had experienced the cleansing power of the gospel of Jesus Christ," wrote Robert J. Matthews. "It is even contradictory for Paul to say these things about himself when in many other instances he declared that Christ had made him free, and that through the power of Christ he was able to walk no longer after the flesh but after the spirit."[9] This is the message of Romans 8:1–10.

In the JST, the context of chapter 7 is changed. Paul was referring to experiences before his conversion while he was still under the law of Moses (see JST Romans 7:14). Paul went on to affirm his current spirituality and that the things he was commanded to do he did do. That which is not right he would not do; but he sought to subdue sin (see JST Romans 7:15–18). Paul then made perhaps his most significant point, that his ability to perform that which is good is found "only in Christ" (JST Romans 7:19). It is "through the assistance of Christ" (JST Romans 7:22) that Paul was able to subdue sin.

From Romans 3:7–8 one might assume Paul was not above lying or teaching that we do evil so that good will come. The JST corrects these impressions by stating that it is the Jews who called Paul's message a lie and others who claimed that Paul taught, "Let us do evil that good may come. *But this is false.*" (JST Romans 3:8).

Is *everything* lawful to Paul? This is the impression one gets as he reads 1 Corinthians 6:12 and 10:23. In the earlier verses of 1 Corinthians 6 and 10, sins and transgressions are discussed. The JST clarifies that "all *these* things are *not* lawful" (JST 1 Corinthians 6:12).

One can get the impression from Romans 9:3 that it was Paul's current wish that he be accursed and separated from Christ. Concerning this passage, Elder Bruce R. McConkie made the following statement: "Before his conversion Paul chose to be accursed, meaning that by failing to accept Christ he was choosing to be accursed, and this was so despite the fact he was born in the house of Israel."[10] This statement sheds significant light on why Joseph Smith added the word *once* (JST Romans 9:3) to Paul's wish that he was cursed from Christ, thus putting it in the past tense.

There are other statements which could be cited that reflect upon Paul's character—for example, his views on marriage and the second coming of Christ. However, many of these will be treated later in this paper. The clarifications of Paul's character made by the Prophet Joseph Smith are a strong evidence of the divine calling of both men.

CLARIFYING POINTS OF DOCTRINE

Marriage and Women

Perhaps more than any other of his writings, Paul's teachings on marriage (found in 1 Corinthians 7) have been misunderstood. Reading this chapter gives the impression that Paul supported the celibate life; that marriage is inferior to the unmarried state. Robert J. Matthews offered the following helpful insights concerning the setting of 1 Corinthians 7 and the contribution to our understanding made by the JST:

> Although the epistle known as First Corinthians is the earliest writing from Paul to the church at Corinth in the present Bible, it is evident from the epistle itself that he had written to them earlier. At least part of the subject matter of that earlier epistle was about morality, marriage relationships, and how to deal with transgressors. Said Paul, in reminding the Corinthians of his earlier epistle, "I wrote to you in an epistle not to company with fornicators" (1 Corinthians 5:9). It is also evident that in response to Paul's former letter the Corinthian church wrote to him about marriage relationships. What is now called First Corinthians was written in reply to their letter. The two earlier epistles are now lost. If we had access to them, both of which predate the present "first" Corinthian letter, we would no doubt be able to more nearly understand Paul's teachings about marriage as presented in 1 Corinthians 7, since his instructions were a follow-up to what had already transpired between him and the Corinthian church. It is at this point that the New Translation [JST] by

Joseph Smith may be the best guide available. Prophet and seer that he was, Joseph Smith placed in the New Translation of 1 Corinthians 7 some background and "bridge" material necessary for a reader to understand Paul's instructions without having access to the two lost epistles.[11]

In the KJV the implication is that it is Paul who said, "It is good for a man not to touch a woman" (1 Corinthians 7:1). This is an unusual statement coming from one who was familiar with the scriptures and the commands to leave parents and become one flesh (see Genesis 2:24; Mark 10:7–9). The JST clarifies this issue by indicating it was the Corinthian Saints who wrote to Paul "*saying*, it is good for man not to touch a woman" (JST 1 Corinthians 7:1). In verse 2 of the JST, we are told that it is Paul who then begins to give his answer at that point. Remember that what we have in chapter 7 are answers to questions which we do not currently possess. One additional point to be made is that much of what Paul wrote on this occasion, he informed us, is his opinion and not a commandment (see 1 Corinthians 7:6, 25).

The crux of what Paul was really responding to is contained in verses 26–33. In the KJV, we are told because of some *present distress* it is good for a man to remain single and that before too long those who have wives will be as though they had none. The person who is unmarried cares for the things of the Lord but the man who is married cares for the things of the world and how he can please his wife (see 1 Corinthians 7:26–33). Now compare those thoughts with the feelings conveyed in the JST:

> I suppose therefore that this is good for the present distress, for a man so to *remain that he may do greater good.*
>
> But *I speak unto you who are called unto the ministry.* For this I say, brethren, the time *that remaineth* is but short, that ye *shall be sent forth unto the ministry.* Even they who have wives, *shall* be as though they had none; *for ye are called and chosen to do the Lord's work.*
>
> But *I would, brethren, that ye magnify your calling.* I would have you without carefulness. For he who is unmarried, careth for the things that belong to the Lord, how he may please the Lord; *therefore he prevaileth.*
>
> But he who is married, careth for the things that are of the world, how he may please his wife; *therefore there is a difference, for he is hindered.* (JST 1 Corinthians 7:26, 29, 32–33.)

Notice that the *present distress* is identified as having to do with missionary work. This throws an entirely different light on the remarks of Paul. He said that it is preferable for a missionary to be single. The missionary can concentrate more on his work and better magnify his calling. This counsel would only apply for the short time he served his mission. Those who had wives and were called on missions were for that period of time as though they had no wives. First Corinthians 7 is not an accurate representation of Paul's complete concept of marriage. It is believed by most scholars that Paul was married.[12] Statements elsewhere in Paul's letters indicate his perspective of marriage: "Nevertheless neither is the man without the woman, neither the woman without the man, in the Lord" (1 Corinthians 11:11). "Marriage is honourable in all, and the bed undefiled" (Hebrews 13:4).

One additional subject which relates to women should be discussed here. Paul is quoted in 1 Corinthians 14:34–35 as telling women to keep silent and not to speak in church. This misconception is in part corrected in the JST, indicating that it is not speaking in church which was in question, but *ruling* or *leading*, which is the responsibility of the priesthood.

Faith, Grace, and Works

As a former debater, this writer used to enjoy finding statements from a single author which were diametrically opposed. These statements could be used in diminishing an opponent's argument in the event that the opponent quoted the same author. Many religious groups have done a similar thing with Paul and his statements on faith, grace, and works. Paul's teachings, that we are "justified freely by his grace" (Romans 3:24) or "that a man is justified by faith alone without the deeds of the law" (JST Romans 3:28), are misunderstood when not harmonized with the whole of Paul's writings. The deeds of the law spoken of so frequently by Paul have reference not to righteous works, with which Paul maintained we should be furnished (see 2 Timothy 3:16–17; Titus 1:15–16), but to the deeds of the law of Moses— a series of performances which were superseded when Christ proclaimed his gospel. This was a lesser law and could not lead one to exaltation.

In Romans 6:14, Paul is quoted as saying that "sin shall not have dominion over you: for ye are not under the law, but under grace." The message conveyed is that sin will not have dominion over us solely because of grace. The two verses prior to verse 14 are a list of sins to which men must not yield. With that in mind, the JST combines works and grace in saying: "For *in so doing* sin shall not have dominion over you for ye are not under the law, but under grace" (JST Romans 6:14).

In perhaps the most completely wedded statement on this subject in the epistles, the JST correctly ties together the three main concepts of faith, works, and grace. "Therefore *ye are justified of faith and works, through grace,* to the end the promise might be sure to all the seed" (JST Romans 4:16). Like the Godhead, these three principles, though separate, distinct, and necessary, are one in their purpose. We are justified only by our faith and works as a result of the grace of God. Faith, works, or grace alone cannot save us.

One additional point on this subject of faith and works is found in the Epistle of James. The JST does much to rearrange the order of James's eloquent discussion in chapter 2. The subject there is the question of whether one can have saving faith without manifesting righteous works. One key addition should be cited: "Thou believest there is one God; thou doest well; the devils also believe, and tremble; *thou hast made thyself like unto them, not being justified*" (JST James 2:19). There is no question that the doctrine of faith without works will rob those who believe in it of eternal life.

Sin and Temptation

Several statements as they now exist in the KJV give false impressions about Paul's and others' teachings on sin and temptation. Following are some examples of these statements and how the JST clarified them.

In a sense, it may be correct to say that "he that is dead is freed from sin" (Romans 6:7). However, our goal to overcome sin is not to do so through death but to overcome sin while in this life. Thus "he that is dead *to sin* is freed from sin" (JST Romans 6:7). As one continues on in Romans 6, Paul seems to say we should thank God we "were the servants of sin" (Romans 6:17). It would seem only logical that we should never be thankful for sin but rather thank God that we "are *not* the servants of sin" (JST Romans 6:17).

From passages in the KJV we are told we are to be "subject to vanity" (Romans 8:20), to "endureth temptation" (James 1:12), and to be joyful when we "fall into . . . temptation" (James 1:2). Though these statements may please those who are weak, Paul would not condone vanity, nor would he encourage us to search out temptation to see how much we can endure. The Prophet Joseph Smith wisely amended these verses to clarify an important principle about tribulation and how we should respond to temptation. In the JST, we are told we are to be "subject to tribulation" (JST Romans 8:20), to "resisteth temptation" (JST James 1:12), and to be joyful when we fall into "many afflictions" (JST James 1:2). Afflictions, as Paul knew so well, can be a refining influence in our lives and thus should be welcomed.

Peter, in his first Epistle, wrote of having fervent charity and then is quoted as saying "charity shall cover the multitude of sins" (1 Peter 4:8). It is certain the chief apostle knew that only by repentance can men receive forgiveness of sins. In the JST, the phrase is given, "charity *preventeth* a multitude of sins" (JST 1 Peter 4:8). Charity is the pure love of Christ and one who possesses it "suffereth long, and is kind, and envieth not, and is not puffed up, seeketh not her own, is not easily provoked, thinketh no evil, and rejoiceth not in iniquity but rejoiceth in the truth, beareth all things, believeth all things, hopeth all things, endureth all things" (Moroni 7:45, 47). Truer words were never said; charity will prevent a multitude of sins.

In another verse from Paul which appears to be a contradiction, the JST changes the command "Be ye angry, and sin not" (Ephesians 4:26) to a thought-provoking question: *"Can ye be angry, and not sin?"* (JST Ephesians 4:26). The KJV of the entire verse could leave one with the impression that anger is appropriate as long as it does not last for more than a day. A final example where the doctrine on sin is clarified is in 1 John where we are told that "He that committeth sin is of the devil"; and that

"Whosoever is born of God . . . cannot sin." In the JST, the concept is changed from committing sin to *continuing in sin*. Concerning this point Elder Bruce R. McConkie stated: "All men sin, before and after baptism, but those saints who strive to keep the commandments, and are continually repenting and returning to the Lord, no longer continue in that course of sinful rebellion against God and his laws which was their lot before they were baptized for the remission of sins. Church members who do so continue in sin are members in name only; they do not receive the companionship of the Holy Ghost, through whose revelations alone can the Lord be 'known' "[13] (See JST 1 John 3:6–9.)

The Second Coming and the End of the World

Though this topic is treated in more detail in another paper, it should receive some treatment here because of its significance in the Epistles. One of the more controversial issues to intrigue mankind throughout the ages is: When will the end of the world be? Paul and Peter have both been represented as believing it would happen in their lifetime. The JST makes some interesting clarifications on this point. Christ did not appear in the "end of the world" to suffer for sins (Hebrews 9:26) but in the "meridian of time" (JST Hebrews 9:26). The message in 1 Corinthians was not for those in Paul's day "upon whom the ends of the world are come" (1 Corinthians 10:11), but the message was for those in Paul's day and *also* "those upon whom the end of the world *shall* come" (JST 1 Corinthians 10:11). Peter is quoted as saying "the end of all things is at hand" (1 Peter 4:7). The JST changes the tone of this statement. "But *to you*, the end of all things is at hand" (JST 1 Peter 4:7). Elder McConkie has said: "As each faithful saint approaches the day of his departure to the paradise of God, it is as though he were prepared for the Lord's second coming; it is as though the end of the world had come in his day."[14]

In letters to the Saints in Thessalonica, one of the major questions with which Paul dealt was the time of the second coming of the Lord. The JST clarifies Paul's message in these letters in four or five ways. The present tense of 1 Thessalonians

4:15, 17 is changed to the future tense; that is, "we which are alive" to *"they* who are alive at the coming of the Lord" (JST 1 Thessalonians 4:15). False information may have been coming to the Saints speaking of the imminence of Christ's second coming. In the JST, the Saints were warned by Paul not to "be troubled by *letter, except ye receive it from us"* (JST 2 Thessalonians 2:2). Paul then speaks of events that must precede Christ's return. The JST, in language stronger than the KJV, affirms that "there *shall* come a falling away" (JST 2 Thessalonians 2:3, see also JST 2 Thessalonians 2:9). It was Satan who was working among the Saints in Paul's time and *"Christ suffereth him to work,* until *the time is fulfilled that he shall* be" bound (JST 2 Thessalonians 2:7).

In the second Epistle of Peter, the JST gives several significant concepts that aid us in understanding Peter's views on the end of the world. Peter speaks of scoffers who will come in the last days who will not only be questioning the coming of Christ but they will be "denying the Lord Jesus Christ" (JST 2 Peter 3:4). In verse 8 of 2 Peter 3, we are told that one day with the Lord is like a thousand years to man. The remarkable thing the JST adds is a purpose for our knowing this fact about the Lord's time frame. It reads: *"But concerning the coming of the Lord,* beloved, I would not have you ignorant of this one thing, that one day is with the Lord as a thousand years, and a thousand years as one day. The Lord is not slack concerning his promise *and coming."* (JST 2 Peter 3:8–9.) Peter urged his readers to not be overly anxious about the time of the Lord's coming, for what is near to God may be a long way off in our reckoning of time.

Joseph made yet further clarifications in Peter's account. The heavens will not pass away (2 Peter 3:10) but they will *shake.* It is not the earth itself which will be burned up, but *"the corruptible works* which are therein" (JST 2 Peter 3:10). Instead of just looking forward to the Lord's coming we should be "looking *unto, and preparing for* the day of the coming of the *Lord"* (JST 2 Peter 3:12). Finally, the JST adds the Lord's promise of preservation to the righteous if they will endure to the end (see JST 2 Peter 3:13).

Christ—His Character and Mission

The contributions considered in this section help define the Savior's character and mission. The principles Christ taught and their importance in leading us to perfection is brought into question in Hebrews 6:1. The Prophet Joseph said the following about this verse:

> The first principles of the Gospel, as I believe, are, faith, repentance, baptism for the remission of sins, with the promise of the Holy Ghost.
> Look at Hebrews 6:1 . . . "Therefore leaving the principles of the doctrine of Christ, let us go on unto perfection." If a man leaves the principles of the doctrine of Christ, how can he be saved in the principles? This is a contradiction. I don't believe it. I will render it as it should be—"Therefore not leaving the principles of the doctrine of Christ, let us go on unto perfection; not laying again the foundation of repentance from dead works, and of faith toward God" [JST Hebrews 6:1].[15]

In striving for perfection, Paul taught, as was discussed earlier, that he found ability "to perform that which is good . . . *only in Christ*" (JST Romans 7:19). In Hebrews 7, Paul spoke of how high priests in Israel offered up sacrifice first for their own sins and then for the sins of the people (see Hebrews 7:27). Christ was such a high priest who did not need to follow this procedure because, as the JST adds, "he knew no sins; but for the sins of the people" (JST Hebrews 7:26). This change is certainly in harmony with other scriptural passages, for Christ "was in all points tempted like as we are, yet without sin" (Hebrews 4:15; see also 1 Peter 2:22).

The proper relationship between Christ and his Father is a subject which requires careful study. The JST of the New Testament Epistles contains additional scriptures which clarify that it is Christ who is the Savior (see JST 1 Timothy 1:1) and that he came to the earth and ascended into heaven "to glorify him who reigneth over all heavens" (JST Ephesians 4:10). The Prophet's renderings in these and other verses help establish the proper understanding of the role and relationship between the Father and his Son Jesus Christ.

Melchizedek

In the JST New Testament Epistles, two additions are made which have specific reference to the great Old Testament high priest, Melchizedek. In Hebrews 5:7–10, the message presented obviously refers to Christ and his mortal ministry. On the JST manuscript a footnote is found referring to verses 7 and 8. It says, "The 7th and 8th verses allude to Melchizedek, and not to Christ." Concerning this footnote Elder McConkie has written:

> Standing alone, and because it is only part of the picture, this footnote gives an erroneous impression. The fact is verses 7 and 8 apply to both Melchizedek and to Christ, because Melchizedek was a prototype of Christ and that prophet's ministry typified and foreshadowed that of our Lord in the same sense that the ministry of Moses did. (Deuteronomy 18:15–19; Acts 3:22–23; 3 Nephi 30:23; Joseph Smith–History 1:40.) Thus, though the words of these verses, and particularly those in the 7th verse, had original application to Melchizedek, they apply with equal and perhaps even greater force to the life and ministry of him through whom all the promises made to Melchizedek were fulfilled.[16]

Joseph Smith knew Melchizedek was a type of Christ (see Hebrews 7:3), and that Christ learned obedience by the things he suffered.[17] Given the nature of this chapter and other related passages, it seems possible that this footnote may have been "awkwardly recorded, and the meaning was intended to be that the verses could allude to both Melchizedek and Christ."[18]

The next addition concerning Melchizedek is found in Hebrews 7:3. In the KJV this verse, in context with verses 1 and 2, presents a dilemma of Melchizedek "being without father, without mother, without descent, having neither beginning of days, nor end of life" (Hebrews 7:3). The JST makes this passage remarkably clear and adds significant understanding: *"For this Melchizedek was ordained a priest after the order of the Son of God, which order* was without father, without mother, without descent, having neither beginning of days, nor end of life. *And all those who are ordained unto this priesthood are* made like unto the Son of God, abiding a priest continually." (JST Hebrews 7:3.) It was not Melchizedek, then, who was without father or mother or beginning of days, but the Melchizedek Priesthood which was formerly called "The Holy Priesthood after the Order of the Son of God" (D&C 107:3). Robert J. Matthews has commented, "It might be thought strange that the priesthood would be spoken of as being without father and mother, since priesthood is not an organic, biological thing; but the contrast is being made with the Aaronic Priesthood, which came down by lineage. Hence, the point is that the priesthood of Melchizedek was not limited to a certain family in Israel."[19]

Further, it was not only Melchizedek who was made like unto the Son of God, but also all those who receive the Melchizedek Priesthood (see JST Hebrews 7:3). As one honors his priesthood and magnifies the callings he receives, he will be prepared to receive exaltation.

Has Any Man Seen God?

In the KJV, there are statements which can and have been used to support both sides of the issue of whether man can see God. In the New Testament Epistles, there are three passages which the JST changes to give a more accurate view of this question. There are many in the world today who say "no man hath seen God at any time" (1 John 4:12). We are told in the JST that no one has seen God "except them who believe" (JST 1 John 4:12), and in Timothy the qualifications for seeing God include those who have "the light and hope of immortality dwelling in them" (JST 1 Timothy 6:16). In a similar vein, we are told that "the things of God knoweth no man, *except he has* the spirit of God" (JST 1 Corinthians 2:11). These clarifications help to harmonize the statements that man can and has seen God (see 3 John 1:11, John 6:46). Moses and the seventy elders of Israel saw God (Exodus 24:9–10). Isaiah (Isaiah 6:1), John (Revelation 4:2), Stephen (Acts 7:55–56), Abraham (Genesis 18:1), and many others have recorded seeing God. These explanations and others found in the JST not only eliminate the contradictions over man's ability to see God, but they provide essential insights into helping understand how one can merit and endure the presence of God.

Salvation for the Dead, or Sufferings?

Hebrews 11:40 has been used by members of the Church in connection with the doctrine of salvation for the dead. In the KJV, it reads: "God having provided some better thing for us, that they [the dead] without us should not be made perfect." The Prophet Joseph Smith on more than one occasion used this verse to teach the doctrine of salvation for the dead.[20] A question arises when the KJV is compared with the JST which says: "God having provided some better things for *them through their sufferings, for without sufferings* they could not be made perfect." This version harmonizes well with the rest of Hebrews 11, which gives accounts of many who were faithful and suffered for the gospel's sake. A reasonable explanation for these two different versions and Joseph's use of them is suggested by Robert J. Matthews.

> One reason may be that in either case the doctrine is true. Since the world and the Church had access to the King James Version, it may be that Joseph Smith used that familiar rendition to undergird the doctrine of salvation for the dead. Because he had obtained the doctrine of salvation for the dead by revelation and not from the printed page of the Bible, he therefore had a certain independence from the Bible and seems to have felt free to use it when it would corroborate true doctrines, even if a particular passage might have been worded differently in its original text. . . . It isn't a matter of "correct" or "incorrect" as much as it is a matter of purpose. The nature of human language is such that there can be no "literal" translation of any extensive or intricate document. Every translation is, in effect, an interpretation. The language is not the revelation; it is the awkward vehicle by which a revelation or a concept is expressed. Thus, texts might often be enlarged or paraphrased by a prophet in order to give a certain emphasis or perspective beneficial to his hearers.[21]

Additional Doctrinal Changes

In 2 Peter 1:19, the JST changes the phrase "we have also a more sure word of prophecy" to read "we have therefore a more sure *knowledge of* the word of prophecy." Whether this verse was meant to refer to *the more sure word of prophecy* which "means a man's knowing that he is sealed up into eternal life, by revelation and the spirit of prophecy through the Holy Priesthood" (D&C 131:5), or that because of the experience on the Mount of Transfiguration, Peter and those with him had a "more sure knowledge of the word of prophecy" is not crucial.[22] The fact is that both concepts are true and can help us in coming to understand 2 Peter 1.

In 1 Corinthians 15:41, Paul speaks of the differing kingdoms in the resurrection. He compares them to three levels: the sun, the moon, and the stars. In the previous verse the names of the kingdoms are given. However, only the celestial and terrestrial are mentioned. In the JST, the Prophet adds the name of the telestial kingdom and thus harmonizes verses 40 and 41.

The false doctrine of predestination is mistakenly attributed to several New Testament passages. In the KJV, Romans 1:6 reads: "Among whom are ye also the called of Jesus Christ." The phrase *the called* gives the impression of predestination. In the JST, Romans 1:5 refers to those who through obedience and faith are called to preach the gospel. Verse 6 reads: "Among whom ye also are called of Jesus Christ." Thus the concept of predestination is removed (see also JST 1 Corinthians 1:23). None of our father's children are predetermined to fail or succeed. The choice is left to each individual.

The law of consecration is a doctrine of the New Testament. On at least two occasions, the JST adds insights concerning this law. In Hebrews 13:5, it is not "conversation" that should be without covetousness but "consecrations." In Romans 13:6-7, the JST teaches that "consecrations" and not tribute should be paid to God's authorized authorities. Tribute or taxes are to be paid, Paul teaches, so that "consecrations may be done in fear to whom fear belongs, and in honor of him to whom honor belongs." The word *fear* in this case means "fright." It may be that fear belongs to the rulers to whom tribute is paid and honor belongs to him in whose debt we will always be.

The most prominent teaching in the New Testament on Christ's mission in the world of spirits is found in 1 Peter 3-4. The JST makes some interesting contributions. In verse 20, the point is clarified that Christ's mission was not just to those who were disobedient in Noah's day: "He went and preached unto the spirits in prison; *Some of whom* were disobedient in the days of Noah" (JST 1 Peter 3:19, 20). In 1 Peter 4:6 the latter part of the verse is changed to clarify that the dead "live in the spirit."

The concept of mediators is taught in the New Testament Epistles; however, some of the passages are vague. The JST makes at least two significant additions in this area of doctrine. In the letter to the Saints in Galatia, the discussion of a mediator is unclear (see Galatians 3:19–20), but in the JST, the concept is explained beautifully. Moses "was ordained by the hand of angels to be a mediator of this first covenant, (the law)" (JST Galatians 3:19). The JST account goes on to explain that Moses "was not a mediator of the new covenant; but there is one mediator of the new covenant, who is Christ" (JST Galatians 3:20). The verse explains that this is according to the promises made to Abraham and his seed. Abraham was told that "in thy seed after thee . . . shall all the families of the earth be blessed, even with the blessings of the gospel, which are the blessings of salvation, even of life eternal" (Abraham 2:11). At least in part, this promise was fulfilled by Christ's mediation and atonement. The other significant change in this area, although not treated here, is found in 1 Timothy 2:4.

CONCLUSION

The Prophet Joseph Smith on one occasion said: "I believe the Bible as it read when it came from the pen of the original writers. Ignorant translators, careless transcribers, or designing and corrupt priests have committed many errors."[23] This being true, the JST makes significant contributions in doctrine and clarity. It will lead one to a better understanding of the New Testament Epistles. A careful analysis of the changes in comparison with the rest of the body of scripture reveals a renewed harmony and clarity in teaching. This is not to say that all corrections have been made or that all misunderstandings have been resolved in the JST of the Epistles. Revelation is an ongoing process of "line upon line," and the Prophet continued to receive new insights concerning the Epistles after he concluded his formal work on the JST in 1833. Some of these insights were recorded in his public teachings. Nevertheless, what we do have in the Joseph Smith Translation of the New Testament Epistles makes it a remarkably useful and inspired work. "It is one of the greatest evidences of the divine mission of the Prophet" Joseph Smith.[24]

Clyde J. Williams is a curriculum writer for the Curriculum and Instruction Division of the LDS Church Educational System.

NOTES

1. The Prophet did not use ancient manuscripts to derive a new translation but relied upon the Holy Ghost to direct the changes he should make. For more information concerning this point see Robert J. Matthews, *"A Plainer Translation": Joseph Smith's Translation of the Bible, A History and Commentary* (Provo, Utah: Brigham Young University Press, 1975), p. 13. (Hereafter referred to as *"A Plainer Translation."*)

2. Joseph Smith, Jr., *History of The Church of Jesus Christ of Latter-day Saints,* ed. B. H. Roberts, 2nd ed. rev., 7 vols. (Salt Lake City: The Church of Jesus Christ of Latter-day Saints, 1964), 1:324. (Hereafter cited as *History of the Church.*)

3. The Prophet referred to his translation of the scriptures as a "branch of my calling." (*History of the Church* 1:238.)

4. Information on the number of changes was compared and compiled from *"A Plainer Translation,"* pp. 418–22, and *Inspired Version Study Guide,* compiled by Frederick M. Edvalson, Jr., and William V. Smith (Provo, Utah: Seventy's Mission Bookstore, 1977), pp. 51–62.

5. Marvin R. Vincent, *Word Studies in the New Testament,* 4 vols. (McLean, Va.: McDonald Publishing Co., n.d.), 4:510.

6. For a more detailed analysis of this change and particularly of Hebrews 9:16 see Richard Lloyd Anderson, *Understanding Paul* (Salt Lake City: Deseret Book Co., 1983), pp. 216–17.

7. See 1 Peter 3:1, 2 in George Ricker Berry, *The Interlinear Greek-English New Testament* (Grand Rapids, Mich.: Zondervan Publishing House, 1979), p. 597.

8. Compare this version with Berry, p. 556.

9. *"A Plainer Translation,"* p. 358.

10. Bruce R. McConkie, *Doctrinal New Testament Commentary,* 3 vols. (Salt Lake City: Bookcraft, 1966–73), 2:275.

11. *"A Plainer Translation,"* pp. 355–56.

12. See Anderson, *Understanding Paul,* pp. 104–5, for a discussion of the likelihood that Paul was married.

13. McConkie, *Doctrinal New Testament Commentary,* 3:386.

14. Ibid., p. 316.

15. *Teachings of the Prophet Joseph Smith,* comp. Joseph Fielding Smith (Salt Lake City: Deseret Book Co., 1972), p. 328. (Hereafter referred to as *Teachings.*) For additional insight on this point see Anderson, *Understanding Paul,* p. 206.

16. McConkie, *Doctrinal New Testament Commentary,* 3:157.

17. See D&C 93:12–14 and *Teachings,* p. 308, where Joseph indicated that to obtain the fulness of the priesthood one must do as Jesus did, which was to be obedient.

18. *"A Plainer Translation,"* p. 384. See also Anderson, *Understanding Paul,* p. 277, note 56.

19. *"A Plainer Translation,"* p. 385.

20. See *Teachings,* p. 356, and Andrew F. Ehat and Lyndon W. Cook, comps., *The Words of Joseph Smith* (Provo, Utah: Brigham Young University, Religious Studies Center, 1980), p. 424.

21. Robert J. Matthews, "I Have a Question," *Ensign,* September 1981, pp. 16–17. This article contains several other helpful insights concerning this issue on Hebrews 11:40.

22. For additional insight on this question see Monte Nyman, "The Sublime Epistles of Peter," in *A Symposium on the New Testament* (Salt Lake City: The Church of Jesus Christ of Latter-day Saints, 1984), pp. 61–62.

23. *Teachings,* p. 327.

24. Bruce R. McConkie, "This Generation Shall Have My Word Through You," *Ensign,* June 1980, p. 56.

12

The JST on the Second Coming of Christ

Keith W. Perkins

As with all of the work of the Prophet Joseph Smith, the Joseph Smith Translation of the Bible adds some very important information to our gospel understanding. There are additional verses which illuminate many aspects of the life and ministry of the Savior that cannot be found in any other book. A classic example of this concerns the period of time following the visit of the boy Jesus at age twelve to the temple in Jerusalem. The present biblical record is almost silent on this stage of Christ's ministry. Luke alone makes any mention of this period: He "came to Nazareth, and was subject unto them. . . . And Jesus increased in wisdom and stature, and in favour with God and man." (Luke 2:51–52.)

For this juncture of Jesus' life, however, three critical verses have been added to the Gospel of Matthew by the Prophet Joseph Smith. Had they been found in the Holy Land, like the Dead Sea Scrolls, these verses would have been proclaimed as one of the greatest biblical discoveries of our age. Not only have these verses been ignored by biblical scholars, which we would expect, but they have generally been ignored by Latter-day Saints, which should not be the case. These verses give us a great deal of insight into the years of preparation by the Son of God.

> And it came to pass that Jesus grew up with his brethren, and waxed strong, and waited upon the Lord for the time of his ministry to come.
> And he served under his father, and he spake not as other men, neither could he be taught; for he needed not that any man should teach him.
> And after many years, the hour of his ministry drew nigh. (JST Matthew 3:24–26.)

As it is with these verses, so it is with our understanding of the second coming of Christ. Truths are taught in the JST that are found nowhere else in scripture, truths which have not only been ignored by biblical scholars but also frequently overlooked by Latter-day Saints. Let us first look at the changes Joseph Smith made in Matthew chapter 24, Mark chapter 13, and Luke chapter 21, which provide great insights into the Second Coming.

One of the most significant changes made by the Prophet in Matthew 24 is the rearrangement of the verses. The following chart shows these changes.

Significant Changes in Verses

Matthew 24	Joseph Smith–Matthew
v. 6	v. 23, 28
v. 7	v. 29
v. 8	v. 19
v. 14	v. 31
v. 15	v. 12, 32
v. 33	v. 39
v. 34	v. 34
v. 35	v. 35
v. 36	v. 40

This rearrangement becomes very significant when it is realized that the Prophet Joseph Smith rearranged the verses so that those signs that apply to the destruction of the temple, Jerusalem, and the Jews following the death of Jesus are placed in the first portion of Matthew 24, while those verses concerning the second coming of Christ are placed together at the end of the chapter.

Another significant change is the many additions made by the Prophet in Mark 13 so that it now reads basically the same as Matthew 24, with a few additions and deletions.

Let us first examine what the Savior said about the destruction of the temple, Jerusalem and the Jews, and see how this can help us as we prepare for his second coming. From the JST we learn very plainly concerning the two questions the apostles were asking Jesus: "Tell us when shall these things be which thou hast said concerning the destruction of the temple, and the Jews; and what is the sign of thy coming, and of the end of the world, or the destruction of the wicked, which is the end of the world?" (JS-M 1:4). Notice that in this version by the Prophet we get the definition of what the Savior meant by the end of the world—the destruction of the wicked.

Jesus further warned them in this chapter of a number of things that would happen prior to both events. Before the destruction of the temple there would be false Christs who would deceive many (v. 6). The apostles would be hated by all nations and eventually they would be killed (v. 7). False prophets would arise who would deceive many (v. 9). Iniquity would abound and the love of many would wax cold (v. 10).

In addition to these signs given both in Joseph Smith-Matthew and JST Mark, Luke 21 also gives us interesting insights into those events that would precede the destruction of the temple of Jerusalem. In discussing how they will be hated by all nations, Jesus gives some additional detail as to how they would be treated. They would be tried in the synagogues before kings and rulers, and finally cast into prisons (Luke 21:12), but there would be something which must have seemed even worse: they would be betrayed by parents, brethren, kinsfolk, and friends—and in some cases these close associates and relatives would cause them to be killed (Luke 21:16). The Lord promised them, however, that their suffering was only a temporary thing—for this life—and in the Resurrection "not an hair of your head [will] perish. In your patience possess ye your souls" (Luke 21:18–19; cf. Alma 40:23).

Next Jesus warned them of the great destruction coming upon Jerusalem and how the former-day Saints would be able to escape this disaster. Both JS-M and JST Mark talk about the abomination of desolation which Daniel had predicted. Contrary to the many things that some have felt this meant, the JST plainly teaches us that it had reference to the destruction of Jerusalem (JS-M 1:12; Mark 13:14). But in Luke 21:20, we are given even further detail on how this time can be determined: "And when ye shall see Jerusalem compassed with armies, then know that the desolation thereof is nigh." In an earlier account of the Savior's prophecy concerning what was coming upon Jerusalem, Luke records, "Thine enemies shall cast a trench about thee, and compass thee round, and keep thee in on every side, And shall lay thee even with the ground, and thy children within thee; and they shall not leave in thee one stone upon another; because thou knewest not the time of thy visitation" (Luke 19:43–44).

Thus the warning of the coming abomination of desolation was very clear: Jerusalem would be encircled by an invading army which would bring about its complete destruction. This prediction was very dramatically fulfilled when in A.D. 70 the city was leveled to the ground by the Romans, and, according to Josephus, the Jewish historian, approximately one million Jews were killed.[1]

Not only did the Lord tell his faithful Saints what was coming upon Jerusalem, but he detailed how they could avoid the impending destruction. He instructed the early Saints that when they saw the signs that he had forwarned them of they were to immediately leave Jerusalem. Those in Judea were to flee into the mountains (see JS-M 1:13). The disaster was coming so rapidly that leaving immediately was essential for their temporal salvation. Those on the housetop were not even to take time to return into the house to take their belongings with them (see JS-M 1:14). Those in the field were not to return back to their own homes to take their clothing (see JS-M 1:15). They were to remember Lot's wife and not look back at what they had to leave (see Luke 17:32).

The Savior expressed concern over those who might be expecting a child at the time and also that their flight not be in the winter or on the Sabbath because of the speed with which they had to flee (see JS-M 1:16–17). He further instructed them that despite the terrible things that had befallen the Jews before (capture by the Babylonians, Assyrians, etc.) the coming destruction would be the worst tribulation that had ever befallen the nation of Israel or ever would befall them at Jerusalem (see JS-M 1:18). All one has to do to see the fulfillment of this prophecy is read of the destruction that came upon Jerusalem as described by Josephus.[2]

Obedient to this command of the Savior, the Jewish converts to Christianity immediately left Jerusalem when the predicted signs came to pass. The Christian historian Eusebius gives us a vivid description of what took place:

> The rest of the apostles who were harassed in innumerable ways, with a view to destroy them, and driven from the land of Judea, had gone to preach the gospel to all nations. The whole body, however, of the church at Jerusalem, having been commanded by a divine revelation, given to men of approved piety there before the war, removed from the city and dwelt at a certain town beyond the Jordan, called Pella. Here, those that believed in Christ, having removed from Jerusalem, as if holy men had entirely abandoned the royal city itself, and the whole land of Judea; the divine justice, for their crimes against Christ and his apostles, finally overtook them, totally destroying the whole generation of these evil doers from the earth.[3]

Thus, by being obedient to the command of the Lord, these early Saints escaped the terrible destruction that came upon Jerusalem. This is very important because the rest of Joseph Smith-Matthew, and the other similar scriptures, tell us what events are going to precede the second coming of the Savior; they also tell us how we can avoid many of the problems that are coming. By learning from the past, we too may escape to a degree those terrible predictions that are connected with Christ's second coming.

Verses 18 through 21 of Joseph Smith-Matthew seem to be the transitional verses between the events associated with the destruction of Jerusalem at the time of the ancient apostles and the second coming of Christ. Verse 21 tells us that prior to the Second Coming there will again be tribulation upon Jerusalem.

Once more there will be false Christs and false prophets who will attempt to deceive the very elect (see JS-M 1:22). President Joseph F. Smith helps us understand the meaning of this verse in a statement of the First Presidency on 2 August 1913, entitled "A Warning Voice."

> At other times people who pride themselves on their strict observance of the rules and ordinances and ceremonies of the Church are led astray by false spirits, who exercise an influence so imitative of that which proceeds from a Divine source that even these persons, *who think they are "the very elect,"* find it difficult to discern the essential difference. Satan himself has transformed himself to be apparently "an angel of light."[4]

There will be wars and rumors of wars. This is not to concern us, for this is exactly what the Savior predicted would precede his coming. But the end is not yet (see JS-M 1:23–24). We are not to follow those who try to deceive us when they say Christ is in the desert or in the secret chambers, for the Second Coming will not be done in secret but will be made known to all the earth (see JS-M 1:25–26).

As it was with the destruction of the temple at Jerusalem, so the Second Coming will be one of great tribulations and persecutions. Nation will be against nation; there will be famines, pestilences, and earthquakes in many places (see JS-M 1:29). But there will also be the gathering of the elect from the four corners of the earth (see JS-M 1:27). There will not only be great physical tribulations but there will be those tribulations within families: iniquity will abound and the love of many will wax cold. We can see how fully this is being fulfilled in our own day. However, if we are not overcome by these problems, the Lord promises us that we will be saved. (See JS-M 1:30.)

Another important sign of the Savior's second coming is the preaching of the gospel to all the world—then the end will come, which is the destruction of the wicked (see JS-M 1:30–31). Sometimes Latter-day Saints seem to feel that we have almost accomplished this goal. But, upon more careful examination, the nations who have at this date had missionaries among them represent approximately one-third of the world. There are some very significant nations that we have yet to reach: China, the Soviet Union, most of India and Africa, as well as all those smaller countries that still have not had missionaries in their midst. Truly we must lengthen our stride and accept with greater enthusiasm the call we received from President Spencer W. Kimball for every worthy young man to go on a mission as well as many, many more of our retired couples.

Once again there will be the abomination of desolation which was predicted by Daniel (see Daniel 9:27; 11:31; 12:11). Will there once again be terrible destruction upon Jerusalem by invading armies? This will undoubtedly be the time when the two prophets (not young missionaries, but General Authorities who hold the sealing power) will be killed, left to lie in the streets for three and one-half days, and then be resurrected (see Revelation 11:3–13). Immediately following this great tribulation, the sun will be darkened, the moon shall not give her light (other sources talk about the moon turning to blood, becoming as blood, bathed in blood; see Joel 2:31; Revelation 6:12; D&C 45:42; 88:87), and the stars shall fall from heaven (see JS-M 1:33) or refuse to give their light (see Isaiah 13:10; Ezekiel 32:7).

This is one of the most universally taught doctrines in all the scriptures, since it is in every standard work of the Church: the Old and New Testaments, the Book of Mormon, Doctrine and Covenants, and the Pearl of Great Price. In the generation that these signs are given, all that Christ has predicted will be fulfilled (see JS-M 1:34). As one reads the account by Josephus of the terrible destruction of the Jews and Jerusalem, one begins to gain an appreciation that the Savior was trying to tell us something about the great tribulation that will once again come upon the earth, this time prior to his second coming.

This will also be the generation in which the times of the Gentiles will be fulfilled; that is, their time for receiving the gospel will be over (JST Luke 21:25, 32). This will not be one grand event, but will cover a long period of time—apparently the entire dispensation prior to the Second Coming. Then will come the time for the Jews to again receive the message of salvation.[5]

Following the great tribulations, which will include the powers of heaven being shaken, there will appear "the sign of the

Son of Man" in heaven. This will cause the tribes of the earth to mourn, while the righteous will rejoice when they shall see the Son of Man coming in "the clouds of heaven, with power and great glory" (JS-M 1:36). One is reminded of the great destruction upon the American Continent prior to the first coming of Christ, and also that following this great tribulation came the great joy of seeing Jesus Christ descending from heaven (see 3 Nephi 8–11). We cannot help but feel that this is simply a type and a shadow of things to come. Will the sign of his first coming—the new star, the day and night and day as though it were one day—be the same sign of his second coming? (see Zechariah 14:6–7).

There are, however, several things that the righteous must do in order to witness the Second Coming. First, we must treasure up Christ's words which he has given us so that we will not be deceived (see JS-M 1:37). Next, we must watch, pray always, and keep the commandments, so that we may be counted worthy to escape the tribulations that will come, and also that we will be worthy to stand before Christ when he comes (see JST Luke 21:37). The Doctrine and Covenants expresses this a little differently, indicating that we should be looking for the signs of his coming, because he "that watches not for me shall be cut off" (D&C 45:39, 44). We must be like the wise virgins who had oil in their lamps; that is, we must take the Holy Spirit as our guide so we will not be deceived (see Matthew 25:1–13; D&C 45:57). No wonder we are given so much detail about the signs of the coming of Christ, so that we will be watching and thus be ready for this great and dreadful day (great for the righteous and dreadful for the wicked). May we be as ready as were the former-day Saints, those who escaped the terrible destruction of Jerusalem because they watched and obeyed.

Before that day the remainder of the elect will be gathered together from "the four winds, from one end of heaven to the other" (JS-M 1:37). To further illustrate this, the Savior told the disciples that two would be in the field, one taken and the other left, and that while two would be grinding at the mill, again one would be taken and one left (see JS-M 1:44–45). Once again the JST clearly explains what Jesus meant by this.

> Where, Lord, shall they be taken [the disciples asked Jesus]. And he said unto them, Wheresoever the body is gathered; or, in other words, whithersoever the saints are gathered, thither will the eagles be gathered together; or, thither will the remainder be gathered together. This he spake, signifying the gathering of his saints; and of angels descending and gathering the remainder unto them; the one from the bed, the other from the grinding, and the other from the field, whithersoever he listeth. (JST Luke 17:36–38.)

To help the apostles understand the signs of the times and their relationship to his coming again on the earth, Jesus gave the parable of the fig tree. When one saw the leaves of the fig tree, he would know that summer was near. So it will be with the elect who are watching for Christ's return to earth: they will know that it is near, "even at the door," by the signs that are given (see JS-M 1:39).

THE TIME OF HIS COMING

No one knows the precise time of the second coming of the Lord, for it will come like a thief in the night to the wicked (see JS-M 1:47). It will be like it was in the days of Noah when the people did not realize the flood was coming until it was there (see JS-M 1:43). For the righteous, however, the coming of the Son of God will not be as a thief in the night: "And again, verily I say unto you, the coming of the Lord draweth nigh, and it overtaketh *the world* as a thief in the night—Therefore, gird up your loins, that you may be the children of the light, and that day *shall not overtake you as a thief* (D&C 106:4–5; emphasis added).

For faithful members of the Church, the coming of the Lord will not be as a thief in the night, but as a woman in travail. Although the expectant mother does not fully know the hour of delivery, she does know the approximate time. So it is for those children of the light who are watching for his return and not sleeping (see 1 Thessalonians 5:2–6). Even though no man nor the angels know the day or the hour, our Heavenly Father knows. One of the interesting insights from the JST is that in discussing who does not know the time of the Second Coming, it is significant that the Son of Man is not one of those so listed (see Mark

13:32 and JST Mark 13:47). This is logical; since the Father and the Son are one, the thought and knowledge of one is the thought and knowledge of the other.

The time of the Second Coming has been of interest to every generation of Saints, former-day as well as Latter-day Saints. Following the death of Jesus, it was obvious that many members of the Church felt that he would return in their lifetime. The same is true of some Latter-day Saints in this last dispensation. It appears that in every generation since this prophecy was given by the Savior, many believed that in their lifetime they would witness the Second Coming.[6] It is essential, therefore, that we learn what the Joseph Smith Translation of the Bible teaches us concerning the time of the Second Coming and in what age he will come.

The Joseph Smith Translation brings out a truth that cannot be found anywhere else in scripture. In Luke 12:36–37, we learn that we are like men who wait for the bridegroom returning from the wedding. We are told that we should be found watching, so that we can be invited to the wedding banquet. It is at this point we learn one of the profound realities from the JST.

> For, behold, he cometh in the first watch of the night, and he shall also come in the second watch, and again he shall come in the third watch.
>
> And verily I say unto you, He hath already come, as it is written of him; and again when he shall come in the second watch, or come in the third watch, blessed are those servants when he cometh, that he shall find so doing. (JST Luke 12:41–42.)

Here is a great truth. It is not wrong that every generation feels it is their day when Christ will come, for according to this scripture, he comes in every watch of the night; that is, in every generation. Indeed, he has come already. Elder Bruce R. McConkie gives an excellent interpretation of this important scripture:

> One of the great incentives which encourages and entices men to live lives of personal righteousness, is the doctrine of the Second Coming of the Messiah. Many revelations speak of the signs which shall precede our Lord's return; others tell of the tragic yet glorious events which shall attend and accom-

pany his return to earth; and still others recite the good and ill which shall befall the living and the dead at that time. All this is preserved in holy writ so that men will be *led to prepare themselves for the day of the Lord,* the day when he shall take vengeance upon the ungodly and pour forth blessings upon those who love his appearing. (D&C 133:50–52; 2 Thessalonians 1:7–10.)

Deliberately and advisedly the actual time of his coming has been left uncertain and unspecified, so that men of each succeeding age shall be led to prepare for it as though it would be in their mortal lives. And for those who pass on before the promised day, none of their preparation will be wasted, for both the living and the dead, speaking in the eternal sense, must prepare to abide the day. . . .

All of the Lord's ministers, all of the members of his Church, for that matter all men everywhere ("What I say unto one, I say unto all"), are counseled to await with righteous readiness the coming of the Lord. However, most men will die before he comes, and only those then living will rejoice or tremble, as the case may be, at his personal presence. *But all who did prepare will be rewarded as though they had lived when he came,* while the wicked will be "cut asunder" and appointed their "portion with the hypocrites" as surely as though they lived in the very day of dread and vengeance.

Thus, in effect, the Lord comes in every watch of the night, on every occasion when men are called to face death and judgment. The phrase, "He hath already come, as it is written of him," pointedly inserted in verse 42, is a witness that even then he ministered among mortal men and that they were judged by their acceptance or rejection of him.[7]

What a thought! No preparation that we make for the second coming of Christ is in vain, for in effect he comes in every generation. If we die prior to his coming, it will be just the same as if we were living on the earth when he finally does return in great glory. When we die, therefore, it is in reality the Second Coming for us. If we are righteous it does not matter whether we come with him in the Second Coming or are caught up to meet him when he descends with the Saints in the greatest reunion of all time.

> And the Lord said unto Enoch: As I live, even so will I come in the last days, in the days of wickedness and ven-

geance, to fulfill the oath which I have made unto you concerning the children of Noah. . . .

And the Lord said unto Enoch: Then shalt thou and all thy city meet them there, and we will receive them into our bosom, and they shall see us; and we will fall upon their necks, and they shall fall upon our necks, and we will kiss each other;

And there shall be mine abode, and it shall be Zion, which shall come forth out of all the creations which I have made; and for the space of a thousand years the earth shall rest. (Moses 7:60, 63–64.)

What a wonderful experience this will be!

Let it not be misunderstood. There will be an actual time when Christ will return to earth again to greet those in the flesh who are so privileged to meet him in that day. There is that day which has been set aside by the Father from the beginning when his Beloved Son will return a second time on earth in a formal second coming. But, the insight we gain from the Joseph Smith Translation of Luke 12 is that no matter when we live or have lived, none of our preparation will be vain. If we have died before he comes we will be with him in the Second Coming. If we are alive at the time we will be caught up to meet him. All will be treated the same in this great event. With this knowledge we need not worry so much about the day of his coming, but rather concern ourselves with our preparation to meet him, regardless of the day. That is the most important thing. Come he will "in the clouds of heaven, with power and great glory," but whether it will be a day of great joy or a day when there will be weeping, wailing, and gnashing of teeth will all depend on us. Our personal preparation will be the deciding factor. May we so prepare that we may be able to receive the greatest reception that will ever be received by any of us: "Well done, thou good and faithful servant: thou hast been faithful over a few things, I will make thee ruler over many things: enter thou into the joy of thy lord" (Matthew 25:21).

Keith W. Perkins is chairman and associate professor of Church History and Doctrine at BYU.

NOTES

1. Flavius Josephus, *Wars of the Jews,* Book VI, chapter 9, in William Whiston, trans., *Josephus: Complete Works* (Grand Rapids, Mich.: Kregel Publications, 1960), p. 587.

2. Ibid., pp. 556-88.

3. Isaac Boyle, ed., *The Ecclesiastical History of Eusebius Pamphilus, Bishop of Caesarea, in Palestine* (Grand Rapids, Mich.: Baker Book House, 1955), p. 86.

4. James R. Clark, comp., *Messages of the First Presidency,* 6 vols. (Salt Lake City: Bookcraft, 1965-75), 4:285 (emphasis added).

5. Bruce R. McConkie, *Doctrinal New Testament Commentary,* 3 vols. (Salt Lake City: Bookcraft, 1966-73), 1:656.

6. Bruce R. McConkie, *The Millennial Messiah* (Salt Lake City: Deseret Book Co., 1982), pp. 33-34.

7. McConkie, *Doctrinal New Testament Commentary,* 1:674-77 (emphasis added).

13

Insights from the JST into the Book of Revelation

Gerald N. Lund

The book of Revelation is one of the most intriguing and controversial books in the biblical library. Most scholars agree that it is one of the most difficult books in either the Old or New Testaments.[1] Typically, modern readers, including Latter-day Saints, find its imagery strange, its prophecies filled with the bizarre and baffling imagery, its message unclear. Not surprisingly, therefore, it is largely left alone and unread.

The title of the book in Greek is *Apocalypsis,* from which we get its other common name, the Apocalypse. *Apocalypsis* is formed from two Greek words—*apo,* a preposition meaning separated or removed from, and *kalypto,* a verb meaning to cover, hide or conceal.[2] *Apocalypsis* literally means to remove or to take away the covering or veil.[3] Hence its title in English, the book of Revelation (or the uncovering or unveiling).

Some would say that without question that title is one of the most ironic or misleading titles in the whole of scripture. There is no book, they say, that is more veiled or unrevealing than this one.

ONE OF THE PLAINEST BOOKS

Even some Latter-day Saints find it difficult to believe that the book reveals or uncovers much truth. One teacher explained the difficulty of the book by noting Nephi's prophecy that when first written, the Bible would include many "plain and precious" truths. However, evil men would remove many of those truths. (See 1 Nephi 13:28; 14:23.) The teacher's conclusion? *All* the plain and precious things in the book of Revelation were removed! That is why we cannot understand it today.

While this sounds plausible and has some attractive elements, it is not justified by other evidence. The Prophet Joseph Smith, in a sermon delivered in 1843, stated that "the book of Revelation is one of the plainest books God ever caused to be written."[4] And his work on the new translation of the Bible bears that out. If the book is obscure and mystifying because of a great loss of original material, the Prophet did not see fit to restore the lost material. While admittedly this is an argument from silence, it is interesting to compare his work on Revelation with his work on some other books thought to be more plain and clearly understood.

For example, the Gospel of Matthew is not generally considered to be a mysterious or difficult book. Yet in his work on that book, the Prophet made changes in 618 of the 1071 verses in Matthew, or 58 percent of the total. In addition to the changes, he added the equivalent of 51 verses of totally new material, which is an expansion of another 5 percent of the total text.[5] Compare these changes with the book of Revelation, where he added only three new verses (JST Revelation 1:7; 2:27; 12:7) and made changes in only 90 of the 394 verses, or 23 percent of the total.[6] In the book of Genesis, as another comparison, the Prophet changed about half the verses and added the equivalent of about 250 new verses,[7] literally pages and pages of new material. Yet the book of Revelation gets only three new verses and relatively few other changes.

Some might think those figures could be the result of the fact that the Prophet worked through the Bible sequentially. Since the book of Revelation is last, it received the least amount of work and therefore reflects the smallest number of changes. Again the evidence does not substantiate this.

As Robert J. Matthews notes, while the Prophet did not generally indicate which portion of the scriptures he was working on at various times, nor how long he spent on any one book, we do have some solid evidence that "in the work of revision the Prophet was moving back and forth in the New Testament rather than working continuously through the Bible in a consecutive order."[8] We find this entry in the Prophet's history: "Upon my return from Amherst conference, I resumed the translation of the Scriptures. . . . Accordingly, on the 16th of February, 1832, while translating St. John's Gospel, myself and Elder Rigdon saw the following vision."[9] Then followed section 76. On 1 March 1832 we find this entry: "About the first of March, in connection with the translation of the Scriptures, I received the following explanation of the Revelation of St. John."[10] Section 77 follows. As Matthews concludes,

> It is unlikely that the work would have progressed consecutively in the short span of two weeks from Chapter 5 of John to the Book of Revelation. A more plausible conclusion suggests that the brethren were not following the New Testament consecutively.[11]

THE BOOK OF REVELATION: MEANT TO BE UNDERSTOOD

We are left with the clear conclusion that John's Revelation was meant to be understood when it was first written, and was meant to be understood today. The Prophet said it was one of the plainest of books, and so it should be. Elder Bruce R. McConkie in response to the question, "Are we expected to understand the book of Revelation?" answered:

> Certainly. Why else did the Lord reveal it? The common notion that it deals with beasts and plagues and mysterious symbolisms that cannot be understood by us is just not true. It is so far overstated that it gives an entirely erroneous feeling about this portion of revealed truth. *Most of the book*—and it is no problem to count the verses so included—*is clear and*

plain and should be understood by the Lord's people. . . . He [the Lord] has withheld the sealed portion of the Book of Mormon from us because it is beyond our present ability to comprehend. We have not made that spiritual progression which qualifies us to understand its doctrines. But he has not withheld the book of Revelation, because it is not beyond our capacity to comprehend; if we apply ourselves with full purpose of heart, we can catch the vision of what the ancient Revelator recorded.[12]

THE WORLD'S CONFUSION

All of this is not meant to imply that the book of Revelation is simple or easily understood. In the quote above, where he talked about it being understandable, Elder McConkie added the qualifying phrase, "if we apply ourselves with full purpose of heart." He went on in the same article to say: "The language and imagery [of the book of Revelation] is so chosen as to *appeal to the maturing gospel scholar, to those who already love the Lord and have some knowledge of his goodness and grace.*"[13]

An understanding of the book comes only when a price is paid in study, pondering and general gospel knowledge. But that alone is not enough. Bible scholars pay the price in terms of time and effort. They study the culture and background. They pore over the original Greek, looking for every nuance and clue. They know the emperors and the historical milieu in which John wrote. They know all of that, and yet there is still no consensus as to what is truly revealed by John.

To illustrate the confusion and babble of interpretive voices, let us just take one example of the world's attempt to explain a highly symbolical passage found in chapter 9 of Revelation. Under the sounding of the fifth trumpet, John saw a "star fall from heaven" and open the "bottomless pit" (Revelation 9:1–2). Out of the pit came a vast cloud of locusts which John says were commanded "that they should not hurt the grass of the earth, neither any green thing, neither any tree; but only those men which have not the seal of God in their foreheads. And to them it was given that they should not kill them, but that they should be tormented five months." (Revelation 9:3–5.)

Note just a sampling of the scholars' attempts to explain what John saw. Adam Clarke, in the first half of the nineteenth century, wrote:

> *Locusts]* Vast hordes of military troops: the description which follows certainly agrees better with the *Saracens* than with any other people or nation, but may also apply to the Romans.
> *As the scorpions of the earth have power]* Namely, to hurt men by *stinging* them. Scorpions may signify *archers;* and hence the description has been applied to *Cestius Gallus,* the Roman general, who had many *archers* in his army. . . .
> *That they should be tormented five months]* Some take these months *literally,* and apply them to the conduct of the Zealots . . . Others consider the *months* as being *prophetical* months, each *day* being reckoned for a *year;* therefore this period must amount to one hundred and fifty years.[14]

Dummelow, another nineteenth-century scholar, did not believe they were men at all. He says, "from the smoke issue *evil spirits with the appearance of locusts.* They are not to hurt green things for they are not really locusts.[15] Tenney cites Mauro who concludes that since trees are used elsewhere as symbols for human greatness or people of eminence (e.g., see Jeremiah 7:20; Ezekiel 31:3), the "grass of the earth" (Revelation 9:4) would be the masses of common people.[16] Clearly nervous about that interpretation, Tenney finally only ventures that the locusts "are really an invasion from another world of malicious embodied spirits whose mission is destruction."[17]

One of the more creative attempts to explain the symbolism is by H. M. S. Richards, Jr., who equates Mohammed, founder of the Islamic faith, to the star that fell from heaven, and the bottomless pit to "the waste of the Arabian desert."[18] He then goes on to explain the symbolism of the locusts:

> I have a copy here of the military command given to this great cavalry army by Abu-bekr, their commander, in A.D. 632, when they were on the verge of entering upon their invasions of Syria. He dispatched a circular letter to the Arabian tribes which reads as follows: "When you fight the battles of the Lord . . . *destroy no palm-trees, nor burn any fields of corn. Cut down no fruit-trees.*"[19]

These are the acknowledged experts in the New Testament and yet still cannot come to a consensus of opinion. But, one asks, doesn't this very confusion disprove your statement that the book of Revelation was meant to be understood? No. What we are saying is that to the world it is a confusing book and that study alone is not enough to open its mysteries to our view.

THE INSTRUMENTALITY OF JOSEPH SMITH

It was Peter who said that "no prophecy of the scriptures is given of any private will of man. For the prophecy came not in old time by the will of man. But *holy men of God* spake as they were moved by the Holy Ghost." (JST 2 Peter 1:20–21; emphasis added.)

It is through the instrumentality of a prophet, the Prophet Joseph Smith, that the correct interpretation of John's vision is to be had. Without it, it is indeed a book covered by a veil, hidden from our view. But with what the Prophet has revealed it becomes understandable. It fulfills and justifies its title as a book of Revelation.

The Prophet gave us access to the mysteries of Revelation through four major means:
1. Latter-day scripture.
2. Non-scriptural sermons and writings.
3. Doctrine and Covenants 77.
4. Joseph Smith Translation revisions of the text of Revelation.

Since the focus of this paper is the contributions of the JST to our understanding of the book of Revelation, we shall skip over the first two quickly, giving only an example or two of each.

One example of a contribution from Latter-day scripture is found in Doctrine and Covenants 130:7–11. There the Prophet explained the meaning of two important symbols used by John, namely the sea of glass before the throne of God (see Revelation 4:6), and the white stone given to the faithful (see Revelation 2:17). Another is found in Moses 4:1–4 and Doctrine and Covenants 76:25–30, which give more information about the war in heaven, which John barely mentions (see Revelation 12:7).

One example of the Prophet's contribution through his non-scriptural sermons or writings is where he said that John "saw the same things concerning the last days, which Enoch saw."[20] That is a significant clue to help us as we interpret the Revelation. Another example is a lengthy sermon given in Nauvoo on 8 April 1843.[21] The whole sermon is an exposition of John's revelation. In a few instances, the Prophet verbally corrected passages in the New Testament, but for one reason or another those changes never made it into the Joseph Smith Translation.[22] Two such changes involved verses in the book of Revelation.[23]

Section 77: The Key to Understanding Revelation

The third area of contribution in which the Prophet Joseph added to our understanding of the book of Revelation is section 77 of the Doctrine and Covenants. In his journal, the Prophet noted, "About the first of March, in connection with the translation of the Scriptures, I received the following on the Revelation of St. John:"[24] Section 77 was then given.

Though not actually part of the JST text, section 77 was given as part of the translation process and therefore must be considered as part of the Joseph Smith Translation contributions. And though not part of the actual text, section 77 certainly ranks as one of the most important, if not the most important, contributions of the Prophet in aiding our interpretation of the book of Revelation.

Section 77 contains fifteen questions and answers about the text of the book of Revelation, though the Prophet gives no indication whether the questions were his or were part of the revelation. Fifteen questions seems at first to be a woefully inadequate amount when one considers the number of questions raised as the text is read. Nevertheless, a careful study of section 77 shows that these fifteen questions do indeed provide the key so we can enter into the "house" of Revelation and begin to explore. Smith and Sjodahl, expanding upon the analogy of the key, say:

> But this Revelation [section 77] is not a complete interpretation of the book. It is a *key*. A key is a very small part of the house. It unlocks the door through which an entrance may be gained, but after the key has been turned, the searcher for treasure must find it for himself. . . . From the key thus given, from the Old Testament prophecies, and from history, ecclesiastical and political, it should be possible to interpret

the rest. As Champollion, by the key furnished in the brief text on the Rosetta stone, was able to open the secrets of Egyptian hieroglyphics, so the Bible student should be able to read the Apocalypse with a better understanding of it, by the aid of this key.[25]

The key lies in the fifteen questions asked and answered in the section.

The Textual Changes

The final contribution of the Prophet to our understanding of the Apocalypse is in the actual work he did on the text of Revelation as part of his inspired translation of the Bible. As was noted above, he deleted from, added to or changed a total of ninety verses. Obviously, not every one of those changes are of equal significance. The committee that worked on the LDS edition of the King James Version included changes for only forty-seven of the ninety verses, or just slightly better than half of the total changes. Taking that as some indication of the number of significant changes, we could say that the Prophet significantly altered only 12 percent of the total verses. Twelve percent is not a staggering proportion, but that percentage does not convey the importance of the contribution made by the Prophet's work on the text of the Apocalypse. Much in the same way as section 77, the verses so changed often become a key to opening our understanding to a passage or even sometimes to a whole concept taught by John.

Now that we have briefly discussed the four areas of contribution made by the Prophet, we shall begin an analysis of the Revelation of John to see how the Prophet has opened this book to our understanding. Since our focus in this paper is primarily on the contribution of the JST to our understanding of Revelation, we shall focus on the contributions of section 77 and the actual textual changes of the JST, though where appropriate we may note contributions from Latter-day scripture or the Prophet's other writings. Space allows discussion of only the most significant of the contributions from all four areas.

THE VISION OPENS: CHAPTER 1

John says it was on Patmos, on a Sunday, that he received the grand and glorious visions recorded in Revelation (vv. 9–10). Chapter 1 provides the prologue to all that follows, and interestingly enough the Prophet made more changes in this opening chapter than in any other chapter except chapter 12. From those changes we learn the following:

1. The Revelation is of John. It is his testimony and witness that is being recorded (see JST Revelation 1:1, 2, 4, 5). This in no way lessens the fact that the source of the vision and inspiration is divine, but the KJV suggests that the revelation is from God to Jesus Christ (see v. 1). The JST clearly identifies it as being given to John, a servant of God, *from* Jesus Christ. Why is this significant? It is another example of how the Savior views his prophets and apostles. They are his servants and he honors them for their faithfulness.

2. The KJV indicates that the revelation was given because "the time is at hand" (v. 3). The JST clarifies what time is meant when it says, "for the coming of the Lord draweth nigh" (JST v. 3).

3. In several places in the opening chapters, reference is made to "seven Spirits" (1:4; 3:1, 4:5) and "seven angels" (1:20; 2:1, 8, 12, 18; 3:1). As is, this makes it sound as though the seven Spirits and the seven angels are different things. But the Prophet changed or explained all references to the seven Spirits and the seven angels to show that the seven Spirits and the seven angels both refer to the leaders of the seven churches (see JST for all of the above verses). John, who at this time is the leader of the Church, is writing to seven branches of the Church in Asia. The JST makes it clear that he specifically addresses the leaders (the bishops or branch presidents, as it were) of each of these branches.

4. Also the JST makes it clear that the seven Spirits (now servants) are the receivers, not the source, of the vision (see JST v. 4).

5. Finally, the Prophet added to the concept of Christ's

second coming that he would come clothed in "the glory of his Father" and be accompanied by "ten thousand of his saints" (JST 1:7). Perhaps here is a good time to note that in Greek the largest named number was ten thousand, which is the word "myriad."[26] Often it is used symbolically to express uncountable numbers.

THE SEVEN LETTERS: CHAPTERS 2 AND 3

Immediately following the opening vision, the Savior, through the angel representing him, dictated seven letters to the seven churches of Asia. Though often neglected in favor of the prophetic visions, these seven letters are choice, individualized pieces of personal revelation. The Prophet made very few changes, the most significant of which include:

1. As noted above, throughout these letters the Prophet changed the wording to make it clear that each letter was addressed to the presiding authority of each church.

2. The bed into which the false prophetess and those who followed after her was to be cast is actually "hell" (see JST 2:22).

3. Those who are faithful in Thyatira are promised that they will be given power over nations and will rule them with a rod of iron, smashing them to pieces like clay pots (2:26–27). This seems contradictory in the KJV. Faithful saints are promised the power to smash the nations to pieces. This symbolism is strongly suggestive of tyranny. The imagery of Nephi's vision shows that the iron rod is a symbol of the word of God (see 1 Nephi 15:23–24) which helps somewhat, but in the JST, the Prophet dropped the imagery of smashed pottery and turned it instead into the idea of a potter shaping and molding vessels. He said that those who were faithful in keeping the commandments would rule the nations "with the word of God; and they shall be in his hands as the vessels of clay in the hands of a potter; and he shall govern them by faith, with equity and justice (JST 2:26–27). This is a very different imagery from that of the KJV.

THE VISION OF HEAVEN: CHAPTER 4

Once the seven letters are finished, John is invited to come into the heavens so that he can see things which will be "hereafter" (4:1). Thus opens the great prophetic vision for which the Apocalypse is famous. John first describes, or rather attempts to describe the majesty and magnitude of the celestial kingdom where God dwells. In a way it is an impossible task—trying to use the finite to describe the infinite. Almost instantly the reader is confronted with a baffling array of symbols, figures and images, some of which, on the surface at least, border on the bizarre.

And here it is that Joseph Smith's work becomes significant, becoming the key to our understanding. While the Prophet made a few textual changes in these chapters, which we will note, the major contribution comes from section 77 of the Doctrine and Covenants. As was mentioned, fifteen questions are asked in that section about the book of Revelation. Seven of the fifteen are questions relating to chapters 4 and 5. From the Prophet's work we learn the following:

1. The earth in its celestialized future state will become like a massive Urim and Thummim to its inhabitants (see D&C 77:1; 130:7–9).

2. Animals from our own world and from other worlds are celestialized and dwell in the presence of God. (See D&C 77:2–3; see also the Prophet's discourse on the meaning of the beasts.[27])

3. The rather bizarre imagery of beasts covered with eyes and wings is actually symbolical of their celestial nature (see D&C 77:4).

4. The seven leaders of the churches as well as twenty-four elders from the seven churches were going to dwell in the presence of God (see JST Revelation 4:5; D&C 77:5). In times of intense persecution and martyrdom, this would have served as a great encouragement to the faithful to stay true to their commitments.

THE SEALED BOOK AND THE SEVEN SEALS: CHAPTER 5

It doesn't take a lot of study of the book of Revelation to come to the conclusion that the imagery of chapter 5 is pivotal to the whole structure of the book. John saw in the right hand of the Father a book (most likely a scroll) which was sealed with seven seals (see 5:1). He also saw that no one in heaven or earth was able or worthy to open the book, except for the Savior (vv. 2–14). Since the rest of the vision describes what John sees as each of the seven seals is opened by the Lamb, an understanding of the sealed book is critical to our whole understanding of the book of Revelation.

And here it is that the Prophet Joseph Smith made his greatest contribution to our ability to unveil the veiled, to reveal the revelation. He answered two significant questions: What is the meaning of the book and what is the meaning of the seals? Certainly more than any other single thing, his answers to those questions (see D&C 77:6–7) become *the key* to gaining access to the "house" of Revelation. From what was revealed in those two verses we then can derive the following:

1. The book in the right hand of the Father represents the history and destiny of the world. It is in his right hand to suggest he controls everything in and about our world. No one except the Savior was worthy to open the book because the atoning sacrifice was what made the whole of world history possible and meaningful.

2. The seven seals represent the seven thousand-year periods which the earth will have during its temporal existence. This not only provides us one of the most specific clues we have as to the closeness of the Second Coming, but it also shows that the book of Revelation is basically structured chronologically, unfolding the earth's history from the time of Adam until the earth is celestialized.

3. Studying that chronological structure carefully, we can see that John's Revelation focuses most heavily on that short period of time between when the last period of a thousand years begins and when Christ comes. Note the amount of time spent on each of the seven seals. The first five (6:1–11) are covered briefly, merely highlighting the thing of greatest import to the covenant people that happened in that time frame. The sixth seal, the one in which we currently live, is expanded considerably (6:12–7:17) but still takes only a few verses of the total. Knowing that the Millennium is the major event of the seventh seal, we might expect John to dwell at great length on that. But the opening of the seventh seal begins in the first verse of chapter 8. The Second

Coming and the Millennium are not seen until chapters 19 and 20. Thus, clearly, the majority of the revelation focuses on that period "after the opening of the seventh seal, before the coming of Christ" (D&C 77:13).

4. This understanding of the time frame aids us greatly in interpreting the symbols used by John. For example, a man on a white horse is seen in 6:2. That same imagery is used of the Savior in 19:11. Therefore, one might think both places refer to the Master, and this is indeed a common interpretation of the scholars.[28] But knowing that the first seal represents the first thousand years of the earth's history (approximately 4000 to 3000 B.C.) makes that interpretation no longer tenable. That single piece of information helps us look for someone or something in that period of time that meets all of the symbolic conditions. With that we conclude it is not Christ but Enoch that is represented.[29] And there are other examples of how this key to the chronology becomes a key to the correct interpretation of the symbolism.

Similarly, the rather ingenious interpretation mentioned above—the locusts not hurting grass and trees being interpreted as the Arab general's order to his troops to leave vegetation alone —can now be rejected, since the events described occurred midway in the fifth seal, and John sees the locusts appear after the opening of the seventh seal.

THE OPENING OF THE SEALS: CHAPTERS 6 TO 11

Again, more through what we learn from section 77 than through actual textual changes, the Prophet greatly adds to our understanding of what John saw as the various seals were opened. Nothing is said about the first five seals, either through section 77 or through JST changes. But when we get to the opening of the sixth and seventh seals—those of our own time, as it were—we are helped immensely and learn the following:

1. The "angel from the east" is Elias (D&C 77:9). This at first may not seem helpful, but we know that the concept of Elias is as a forerunner, and that here it refers to the restoration of the

gospel in the last days.[30] Applying that interpretation to John's vision makes perfect sense. Before the angels of destruction are loosed, the servants of God will be sealed and thus saved from destruction, through the restoration of the gospel, with its priesthood and ordinances. Commenting on these very verses, the Prophet later explained that the sealing "signifies sealing the blessing upon their heads, meaning the everlasting covenant, thereby making their calling and election sure. When a seal is put upon the father and mother, it secures their posterity, so that they cannot be lost, but will be saved by virtue of the covenant of their father and mother."[31]

2. The Prophet clearly indicates that the twelve thousand sealed from each of the twelve tribes is not just a symbolic representation of the forces of righteousness, as some scholars maintain. They are a great missionary force of the sixth seal (see D&C 77:10). Joseph Smith shows us that they are ordained high priests chosen from among every nation to carry forth the gospel and bring as many as will come to the true Church (see D&C 77:11). (In another revelation the Prophet indicated that these 144,000 would also stand on Mt. Zion with the Savior. See D&C 133:18 and compare with Revelation 14:1–5.)

The Prophet also said, shortly before his death, "I attended prayer-meeting with the quorum in the assembly room, and made some remarks respecting the hundred and forty-four thousand mentioned by John the Revelator, showing that the selection of persons to form that number had already commenced."[32] This statement would seem to indicate that this great body of missionaries may be composed of mortals and immortals together.

3. Though the Prophet did not give us specific help in interpreting the various images mentioned under the sounding of the seven trumpets that begin in chapter 8, two things he revealed are of great help as we study this section of Revelation. First, he revealed that the trumpets represent the judgments of God which will prepare the world and cleanse it for the millennial reign of Christ (see D&C 77:12). Second, he clearly specifies that these trumpets (or judgments) happen in the seventh seal (see D&C 77:12–13). Since the evidence suggests we have not yet entered that last period of a thousand years, this prophecy is yet future to

us. In fact, once the judgments happen it may be that the imagery used by John in this section will become much more clear. It also tells us that any attempt to tie these judgments with past historical events is not justified.

4. In chapter 10, there is a brief pause in the description of the judgments in which John is given a little book to eat. This seems puzzling at first, but again the information revealed through the Prophet Joseph Smith helps us with the interpretation. He explains that the book is symbolic of the mission of John himself during these great events, which mission is to help gather the tribes of Israel (see D&C 77:14). We know from scripture that John is privileged to continue his ministry on the earth until the Savior returns (see John 21:22–23; D&C 7). It is almost as though the Lord says to John in chapter 10, "Since you will still be living at the time all these things I have shown you are transpiring, would you like to see what you will be doing?" At a conference of the Church in June 1831, the Prophet confirmed that the "little book mission" was being fulfilled when he said that "John the Revelator was then among the ten tribes of Israel who had been led away by Shalmaneser, king of Assyria, to prepare them for their return from their long dispersion."[33]

6. Finally, we learn from the Prophet's revelations that the "two witnesses" seen by John as playing a pivotal role in the great battle of Armageddon were two prophets raised up to the Jewish nation (not necessarily Jewish themselves, as some have maintained) in the last days, who would work among the Jewish people in their homeland (see D&C 77:15). Elder Bruce R. McConkie said that these two prophets would be "followers of that humble man, Joseph Smith. . . . No doubt they will be members of the Council of the Twelve or of the First Presidency of the Church."[34]

THE CHURCH AND KINGDOM OF GOD

After the sounding of the seven trumpets of judgment, John heard "great voices in heaven, saying, The kingdoms of this world are become the kingdom of our Lord, and of his Christ" (JST Revelation 11:15). Then, much as a teacher pauses in the course of his lecture to explain an important point, the Lord pauses in his vision of the judgments to explain some significant things about these kingdoms he has just mentioned.

Chapter 12, where this explanation begins, was altered more by the Prophet in his revision of the book of Revelation than any other chapter. He changed most of the verses, rearranged the order of them, and added one new verse—the only place where a significant amount of new material is added in all of Revelation (see JST Revelation 12:7).

While there is much we could study in these changes, space permits us to focus only on the most important insight derived from those changes. Chapter 12 contains three great figures or signs "in the likeness of things on the earth" (JST v. 1)—a woman who is pregnant, a man child to whom she gives birth, and a great red dragon. The dragon is clearly identified as Satan (see JST v. 8). Most commentators agree that the woman represents the Church of Jesus Christ, a fact which Joseph Smith definitely confirmed (see JST v. 7). But it is the man child that has caused commentators the most difficulty. We are told in both the KJV and the JST that the man child is to rule all nations with the rod of iron and that he will be caught up to the throne of God (see v. 5; JST v. 3). Nearly identical imagery is used in 19:15, and so most scholars assume the man child is none other than the Savior.

But in chapter 12, if that is the correct interpretation, there is a problem with the imagery. The woman is pregnant with, or in other words gives birth to, the man child. But if the woman is the Church and the man child the Savior, this is contrary to what we know to be true. The Church does not bring forth Christ. Just the opposite is true.

Others have suggested, since it is specified the child is male, that the baby represents the priesthood. But again we have the same problem. The Church does not give birth to the priesthood, but just the opposite.

One simple phrase added by the Prophet in this chapter brings the whole matter into perfect clearness. In fact, it becomes a key to our understanding of this whole section on the kingdoms of the world and of Christ. He changed verse 8 in the KJV to read,

"And the dragon prevailed not against Michael, neither the child, nor the woman *which was the Church of God,* who had been delivered of her pains, and *brought forth the kingdom of our God and his Christ*" (JST v. 7; emphasis added).

Sometimes in the Church we use the phrase "the kingdom of God" to refer to the Church itself, but technically it has a more specific meaning. Elder Joseph Fielding Smith said:

> After Christ comes, all the peoples of the earth will be subject to him, but there will be multitudes of people on the face of the earth who will not be members of the Church; yet all will have to be obedient to the laws of the kingdom of God, for it will have dominion upon the whole face of the earth. These people will be subject to the *political government,* even though they are not members of *the ecclesiastical kingdom which is the Church.*
> This government which embraces all the peoples of the earth, both in and out of the Church, is also sometimes spoken of as the kingdom of God, because the people are subject to the kingdom of God which Christ will set up.[35]

Now the imagery is consistent and logical. Eventually there will be a political kingdom led by Jesus Christ which will rule all nations with the word of God. That political kingdom will grow out of, and is made possible by (that is, is given birth by) the Church of Jesus Christ. And since the creation of the political kingdom of Christ signals the end to the kingdoms of the world, it is little wonder that Satan seeks to destroy the man child. During the meridian of time, the Church was not able to bring forth that political kingdom, but itself was taken into the wilderness, or went into apostasy (see JST Revelation 12:14; D&C 86:3). The man child, or the political kingdom was thus taken to heaven to await the day of the Restoration.

Such a clear and reasonable explanation of this chapter is made possible only through the JST and the instrumentality of the Prophet Joseph Smith.

CONCLUSION AND SUMMARY

In Nephi's grand and glorious vision, he was privileged to see from his own time down through the stream of history to the end of the world. He was allowed to write most of the things he saw, including some things fulfilled in our own generation (e.g., see 1 Nephi 14:12). But at the point where he began to see things still future to us, he was told that he could write no more of them, even though he would be allowed to see them. He was told that he could not write them because it was a stewardship that belonged to another (see 1 Nephi 14:20–21, 25). It belonged to one of the apostles of the Lamb, and, said Nephi, "I . . . heard and bear record, that the name of the apostle of the Lamb was John" (1 Nephi 14:27).

The fulfillment of that stewardship is found in what we call the Apocalypse, or the book of Revelation. It was written for our time and primarily about our time. It is a book of eminent importance to Latter-day Saints.

And it is through the instrumentality of the Prophet Joseph Smith, and especially his work on the new translation of the scriptures, that the book of Revelation has become just that for us. It is a book that stands revealed, as the Prophet said, as "one of the plainest books God ever caused to be written."[36]

Gerald N. Lund is director of the Curriculum and Instruction Division in the LDS Church Educational System.

NOTES

1. Canon Leon Morris, *The Revelation of St. John* (Grand Rapids, Mich.: Wm. B. Eerdmans Publishing Co., 1969), p. 15.

2. Joseph Henry Thayer, *Greek English Lexicon of the New Testament,* s.v., *apo* and *kalypto.*

3. Ibid., s.v., *apokalypsis.*

4. *Teachings of the Prophet Joseph Smith,* comp. Joseph Fielding Smith (Salt Lake City: Deseret Book Co., 1938), p. 290. (Hereafter cited as *Teachings.*)

5. Joseph Smith, *Joseph Smith's "New Translation" of the Bible* (Independence, Mo.: Herald Publishing House, 1970), pp. 236–317.

6. Ibid., pp. 513–23.

7. Ibid., pp. 27–116.

8. Robert J. Matthews, *Joseph Smith's Revision of the Bible* (Provo, Utah: Brigham Young University Press, 1969), p. 10.

9. Joseph Smith, *History of The Church of Jesus Christ of Latter-day Saints,* 7 vols. (Salt Lake City: The Church of Jesus Christ of Latter-day Saints, 1946), 1:245. (Hereafter cited as *History of the Church.*)

10. Ibid., 1:253.

11. Matthews, *Joseph Smith's Revision,* p. 10. For additional evidence see his whole discussion, pp. 8–13.

12. Bruce R. McConkie, "Understanding the Book of Revelation," *Ensign,* September 1975, p. 87 (emphasis added).

13. Ibid., p. 89 (emphasis added).

14. Adam Clarke, *Bible Commentary* (Nashville, Tenn.: Abingdon Press, n.d.), 3:1001 (emphasis added).

15. J. R. Dummelow, *A Commentary on the Holy Bible* (New York: Macmillan Publishing Co., 1936), p. 1080 (emphasis added).

16. Merrill C. Tenney, *Interpreting Revelation* (Grand Rapids, Mich.: Wm. B. Eerdmans Publishing Co., 1957), p. 75.

17. Ibid.

18. H. M. S. Richards, Jr., *What Is in Your Future?* (Los Angeles: Voice of Prophecy, 1972), p. 23.

19. Ibid., pp. 23–24 (emphasis added).

20. Smith, *Teachings,* p. 84.

21. Ibid., pp. 287–94.

22. Robert J. Matthews, *"A Plainer Translation": Joseph Smith's Translation of the Bible: A History and Commentary* (Provo, Utah: Brigham Young University Press, 1975), pp. 210–12.

23. Ibid.

24. Smith, *History of the Church,* 1:253.

25. Hyrum M. Smith and Janne M. Sjodahl, *Doctrine and Covenants Commentary,* rev. ed. (Salt Lake City: Deseret Book Co., 1951), p. 478.

26. Thayer, s.v., *myrios.*

27. Smith, *Teachings,* pp. 287–94.

28. See for example, Dummelow, *Commentary,* p. 1078; R. C. H. Lenski, *The Interpretation of St. John's Revelation* (Minneapolis: Augsburg Publishing House, 1963), pp. 221–22.

29. Bruce R. McConkie, *Doctrinal New Testament Commentary,* 3 vols. (Salt Lake City: Bookcraft, 1966–73), 3:476–77. (Hereafter cited as *DNTC.*)

30. Ibid., 3:491–92.

31. Smith, *Teachings,* p. 321.

32. Smith, *History of the Church,* 6:196.

33. Ibid., 1:176, note.

34. McConkie, *DNTC,* 3:509.

35. Joseph Fielding Smith, *Doctrines of Salvation,* 3 vols. (Salt Lake City: Bookcraft, 1954–56), 1:229.

36. Smith, *Teachings,* p. 290.

14

Major Doctrinal Contributions of the JST

Robert J. Matthews

It is a privilege to participate in a symposium devoted to a wider understanding of Joseph Smith's translation of the Bible. I am reminded of the words of President Brigham Young when he spoke of his high regard for the Prophet Joseph Smith. He said: "Would he not take the scriptures and make them so plain and simple that everybody could understand?"[1] President Young was never too busy to stop whatever he was doing and listen to the Prophet Joseph. He considered the Prophet's words and opinions to be of unequaled worth. Said he on various occasions: "An angel never watched him closer than I did, and that is what has given me the knowledge I have today. I treasure it up, and ask the Father, in the name of Jesus, to help my memory when information is wanted."[2] In 1868: "[I never let] an opportunity pass of getting with the Prophet Joseph and of hearing him speak in public or private, so that I might draw understanding from the fountain from which he spoke."[3] And in 1877:

> From the first time I saw the Prophet Joseph I never lost a word that came from him concerning the kingdom. And this

is the key of knowledge that I have today, that I did hearken to the words of Joseph and treasured them up in my heart, laid them away, asking my Father in the name of his son Jesus to bring them to mind when needed. . . . I was anxious to learn from Joseph and the Spirit of God.[4]

The reason President Young was so willing to listen was that he knew Joseph Smith offered something no one else could offer. We feel the same way about the Prophet and we honor his blessed name and memory. We know what Joseph Smith can tell us about the Bible is very significant.

To do well in this presentation is important to me, and I have sought sincerely for the guidance of the Spirit of the Lord to direct my preparation and delivery. My motive for wanting to do well is prompted by the feeling that if I do not do well it might reflect adversely upon the reputation of the Joseph Smith Translation of the Bible. Or at least it might give the impression that the translation is not very important or has little to offer. For that reason, I deeply wish to have the power of expression and clarity of speech so that the Spirit of God will carry into your hearts the testimony and conviction that Joseph Smith's translation of the Bible is a unique production, divinely inspired, worthy of study and of importance to every soul who wants to understand the gospel of Jesus Christ. I alone am responsible for what I say here, but I believe it to be correct.

ADVANTAGES OF THE JOSEPH SMITH TRANSLATION

The reader of the Joseph Smith Translation of the Bible will be thrice blessed. First, he or she will gain an insight into the Prophet's understanding of various scriptures; second, he or she will learn many things about the gospel not found in other sources; and third, he or she will obtain a clue as to the meaning and content of the Old and the New Testaments in their original form.

As one takes in his hands a printed copy of the Joseph Smith Translation, he has to wonder how and what it is, and what it has to offer that other Bibles do not have. It has been my experience that while other editions of the Bible contain much of the historical part of the ancient record, they are often flat or weak on doctrinal matters. Or to say it another way, the other Bibles generally tell *what,* whereas the JST not only tells *what* but also tells *why.* As we proceed with this discussion, I hope to be able to demonstrate some of the doctrinal contributions of the JST and how it often adds not only new historical perspectives and information, but also tells *why* certain things are so. That is, it gives the *doctrinal* substance or foundation.

HISTORY OF THE BIBLICAL TEXT

First, let us read an excerpt from 1 Nephi. This is the Book of Mormon explanation about the history of the Bible text.

And I, Nephi, beheld that the Gentiles that had gone out of captivity were delivered by the power of God out of the hands of all other nations. [These are the early colonists of America.]

And it came to pass that I, Nephi, beheld that they did prosper in the land; and I beheld a *book,* and it was carried forth among them.

And the angel said unto me: *Knowest thou the meaning of the book?*

And I said unto him: I know not.

And he said: Behold it proceedeth out of the mouth of a Jew. And I, Nephi, beheld it; and he said unto me: *The book that thou beholdest is a record of the Jews,* which contains the covenants of the Lord, which he hath made unto the house of Israel; and it also containeth many of the prophecies of the holy prophets; and it is a record like unto the engravings which are upon the plates of brass, save there are not so many; nevertheless, they contain the covenants of the Lord, which he hath made unto the house of Israel; wherefore, they are of great worth unto the Gentiles.

And the angel of the Lord said unto me: Thou hast beheld that the book proceeded forth from the mouth of a Jew; and when it proceeded forth from the mouth of a Jew it contained the *fulness* of the gospel of the Lord, of whom the twelve apostles bear record; and they bear record according to the truth which is in the Lamb of God.

Wherefore, these things go forth from the Jews in purity unto the Gentiles, according to the truth which is in God.

And after they go forth by the hand of the twelve apostles of the Lamb, from the Jews unto the Gentiles, thou seest the formation of that great and abominable church, which is most abominable above all other churches; for behold, they have taken away from the gospel of the Lamb many parts which are plain and most precious; and also many covenants of the Lord have they taken away.

And all of this have they done that they might pervert the right ways of the Lord, that they might blind the eyes and harden the hearts of the children of men.

Wherefore, thou seest that after the book hath gone forth through the hands of the great and abominable church, that there are many plain and precious things *taken away from the book,* which is the book of the Lamb of God.

And after these plain and precious things were taken away it goeth forth unto all the nations of the Gentiles; and after it goeth forth unto all the nations of the Gentiles, yea, even across the many waters which thou hast seen with the Gentiles which have gone forth out of captivity, thou seest—because of the many plain and precious things which have been taken *out of the book,* which were plain unto the understanding of the children of men, according to the plainness which is in the Lamb of God—because of these things which are taken away out of the gospel of the Lamb, an exceedingly great many do stumble, yea, insomuch that Satan hath great power over them. . . .

Neither will the Lord God suffer that the Gentiles shall forever remain in that awful state of blindness, which thou beholdest they are in, because of the plain and most precious parts of the gospel of the Lamb which have been kept back by that abominable church, whose formation thou hast seen.

And it came to pass that I beheld the remnant of the seed of my brethren, *and also the book of the Lamb of God, which had proceeded forth from the mouth of the Jew,* that it came forth from the Gentiles unto the remnant of the seed of my brethren.

And after it had come forth unto them I beheld *other books,* which came forth by the power of the Lamb, from the Gentiles unto them, unto the convincing of the Gentiles and the remnant of the seed of my brethren, and also the Jews who were scattered upon all the face of the earth, that the records of the prophets and of the twelve apostles of the Lamb are true.

And the angel spake unto me, saying: These *last records,* which thou hast seen among the Gentiles, *shall establish the truth of the first, which are of the twelve apostles of the Lamb,* and shall make known the plain and precious things which have been taken away from them; and shall make known to all kindreds, tongues, and people, that the Lamb of God is the Son of the Eternal Father, and the Savior of the world; and that all men must come unto him, or they cannot be saved. (1 Nephi 13:19–30, 32, 38–40; emphasis added.)

We could add to that the words of the Lord to Moses:

And now, Moses, my son, I will speak unto thee concerning this earth upon which thou standest; and thou shalt write the things which I shall speak.

And in a day when the children of men shall esteem my words as naught and take many of them from the book which thou shalt write, behold, I will raise up another like unto thee; and they shall be had again among the children of men—among as many as shall believe. (Moses 1:40–41.)

We reverence the Bible. You note that the angel asked Nephi if he knew the meaning of the book. When he said he did not, the angel explained that it was a record of the Jews, the Jewish prophets and the Twelve Apostles (Old and New Testaments), that it contained the covenants of the Lord to the house of Israel and they were of great worth to both Israel and the Gentiles. This Jewish record in its original purity "contained the fulness of the gospel of the Lord, of whom the twelve apostles bear record." We revere the Bible as a sacred record, not only for its history but as a witness for Jesus Christ, and because it contains many parts of his gospel and the plan of salvation. But we recognize, as the angel pointed out to Nephi, that the Bible has not come to us in its original completeness, and some things are lost from it. We should take special note, however, that not only do the scriptures speak of a *loss,* they also promise a *return,* a restoration of the lost material because it is so vital to salvation.

My intent is to discuss the doctrinal contributions of the JST. There are so many that even in one entire symposium we could not touch them all. We will cover a few that seem to be basic and which are representative, hoping that in so doing it will be like standing on a mountain peak on a clear day, where you can see almost forever, with the long view before us kindling an intense desire to explore not only all of the other peaks but also the valleys. Each of us will have to discover those things for ourselves, with our own books. We are thrilled, we are fed spiritually, and our interest grows when we make our own discoveries.

First let us consider the fact that the gospel of Jesus Christ was taught to Adam.

THE GOSPEL TAUGHT TO ADAM

We learn from the JST that the gospel, with its ordinances and the holy priesthood, was taught to Adam and was had among all the early patriarchs, from Adam to Abraham. This concept is only hinted at in the King James Version and other translations. Instead of it being forthrightly stated and the crux of the message, it is at best something that an alert student of the Bible might arrive at circumstantially or by inference, but it is never taught convincingly. By contrast, in the JST the central message is that Adam was taught the gospel by an angel from heaven and also by other revelations from God. The JST states that Adam personally asked the Lord why repentance and baptism in water were necessary. The record goes on to show that subsequently Adam himself was baptized in water and received the Holy Ghost. This is an unmistakable message and the JST is more clear upon that subject than anything that can be found in any other source. I will read part of it from chapter 6 of JST Genesis:

> But God hath made known unto our fathers, that all men must repent.
> And he called upon our father Adam, by his own voice, saying, I am God; I made the world, and men before they were in the flesh.
> And he also said unto him, If thou wilt, turn unto me and hearken unto my voice, and believe, and repent of *all thy transgressions,* and be baptized, even in water, in the name of mine Only Begotten Son, who is full of grace and truth, which is Jesus Christ, the only name which shall be given under heaven, whereby salvation shall come unto the children of men; and ye shall receive the gift of the Holy Ghost, asking all things in his name, and whatsoever ye shall ask it shall be given you.
> And our father Adam spake unto the Lord, and said, *Why is it that men must repent, and be baptized in water?*

And the Lord said unto Adam, Behold, I have forgiven thee thy *transgression* in the garden of Eden.

Hence came the saying abroad, among the people, that the Son of God hath atoned for original guilt, wherein the sins of the parents cannot be answered upon the heads of the children, for they are whole from the foundation of the world.

And I have given unto you another law and commandment; wherefore teach it unto your children, that all men, everywhere, must repent, or they can in no wise inherit the kingdom of God.

For no unclean thing can dwell there, or dwell in his presence; for, in the language of Adam, Man of Holiness is his name; and the name of his Only Begotten is the Son of Man, even Jesus Christ, a righteous judge, who shall come in the meridian of time.

Therefore I give unto you a commandment, to teach these things freely unto your children, saying, that by reason of transgression cometh the fall, which fall bringeth death; and inasmuch as ye were born into the world by water and blood, and the spirit, which I have made, and so become of dust a living soul;

Even so ye must be born again, into the kingdom of heaven, of water, and of the Spirit, and be cleansed by blood, even the blood of mine Only Begotten; that ye may be sanctified from all sin; and enjoy the words of eternal life in this world, and eternal life in the world to come; even immortal glory.

For, by the water ye keep the commandment; by the Spirit ye are justified; and by the blood ye are sanctified.

And now, behold, I say unto you, this is the plan of salvation, unto all men, through the blood of mine Only Begotten, who shall come in the meridian of time.

And it came to pass, when the Lord had spoken with Adam our father, that Adam cried unto the Lord, and he was caught away by the Spirit of the Lord, and was carried down into the water, and was laid under the water, and was brought forth out of the water; and thus he was baptized.

And the Spirit of God descended upon him, and thus he was born of the Spirit, and became quickened in the inner man.

And he heard a voice out of heaven, saying, Thou art baptized with fire and with the Holy Ghost; this is the record of the Father and the Son, from henceforth and for ever;

And thou art after the order of him who was without beginning of days or end of years, from all eternity to all eternity.

Behold, thou art one in me, a son of God; and thus may all become my sons. Amen. (JST Genesis 6:51–56, 59–65, 67–71; emphasis added.)

You may recognize that passage as part of the book of Moses from the Pearl of Great Price. As you know, the book of Moses is an extract from the JST of Genesis. This material was revealed to Joseph Smith and was in the JST for years before there was a publication called the Pearl of Great Price.

The Book of Mormon and the Doctrine and Covenants inform us that all of the prophets from the beginning knew of Christ (see Jacob 4:4; 7:11; D&C 20:25–28), but the uniqueness of the JST is that it actually presents the details and puts the gospel into the narrative of the Old Testament setting. The passage we just read from JST Genesis was really from a discourse by Enoch, seven generations after Adam, which shows that this clear exposition of the Fall, the Atonement, the mission of the Savior, and the very gospel of Jesus Christ was had among the early patriarchs in written form as well as by word of mouth.

As an extension to and a corollary to the antiquity of the gospel and its presence in the very beginning of this earth, we learn from the JST that each of the ancient dispensations were connected and associated by the gospel and the covenants, and that there is continuity and order in the kingdom of God. There is no difficulty in the entire plan of salvation being revealed from the very beginning of man on the earth, because the plan is older than the earth. In fact, the earth was created in cooperation with the provisions of the plan of salvation.

CONTINUITY IN THE OLD TESTAMENT

If one had only the Bible translations known throughout the world, there would be no hint that the ancient patriarchs had the fulness of the gospel or that there was a continuity in the way the gospel was handed down and communicated from one generation to another. In other Bibles, the first time the word *covenant* appears is with Noah in Genesis 6:18, which reads as follows: "But with thee will I establish my covenant; and thou shalt come into the ark, thou, and thy sons, and thy wife, and thy sons' wives with thee."

In the King James Version there is no hint of any covenant between God and Adam, or any of the patriarchs between Adam and Noah, a space of some fifteen hundred years. And even the covenant that *is* mentioned in connection with Noah is not spoken of as a gospel or a priesthood covenant. And there is no visible connection between Adam, Enoch, Noah, Melchizedek and Abraham. By contrast, the JST speaks of Adam having the priesthood and the gospel, and this continues to Enoch, and then to Noah, and then to Melchizedek, and then to Abraham—the same covenant, the same priesthood, the same gospel. I will briefly read a few of these from the JST.

> And thus the gospel began to be preached from the beginning, being declared by holy angels, sent forth from the presence of God; and by his own voice, and by the gift of the Holy Ghost.
>
> And thus all things were confirmed unto Adam by an holy ordinance; and the gospel preached; and a decree sent forth that it should be in the world until the end thereof; and thus it was. Amen. (JST Genesis 5:44–45.)
>
> And then began these men to call upon the name of the Lord; and the Lord blessed them; and a book of remembrance was kept in the which was recorded in the language of Adam, for it was given unto as many as called upon God, to write by the Spirit of inspiration;
>
> And by them their children were taught to read and write, having a language which was pure and undefiled.
>
> Now this same priesthood which was in the beginning, shall be in the end of the world also.
>
> Now this prophecy Adam spake, as he was moved upon by the Holy Ghost. (JST Genesis 6:5–8.)

Next from Enoch:

> And death hath come upon our fathers; nevertheless, we know them, and cannot deny, and even the first of all we know, even Adam; for a book of remembrance we have written among us, according to the pattern given by the finger of God; and it is given in our own language.
>
> And as Enoch spake forth the words of God, the people trembled and could not stand in his presence.
>
> And he said unto them, Because that Adam fell, we are; and by his fall came death, and we are made partakers of misery and woe. (JST Genesis 6:47–49.)

Then from Noah:

> But with thee will I establish my covenant, even as I have sworn unto thy father, Enoch, that of thy posterity shall come all nations.
>
> And thou shalt come into the ark, thou and thy sons, and thy wife, and thy sons' wives with them. (JST Genesis 8:23–24.)

You will recall that we read earlier the corresponding verse from the KJV which mentioned a covenant with Noah but it did not say what the covenant was. In the JST the statement is clarified to show that it is the same covenant that was given to Enoch, which was the same as was given to Adam, and so forth. Let us read from JST Genesis the instructions from the Lord to Noah:

> And God spake unto Noah, and to his sons with him, saying, And I, behold, I will establish my covenant with you, *which I made unto your father Enoch, concerning your seed after you.*
>
> *And I will establish my covenant with you, which I made unto Enoch, concerning the remnants of your posterity.*
>
> And the bow shall be in the cloud; and I will look upon it, that I may remember the everlasting covenant, *which I made unto thy father Enoch; that, when men should keep all my commandments, Zion should again come on the earth,* the city of Enoch which I have caught up unto myself.
>
> And this is mine everlasting covenant, that when thy posterity shall embrace the truth, and look upward, then shall Zion look downward, and all the heavens shall shake with gladness, and the earth shall tremble with joy;
>
> And the general assembly of the church of the first-born shall come down out of heaven, and possess the earth, and shall have place until the end come. *And this is mine everlasting covenant, which I made with thy father Enoch.* (JST Genesis 9:15, 17, 21–23; emphasis added.)

This instruction is given to Abraham in JST Genesis 13:13: "And remember the covenant which I make with thee; for it shall be an everlasting covenant; and thou shalt remember the days of Enoch thy father." Then to Melchizedek:

> Now Melchizedek was a man of faith, who wrought righteousness; and when a child he feared God, and stopped the mouths of lions, and quenched the violence of fire.

> And thus, having been approved of God, he was ordained an high priest after the order of the covenant which God made with Enoch.
>
> It being after the order of the Son of God; which order came, not by man, nor the will of man; neither by father nor mother; neither by beginning of days nor end of years; but of God. (JST Genesis 14:26–28.)

And in JST Genesis:

> And it came to pass, that Abram fell on his face, and called upon the name of the Lord.
>
> And God talked with him, saying, My people have gone astray from my precepts, and have not kept mine ordinances, which I gave unto their fathers;
>
> And they have not observed mine anointing, and the burial, or baptism wherewith I commanded them;
>
> But have turned from the commandment, and taken unto themselves the washing of children, and the blood of sprinkling;
>
> And have said that the blood of the righteous Abel was shed for sins; and have not known wherein they are accountable before me.
>
> But as for thee, behold, I will make my covenant with thee, and thou shalt be a father of many nations.
>
> And I will establish a covenant of circumcision with thee, and it shall be my covenant between me and thee, and thy seed after thee, in their generations; that thou mayest know for ever that children are not accountable before me until they are eight years old.
>
> And thou shalt observe to keep all my covenants wherein I covenanted with thy fathers; and thou shalt keep the commandments which I have given thee with mine own mouth, and I will be a God unto thee and thy seed after thee. (JST Genesis 17:3–8, 11–12.)

All of these references, including the verse content, are available in the footnotes or the appendix in the new LDS edition of the King James Version. As you can plainly see, there is a *continuity* in the account of the JST Genesis that is not found in any other Bible. The JST gives an account of the early patriarchs in gospel context and setting, with the fulness of the gospel, the priesthood, and faith in Jesus Christ and the same covenant. These ancient patriarchs knew of each other and had a common bond, a common faith—a oneness that we would never have suspected or known about or understood without the Joseph Smith Translation of the Bible. This is the same concept taught so clearly in the first and second lectures in *Lectures on Faith,* and the JST is no doubt the source for the doctrine in these lectures.

THE JST AND THE PLATES OF BRASS

We read earlier from 1 Nephi 13 that many plain and precious things had been taken away out of the record of the Jews (the Bible) and that many covenants of the Lord had been lost in that process. We have just observed by reading these last few passages a small amount of what Nephi was referring to and we can see that the covenant is being restored. Nephi said the Jewish Bible, before it was altered, was like unto the record of the plates of brass (see 1 Nephi 13:23). We read also that the Lord would bring forth *other books* to make known the plain and precious things that had been lost from the Bible. The JST would surely be one of those *other books,* along with the Book of Mormon, the Doctrine and Covenants, and the Pearl of Great Price. It would follow, therefore, that the JST reads more like the plates of brass than does any other Bible we know about. Another example is 2 Nephi 2:17 in which Lehi tells how Lucifer became the devil. This is similar to JST Genesis 3:1–5. Further, Lehi tells us that Adam and Eve would have had no children (see 2 Nephi 2:22–25). JST Genesis 5:11 says the same. Lehi said he read these things from the brass plates. There can be no question that the JST is closer to the plates of brass than is any other Bible.

Joseph Smith could not have restored these things without the spirit of revelation. He had that spirit. He held the keys of salvation. Let us read what the Lord said about this in the Doctrine and Covenants:

> And I have sent forth the fulness of my gospel by the hand of my servant Joseph; and in weakness have I blessed him;
> And I have given unto him the keys of the mystery of those things which have been sealed, even things which were from the foundation of the world, and the things which shall

come from this time until the time of my coming, if he abide in me, and if not, another will I plant in his stead.

Wherefore, watch over him that his faith fail not, and it shall be given by the Comforter, the Holy Ghost, that knoweth all things.

And a commandment I give unto thee [Sidney Rigdon]— that thou shalt write for him [Joseph Smith]; and the scriptures shall be given, even as they are in mine own bosom, to the salvation of mine own elect. (D&C 35:17–20.)

FUNDAMENTAL DOCTRINES

There are some very basic doctrines that are prominent in the JST that are not presented so clearly in other Bible translations. In some cases the JST material is completely new, as in the early chapters of Genesis, detailing the secret oaths of Cain (see JST Genesis 5) and the ministry of Enoch (see JST Genesis 6–7). In most instances, however, the JST consists of enlargement or clarification of existing material, as is the case in the Epistles or the Sermon on the Mount.

Often there is a third level of benefit that comes as a result of the enlargements and additions. This arises because of the fact that the more we know, the more we are *able* to know. Thus, many of the clarifications in the JST are valuable not only in their own right, but because they supply key information enabling us to understand and see new significance to other passages that were not textually changed in the JST. This is the case with John 8:1–11 about the Pharisees condemning a woman taken in adultery. There are no clarifications in the JST in this passage relative to the Pharisees. But substantial clarification in JST Luke 16:13–19 sets a pattern for the hypocritical life of the Pharisees that sheds much light on the Savior's statement: "He that is without sin among you, let him first cast a stone at her" (John 8:7).

The JST has everything any other Bible has, and the JST supplies additional information about the nature of God, of man, the origin of Satan, the premortal existence, the grand council and war in heaven (see JST Genesis 3:1–5; JST Revelation 12:6–10) and the gospel being taught to Adam and the early patriarchs.

In the JST God does not need to repent (cf. Genesis 6:6 with JST Genesis 8:15; also cf. Jonah 3:10 wth JST Jonah 3:10), nor does he harden men's hearts (cf. Exodus 7:3, 13 with JST Exodus 7:3, 13; Isaiah 63:17 with JST Isaiah 63:17). Little children are saved by the atonement of Jesus Christ (JST Genesis 6:56; JST Matthew 18:10–11; 19:13).

One of the major contributions of the JST is the insight it gives about the personality and ministry of Jesus Christ. Jesus is more alert, more compassionate with sinners and more stern with the perfidious Jewish rulers, and is reflected as a greater person in the four Gospels of the JST than he is in any other Bible translation.

Little information is given in any Bible about the ministry of Enoch, and there is no mention of his city or of a people called Zion; but in the JST there is eighteen times more column space than is given to Enoch and his preaching in the KJV, and it says much about his city Zion. This marvelous information about Enoch was revealed to Joseph Smith in November and December 1830 and forms an example and pattern for the building of Zion in our dispensation.

In like manner, little is given of Melchizedek in any other Bible; much is given of him in JST Genesis 14:16–40 and JST Hebrews 7:13.

On 7 March 1831 the Prophet received a revelation now identified as Doctrine and Covenants 45, a major topic of which is the second coming of the Lord. In this divine communication the promise is given that through the translation of the New Testament the Lord will yet reveal to the Prophet (and thus to the Church) much more about the Second Coming. The passage is as follows:

> And now, behold, I say unto you, it shall not be given unto you to know any further concerning this chapter, until the New Testament be translated, and in it all these things shall be made known;
> Wherefore I give unto you that ye may now translate it, that ye may be prepared for the things to come.
> For verily I say unto you, that great things await you. (D&C 45:60–62.)

Just what "chapter" is meant, we do not know, but given the subject matter of Doctrine and Covenants 45, this revelation clearly indicates that the JST will give considerable information relative to the Lord's second advent.

Another major contribution of the JST is its emphasis on the first principles of the gospel. Many of the clarifications and inserts, both in Genesis 5, 6 and 7 and in the four Gospels, emphasize the messiahship of Jesus, faith, repentance, baptism in water, and the need we have for the influence and power of the Holy Ghost. We have dealt with the Genesis passages earlier in this article. Other passages are found in JST John 1; JST Mark 1:1–6; JST Matthew 3; Luke 3.

A PROBLEM OF TRANSMISSION

Now, why are these concepts and clarifications not in the Bibles the world uses? Were not the ancient biblical writers, apostles and prophets able to express themselves more clearly than the present Bible record shows? If the current Hebrew and Greek manuscripts of the Bible are anywhere near being correctly recorded, then we have to conclude that either those ancient writers did not have a clear knowledge of the gospel of Jesus Christ, or if they did they did not tell it.

I cannot believe that they did not know it nor can I believe they did not tell it—or write it. What I do believe is that their writings as found in all known ancient manuscripts have been altered and diluted so that what presently is regarded as their writings no longer contains many of the plain and precious and the "more particular parts of the gospel" that once were there.

The major problem, it appears, is not one of *translation* but of *transmission*. There are today able scholars who know well the ancient languages and who have the ability to translate clearly what is on the manuscripts. They do a great service in citing many technical points and updating the changes in language and clarifying different words and passages. But that is not the heart of the problem. The pivot on which the whole subject turns is the absence of an adequate manuscript. There is no way that a translator using existing biblical manuscripts can get out of them the fulness of the gospel, with plain and extensive statements about the nature of God, man, the devil, premortal existence, the Second Coming, the Resurrection, and so forth. There simply is no way that a translator can make current biblical manuscripts read the way that the Book of Mormon, the Doctrine and Covenants, and the Pearl of Great Price teach these same doctrines. What is it then? Did the Bible prophets—Moses, Enoch, Abraham, Paul, Matthew, John, and others—not know the gospel as clearly as the Book of Mormon prophets, or is it that the records of the Bible prophets have not been preserved in complete clarity and accuracy?

Thus, logically we are forced to conclude that if the current available biblical manuscripts are correct, either the ancient biblical writers did not know the gospel in its clarity, or if they knew it, they did not write it. The testimony of the Book of Mormon, however, is that they *did* write it, but (1) much of it has been lost through faulty transmission, both wilful and accidental, and (2) much of it has now been restored through the Joseph Smith Translation, the Book of Mormon, and the other revelations.

Frequently people ask me if the Joseph Smith corrections are supported in the Hebrew and Greek manuscripts. An answer to that seems to be that *if* the JST offered no more than the biblical manuscripts or if it were completely supported by them, there would have been no need for a JST. Of course it is *not* supported by the manuscripts. That reminds me of an experience I have every now and again when I go for a hair cut. Often some unappreciative young man has preceded me in the chair who has more hair than three men ought to have. Generally some comment is made about my own contrasting lack of hair, and I say to the barber, "Make me look like him." The barber laughs, and the answer is always the same. He looks at me and says, "It is too late for that." And that is why the existing Hebrew and Greek manuscripts cannot provide the light and truth that once were there, and why there had to be a restoration of the Bible if a correct Bible were to be had. Present Bible manuscripts simply do not have the luxuriant supply of doctrine that the original had. It is too late for them to do so. They lost it centuries ago.

JOSEPH SMITH: A RESTORER

Since all the other things of this dispensation are true: the First Vision, Book of Mormon, restoration of the Aaronic and Melchizedek priesthoods, temple endowments, and so forth—the whole package of the Restoration—it is inevitable that the Prophet would also make a divinely inspired correction and supplemental edition of the ancient Bible. *Not* to have done so would have been the surprising thing. Not to have corrected and restored the Bible would have left Joseph Smith's mission incomplete.

Revelation is progressive, and one revelation builds upon another. For example, as part of the JST the Prophet made a manuscript correcting certain passages in the book of Revelation. Then more information is given about the book of Revelation in Doctrine and Covenants 77, and still more application and explanation is given in Doctrine and Covenants 88.

This reflects a very real relationship of the JST to the Doctrine and Covenants, for much of the doctrine of this dispensation came to Joseph Smith while he was translating the Bible.

How can anyone take *lightly* what Joseph Smith says about the Bible and about scripture? If he were a great athlete, or a coach, or a famous actor, his opinion would be sought throughout the nation on all kinds of things—what cereal he preferred for breakfast, what toothpaste he used, and the car that he drives, and those are not even areas of such a person's expertise. Yet scripture and the Bible, and the gospel and its restoration, are mainstream and of central importance to a prophet—the Prophet Joseph Smith—and his opinion and teachings on such matters ought to be given the highest priority by anyone who wants to understand the scriptures.

THE "APOLLOS PRINCIPLE"

The need for using all of the standard works when interpreting the Bible is illustrated in what I am pleased to call the "Apollos Principle." Apollos, as you know, was a bright and capable man from Alexandria. He was a believer and very gifted in speech. The following is recorded of him in Acts:

> And a certain Jew named Apollos, born at Alexandria, an eloquent man, and mighty in the scriptures, came to Ephesus.
> This man was instructed in the way of the Lord; and being fervent in the spirit, he spake and taught diligently the things of the Lord, knowing only the baptism of John.
> And he began to speak boldly in the synagogue: whom when Aquila and Priscilla had heard, they took him unto them, and expounded unto him the way of God more perfectly.
> For he mightily convinced the Jews, and that publickly, shewing by the scriptures that Jesus was Christ. (Acts 18:24–26, 28.)

I will paraphrase the passage so as to illustrate the point:

> And a certain *teacher,* named Apollos, born in *Salt Lake City* [or anywhere], an eloquent man, and mighty in the scriptures, came to *the Church Educational System.*
> This man was instructed in the way of the Lord; and being fervent in the spirit, he spoke and taught diligently the things of the Lord, knowing only the *King James Version.*
> And he began to speak boldly in the *classrooms and in firesides:* whom when his *supervisors* and *teacher trainers* had heard, they took him unto them, and expounded unto him the way of God more perfectly, *using the Book of Mormon, Doctrine and Covenants, Pearl of Great Price, the JST, and the teachings of Joseph Smith and of the living prophets.*
> And *afterwards* he mightily convinced the *students,* and that publicly, shewing by the scriptures that Jesus was Christ.

We see that Apollos had many of the valuable tools and skills helpful to be a great teacher. He was fervent, dedicated, eloquent, and had a knowledge of the scriptures. But as long as he was acquainted with only a portion of the scriptures, he could not put his great skills to fully benefit the work of the Lord. We need not only eloquence, skill, and dedication; we need the sources, the facts, and the substance of latter-day revelation if we wish to properly teach and interpret the Bible.

We now have a second chance. The JST was offered to the Saints in its entirety in the early days of the Church. They did not reject it; they just *neglected* it. As a church we therefore essentially lost it for about a century. We now have it again in the new

LDS edition of the Bible. We should be careful to not neglect and lose it again. It is an idea whose time is *come.*

TESTIMONY

The JST is a witness for Jesus Christ. It is a witness for the divine calling of Joseph Smith as a prophet and apostle of Jesus Christ. Many people seem to go about it backwards. They want to test Joseph Smith by the content of the inadequate manuscripts. Actually the restoration of the gospel in this dispensation is as great as any other dispensation and can stand on its own record. Joseph Smith had an independent revelation of his own. The Book of Mormon and the JST are the proper standards by which to measure the accuracy of the ancient Bible. We are not measuring the prophets, but the quality of the ancient record that tells about them. I think we should be more like President Brigham Young and not ignore the Prophet's teachings.

I am grateful for the opportunity to have all the books—all of the standard works—and a testimony of the Spirit. I have a testimony that what I have said is true. Studying the scriptures will not always answer all our personal problems, but it will increase our *spirituality,* and with that increased spirituality we can then see our way more clearly to gain the inspiration from the Lord for our immediate problems. In the name of Jesus Christ. Amen.

Robert J. Matthews is dean of Religious Education and professor of Ancient Scripture at BYU.

NOTES

1. Brigham Young, *Discourses of Brigham Young,* comp. John A. Widtsoe (Salt Lake City: Deseret Book Co., 1941), p. 459.

2. Brigham Young Papers, 8 October 1866 sermon.

3. Brigham Young, *Journal of Discourses,* 12:269–70.

4. Sermon given 21 May 1877; printed in *Deseret News,* 6 June 1877.

15

The JST: Retrospect and Prospect—A Panel

Moderated by Robert J. Matthews

Those who attended this symposium were invited to submit questions in writing. These were then read to the panel and responses were made.

QUESTION: Is the Inspired Version as published by the Reorganized Church consistent with the original manuscript?

ROBERT J. MATTHEWS: To that I can answer confidently, yes. Now, another way of asking that question is, is the printed Inspired Version accurate; is it reliable? The answer is yes. That's something we didn't know for a long time. I would have to say it this way: if the manuscript is correct, then the published Inspired Version is correct, for they have followed the manuscript closely. There are a few corrections in spelling and grammar, and a few other things that are very minor, but I have gone over that manuscript several times and I am somewhat familiar with it; in my judgment and experience, yes, it has been published accurately.

QUESTION: Why did Joseph Smith make a new translation of the Bible?

ROBERT L. MILLET: Well, with all that we've said in the last two days, I suppose that no one has come out directly and said Joseph Smith made a translation for the following reasons. I think there are, however, a few things we should keep in mind. Though we do not have the actual revelation in our possession commanding the Prophet to begin the translation, what we do have is occasional references to the fact that he and his scribes had been appointed to the task. He makes that clear in the vision of the glories ("While we were doing the work of translation, *which the Lord had appointed* unto us" [D&C 76:15; emphasis added]). So one reason would be very simple: the Lord commanded them to.

Second, this labor seemed to serve as a type of spiritual education for the Prophet himself. Unfortunately, some misunderstand the whole reason Joseph Smith is doing the translation. I have had numerous people ask me: "Isn't Joseph Smith just 'Mormonizing' the Bible?" I assume they mean by that, isn't he taking presently existing LDS doctrine, reading that into the Bible, and making it into a Mormon book of scripture? The problem with that line of reasoning is that historically that makes very little sense; there wasn't a great deal of Mormonism with which to Mormonize the Bible in June of 1830. The Prophet had translated the Book of Mormon, and certainly knew a number of things. What Joseph did was learn as he went. This proved to be a part of his education, as well as the education of the Church. So that would be a second reason, the spiritual education of the Prophet.

The third thing that I would say is that the Joseph Smith Translation demonstrates to us how it was that revelation came to Joseph Smith, in some cases line upon line and precept upon precept. Even as he was able to review and revise some things, we see that revelation frequently comes in such a manner—bit by bit. In a sense the JST becomes a pattern or a type for every member of the Church. We don't go to the scriptures to read into them what we already know; rather, we go to the scriptures to learn. So it becomes a type for how to receive revelation ourselves.

QUESTION: Did Joseph Smith actually finish the translation, and if not, how much did he do?

MONTE S. NYMAN: He did not finish the translation. I know that it is written in Church history that he finished it in July of 1833. We have no idea the percentage of completion. I think he did a pretty thorough job in the early parts of Genesis and in some parts of the New Testament, but if we consider the Old Testament prophets, that is another matter. I look at the prophet Isaiah, and realize that many areas are untouched. There is no way of knowing whether he did 10 percent or 20 percent or some other percent. What he did, he did well. But because of time and other factors, there was much that he did not get around to doing.

ROBERT J. MATTHEWS: I don't think Brother Nyman will mind if I add a postscript to that. As you probably know, in the process of translation, Joseph Smith used two different systems —actually three. When they first began to translate, they wrote the scriptures out entirely—the whole thing, even passages and whole chapters in which there were no alterations to be made. Along the way the Lord, in Doctrine and Covenants 93:53, said to the Prophet, "Hasten to get the work done." That's a gentle nudge, a way of saying, "Can't you do it a little faster?" So they adopted a faster system. The faster system was to only record the *passage,* just the verse that needed to be changed. Then, after a while they made an even quicker system; that is, they only wrote down on the paper the *word(s)* that needed to be changed. They would then put a little mark in the Bible where that word was supposed to go. That's faster still. Now, I don't know just exactly why it is, but in harmony with what Monte was saying, those passages that were written out in full generally have more changes than those passages which were done the faster way. For whatever it is worth, that is just a mechanical observation indicating that perhaps the procedure had something to do with how many changes were made.

QUESTION: Why has no other Prophet in the Church completed the translation of the Bible?

JOSEPH F. McCONKIE: I think the obvious key here is that in all things wherein we do the Lord's work we have to be called of the Lord to do it. There are undoubtedly prophets who are spiritually and intellectually qualified to do that work, but they haven't received the call to do it. Let me suggest to you a classic case study that illustrates the principle. In 1 Nephi chapter 14 we read about Nephi having had the same revelation that John the Revelator had, the one recorded in the book of Revelation. Nephi desired to write it, and surely there is no question about his competency and ability to do it. He was about to do it when, in effect, the Lord said, "Nothing doing; I've already given that assignment to another by the name of John." Maybe John was still making major preparations in the preexistence, I don't know. But John was due to come along in six hundred years and write the vision, and it was his mission and his commission. For that reason Nephi was told not to do it. Now, without question there are prophets who have been trained from eternity and who will come forth at the right point in time to do that work.

QUESTION: Why does the Church, meaning The Church of Jesus Christ of Latter-day Saints, not accept Joseph Smith's translation of the Bible? (That is a trick question, so be careful.)

ROBERT A. CLOWARD: The simplest answer is that we *do* accept the Joseph Smith Translation. But if I can complicate it a little bit, let me go on from there. Since the translation was made, there are parts of it that have been more available to the Church. From 1832 to 1851 parts of it were published in various periodicals. In 1851 the first edition of the Pearl of Great Price was published in Liverpool, England, including parts of what we now call the book of Moses and chapter 24 of Matthew, which were taken directly from the Joseph Smith Translation. As a Church, we have had since that time, and now have as part of our canon or standard works, those portions of the Joseph Smith Translation. I think that it is a fortunate thing that the name Pearl of Great Price was put on that book and if I can apply a parable, I can see a process going on in the Church today that goes back to the parable the Lord gave on a pearl of great price. You remember the parable about a pearl hidden in a field. When it was discovered where the pearl was, a man went and sold all that he had and he purchased the field. I see the Joseph Smith Translation as being a pearl for our day, and one at a time members of the Church are discovering where the field is. They are putting in the study and the work that it takes to purchase the field and find the pearl and receive the worth that it represents. Though we do accept the translation, the process of making it part of individual lives is a process of individuals encountering and studying and finding the worth of Joseph Smith's work.

QUESTION: For a number of years we have called Joseph Smith's work with the Bible the Inspired Version. Why have we now begun to call it the Joseph Smith Translation?

GERALD N. LUND: Joseph Smith himself in several places in his history refers to it by the word *translation*. His most typical title is the "New Translation of the Bible." When the Reorganized Church published an edition in 1936, they chose to call it the Inspired Version. Both words are accurate; a *version* of the Bible is obviously an appropriate title, and it is clearly an *inspired* version. As I understand it, when the Scriptures Publications Committee talked about putting the JST corrections in the new LDS edition of the Bible, they chose to go with the phrase that the Prophet preferred and call it the "translation," and therefore it became the Joseph Smith Translation.

One other reason might have had a practical basis: If within the footnotes it was listed as IV, many might misunderstand that designation as being a Roman numeral IV. JST is easier to pick up in the reading.

ROBERT J. MATTHEWS: Also, had they called it the New Translation, as the Prophet did, NT looks surprisingly like New Testament when it is in the footnotes. For those reasons it was called the Joseph Smith Translation. Now, one thing we learn and feel a reverence for is scripture. We feel much reverence for the words of the prophets, any of the prophets. Calling it the JST is no careless, reckless, thing. That suggestion itself was taken by the Scriptures Publications Committee, which consists of Elders Monson, Packer, and McConkie, to a meeting in the temple with the First Presidency and the Quorum of the Twelve and it was there officially adopted. That piece of work, the work that Joseph Smith did, was officially adopted by that group in the temple as the Joseph Smith Translation, to be officially abbreviated JST.

QUESTION: Why did Joseph Smith in his sermons sometimes quote the King James Version on passages that he had already corrected in his translation?

CLYDE J. WILLIAMS: First of all, I think the fact that Joseph did not have and the people of his time did not have a complete published edition or version of the JST would make it very difficult for a congregation to know exactly what he was referring to. That is one possible reason. Another factor may have been the particular audience to which he was speaking—what their needs were, and their background. Let me give you an example from Doctrine and Covenants 128, where we find a rather interesting passage. The Prophet Joseph has just quoted Malachi and, as you know, Malachi 4:5–6 is quoted different ways in two or three different places in our scriptures. After quoting that passage he makes this statement, "I might have rendered a plainer translation to this but it is sufficiently plain to suit my purpose as it stands" (D&C 128:18). And then he moves on. The point is that often what was needed to be drawn from a particular passage could be supplied by the King James Version, so he would quote it as it was recorded there because the people were familiar with it and had access to that passage.

Another example might be Hebrews 11:40, where we find in the King James Version what appears to be reference to doing work for the dead. "They without us cannot be made perfect," and so on. In the JST it is changed in such a way as to refer to sufferings. As you read chapter 11 in Hebrews and all that is found there, it is obvious that the context and flow of that chapter has to do with those who have endured suffering and how it literally perfected them. And so the JST change does fit the context. Yet on later occasions Joseph Smith would refer to that passage and would use it in the context of work for the dead. I think the point here is that the principle in either case is true. The Prophet Joseph Smith did not feel himself bound by any particular written word, but rather to be bound by revelation and true principles.

QUESTION: What evidence do we have that Joseph Smith intended to publish his translation of the Bible and if there is such evidence, why didn't he do it?

KEITH W. PERKINS: Probably two reasons: Money and time. In Doctrine and Covenants 43:12–13 the Lord was very plain that the Saints, if they wanted to learn the mysteries of the kingdom from the Prophet Joseph, needed to help him financially and temporally. It is interesting that the Latter-day Saints expected Joseph Smith to be a prophet, seer, revelator, mayor, administrator, general, translator, and yet support his family financially, build his home, chop his wood. And so the Lord had to remind them that if they wanted Joseph to have the time to do the work that was necessary for more doctrine, then they must help him by giving him money, food, and other items. Unfortunately, that was not done as often as it should have been done. As a result, we did not get as much as we might have obtained. Section 94 talks about buildings that were to be established in Kirtland. One of those buildings was to be for publication, and part of that publication the Lord said was to be the Joseph Smith Translation. Section 104 talks about publishing the scriptures, again referring to the New Translation. Incidentally, in the manuscript for section 104, reference is made to the copyright which was to be obtained for the New Translation of the Bible. That copyright has never been found, but it apparently was obtained.

Finally, the Lord said in Doctrine and Covenants 124:89 that William Law had a responsibility to give of his means so that the New Translation could be published. In Church history, as some of you know, William Law began to lose his testimony and in fact did not follow the Lord's counsel in this regard. I suppose had William Law done what he should have done, we would have had the printed translation much sooner. Instead, we have had to wait over 125 years before we could get it printed in our own literature, and it was a great loss. But certainly the Lord *intended* that they publish it. Back in 1833 Joseph Smith wrote a letter to W. W. Phelps, who was publishing some of the translations in the *Evening and Morning Star;* Phelps was instructed not to publish any more, because the Prophet intended to publish the Book of Mormon and the JST New Testament together in a book. But that was never done; he didn't have time to finish it.

QUESTION: How should I use the JST in teaching the gospel?

GEORGE A. HORTON, JR.: I think the answer to that may be obvious to every one of us. We should use it in the best manner we possibly can, just as we would teach with any other scripture. The first thing to do is be aware that there are contributions in the Joseph Smith Translation that might be appropriate to any given subject. In a sense, it is like putting the picture of a puzzle together. We might think of having stacks of miscellaneous parts to put in this great picture. As we put the puzzle together, we learn that the more pieces we can put into the puzzle, the more plain, clear, and beautiful the picture is going to appear. So we're going to look for every one of those pieces and some of them are going to be JST pieces.

In December of 1974 there was a *Church News* editorial that essentially gave the members of the Church the notion that it was appropriate to use the JST in both teaching and writing about the doctrines of the Church. It did, however, add one little suggestion. The article said it would be appropriate that if the matter under study is already in our canonical scripture, we should quote that first. In other words, if there is something in the book of Moses, quote the book of Moses first rather than quote the same verse out of the Joseph Smith Translation. Once one has used all of the sources that are now available (those actually canonized as scriptures), then he is free to go to any other source that is available. The only thing I could add to that is that we should do so with testimony, with the Spirit and with knowledge that those things were inspired, that the Lord gave them for a purpose. Thus, if we can find any help in the JST, it obviously would have some significance and would be appropriate in our teaching.

QUESTION: Would you recommend that missionaries use the JST in teaching the gospel?

GEORGE A. HORTON, JR.: If I were standing in front of my own branch over at the MTC and a missionary asked me, "Should we use the JST?" I suspect that my immediate answer would be, probably not, at least not to begin with. I believe the role of the missionary is not to teach some of the deeper doctrines of the Church. The first thing he should do is bear testimony of the Lord and the restoration of the gospel through the Prophet Joseph Smith. Once that is established, I suppose that if they have an investigator or, even better, a member of the Church who has accepted the message of the Restoration, who has a testimony of the Prophet, who knows about the Book of Mormon and who has read the Book of Mormon, then perhaps they are ready to go on to some of these other things. But I think it would be counterproductive if they were to immediately turn to the JST. Now, they might ease into the JST once they've established the Prophet as the divine representative. If a person is accepting of that, then they are on good ground. There is that little caveat in the first chapter of the book of Moses where the Lord said that these things are to be given to those who believe. With that caution in mind, I might introduce it, but I'd only bring it up as they had gone from step to step in the faith to where they were ready to receive it.

QUESTION: Why is it that we don't have more than eight chapters of Moses in the Pearl of Great Price? Did not Franklin D. Richards, who compiled the Pearl of Great Price in 1851, have access to more than that?

ROBERT J. MATTHEWS: It appears that Franklin D. Richards did not have more than that. In fact, if you examine a Pearl of Great Price as published in 1851, the material that we now call

Moses is put in sketchily and piecemeal, a part here and a part on another page and a part on another page; none of it is called the book of Moses. It is just called excerpts from another translation. It was not until Elder Orson Pratt organized the material and brought it forth in the Pearl of Great Price in 1879 that it began to look like our present book of Moses. Now it would seem entirely appropriate—and perhaps the time will come—when the book of Moses and the Pearl of Great Price might be extended. It would seem consistent to me that it ought to be extended at least down to Abraham, then you could pick up with the book of Abraham as the next item in the Pearl of Great Price. As indicated earlier, scriptures are sacred and used with care. Obviously, that sort of thing would have to be recommended and approved by the First Presidency and the Quorum of the Twelve. Since I am not a steadier of the ark, I don't know when that will ever come up, but someday you might see it.

QUESTION: Who is responsible for the little informational headings preceding each chapter in the Bible, the Book of Mormon, the Doctrine and Covenants and the Pearl of Great Price?

ROBERT J. MATTHEWS: I would be glad to tell you who did that, but first let me say one other thing. The Scriptures Publications Committee used many people for many things. It was somewhat agreed that it was a group project and that although individuals worked on certain things, it would not be noised abroad that this person did this thing and that person did another thing. So that is why you cannot find in any published works who did what. I think it would be no breach of etiquette or of confidentiality if I were to say with pleasure that Elder Bruce R. McConkie produced those headings. Now I don't know anybody else who could do it so well. All of the headings are definitive and interpretive; they are a valuable part of the new edition of the scriptures. Occasionally people say to me, "We have a marvelous topical guide" (and let me say that there are people here who helped on the topical guide), "there are a lot of other good things in this new edition of the scriptures, but there is no commentary." It struck me one day that the commentary is in the chapter headings. In fact, try this exercise sometime. Start with Genesis and just read the headings—Genesis 1, then Genesis 2, Genesis 3, and do this for about fifteen chapters. You'll see that those headings are not only good for the chapter in which they are placed, but they are consecutive and relate well to one another.

QUESTION: Last night you referred to Doctrine and Covenants 35:18 (in which the Lord informs Sidney Rigdon that Joseph Smith had been given the keys of the mysteries of those things that were sealed). Does that mean that no more mysteries will be revealed until Joseph returns?

ROBERT J. MATTHEWS: I don't think that is what it means, although I do believe that most of the doctrine for this dispensation was revealed through the Prophet Joseph Smith. Elder McConkie alluded to that in his address. In Doctrine and Covenants 5:10 we are told that this generation shall receive the Lord's word through the Prophet Joseph Smith. That does not limit the word to him, but it does indicate that he laid the doctrinal foundation.

QUESTION: Can and should we purchase Joseph Smith's translation of the Bible to use in teaching classes in the Church? Would it be appropriate to do so?

ROBERT J. MATTHEWS: I think everybody on the stand here behind me and two-thirds of you there in the congregation would say "Yes, you can"; "Yes, you should"; "Yes, it would be appropriate." Now, that leads to another question.

QUESTION: How many excerpts or corrections in the Joseph Smith Translation were included in the new LDS edition of the Bible; and why were not all of them included?

ROBERT J. MATTHEWS: In the LDS edition of the King James Bible, there are close to 700 actual verses from the JST in the footnotes and in the appendix. There seemed no need to include in the footnotes the text to the book of Moses or the text to chapter 24 of Matthew, since it was felt that everyone who had the new LDS edition of the Bible would also have a Pearl of Great Price. It seemed to be a saving of space not to include the text of Moses and chapter 24 of Matthew in those footnotes. If we count close to 700 verses that are there, plus the 400 in the book of Moses and 70 or so in chapter 24 of Matthew, we have around 1150 passages or verses available to us from the JST. That gives a clue as to how many we have.

Now, why were they not all included? I can give you two of the reasons. First, the book was getting large anyway. Second, we do have essentially all the changes that are obviously, plainly doctrinal. This was a matter of judgment. Another practical consideration was that the Reorganized Church has the original manuscript, and they have it copyrighted. They own it as far as the laws of the land can establish that. It seemed to be a bit of prudence not to go to them and say, "We want you to give all of the JST to us." So what was done was this: a selection was made of about 700 verses, a list of those verses was prepared, and it was presented to the RLDS historian. We indicated that we were planning a new edition of the Bible, had intentions to use some JST footnotes, and were going to fit these into the text. The RLDS Church historian felt that this would be a great idea. When the job was done, we wanted some agreement between the publishing houses, the Herald House for the Reorganized Church and Deseret Book Company for the LDS Church. A legal contract was drawn up and the RLDS Church was gracious and even pleased that we wanted to use the JST. You see, that's a good sign, and it left a sweet feeling, a good taste in their mouth. They were not asked for everything, but I do think we have everything that is doctrinally significant.

QUESTION: What is the present position of the RLDS Church with regard to the Inspired Version?

ROBERT J. MATTHEWS: Let me preface this with some comparisons. I cannot speak for the RLDS Church. Officially they hold the JST in honor and respect. But I think I have detected some slippage among them in some areas. The RLDS Church has taken a dim view of the book of Abraham. In fact, if you study the RLDS history you can see them progressively accepting the book of Abraham less and less until now they reject it altogether. Some of them have shown a trend in that direction somewhat with the Book of Mormon. They haven't rejected it, but they have begun to discount its doctrinal and historical value. There is sometimes a difference between one member and another member. It would be hard to say that all Latter-day Saints believe this thing or that all Latter-day Saints don't believe that thing. The same is true with the Reorganized Church; they don't all believe alike, but there is a good number among them (some among their leadership) who have taken a lesser view of the Book of Mormon. Along that line, now that we've established a pattern, "What is the present position of the RLDS church in relation to the Joseph Smith Translation?"

The relationship as far as I can tell is that it too might be going the way of the book of Abraham and the Book of Mormon. How could it help but do that? The thing about the JST that makes it better than any other Bible is the doctrine. But after a hundred years, it seems they are getting a little careless in the way in which they deal with the doctrine, and therefore it seems to me that the JST is not held today by the RLDS in as high esteem as it was a hundred years ago. Now, you may have a neighbor who is an RLDS member and he might say that this isn't true. Well, it may not be true in his mind, but the JST does not seem to have quite the same shine and glitter and luster among the RLDS officials today that it did a hundred years ago. Have they rejected it? No, but I think they have rejected, or at least neglected some of the concepts that are within it.

CONCLUSION

I would like to thank Brother Nyman and Brother Millet and many others. They shouldered the responsibility for this symposium. There are many others: Brother Millet and Brother Alan Parish did much by way of advertising; the members of this panel, who have delivered lectures and who have worked so hard, have put a great amount of work into the production of this symposium. I think you should know that I did not suggest this symposium. I hesitated for at least two seconds before I said yes after it *was* suggested. I believe it was a thing that was needed. I'm glad we did it. I hope you're glad we did it. There will be a publication that will come out of this sometime in the near future. Now, to all of those who labored so hard and to all of you who came who made it a success, we give our thanks.

Let me reflect on a change that has taken place in my short lifetime. Twenty-five or thirty years ago, if you were to announce you were going to speak at a fireside on the Joseph Smith Translation of the Bible, people looked at you as if you were a little strange; they would hope that the blinds would be drawn and the door would be locked and that no one would see them come or leave. There was a cloud hanging over the New Translation and as much misunderstanding as there has ever been, I suppose, about anything. I have seen that cloud gradually dispel. The fact that it is now a prominent part of the new LDS edition of the Bible surely shows that it has gained its proper place or at least is on its way. It is gaining a place in the hearts and the understanding of the membership of the Church. It could not have been in our new Bible if the First Presidency and the Twelve had not permitted it to be so. Now, that indicates a change that has taken place through the years.

Because we have access to the manuscript and because we now know more about the JST and the background than we did before, we now appreciate the Prophet Joseph Smith in an additional dimension. We've always known about him in some other ways: the First Vision, the Book of Mormon, Doctrine and Covenants, priesthood, temples. Now we have all of those and yet see him in an additional dimension. We also understand the Book of Mormon better than we used to because of the JST. We understand the Doctrine and Covenants better than we used to. We understand Church history better than we used to. We understand the Bible better than we used to, and so it truly is an improvement and a light that is growing brighter. As to the future for the JST, I believe that it has only one way to go: it will become stronger and greater and better appreciated, it will be read by more people, and will contribute to the understanding of the gospel and thus to the salvation of many people. I would say that the future for the JST is not only rosy, it is bright!

The JST represents an idea or a concept whose day has come, and I invite all who want to know more about the gospel to consider studying the Joseph Smith Translation. Because it is scripture and because it came from the Lord through the Prophet Joseph Smith, I would say pray about it. Then, when we get that under our belts and neckties and understanding, we will be a little more ready when other things come forth from the Lord. I believe it was time in the economy of the Lord that this book should become known to the Latter-day Saints. More could be said about that, but we don't have time to say it, so I pray that the blessings of the Lord might be upon us.

I bear testimony that we're living in a new era, a progressive era, a reflection of President Kimball's statement in April 1979 conference that we had "paused on some plateaus long enough. Let us resume our journey forward and upward." With that suggestion and with this opportunity that lies before us to become better acquainted with the scriptures, I say that we are living in a very special day. The faster we become acquainted with the word of the Lord that he has already given us, the sooner more will come. In the name of Jesus Christ. Amen.

Subject Index

A

Abijam, king, 97
Abimelech, 65
Abominable church, 125
Abraham, book of. *See* Book of Abraham
Adam and Eve, 58–59, 64, 276–78
Adam-ondi-Ahman, 67
Adonai, 77
Adultery, committed in heart, 181
Afflictions, 225
Ahaziah, 99
Ahijah, 96
Ale (Hebrew word), 115
Almsgiving, 183–84
Amos (Old Testament book), 141–43
Anger, 179, 225
Animals, 261
Apocalypsis (Greek word), 251
"Apollos Principle," 287–89
Apostles, 1, 167, 187, 189
Ariel, 125
Articles of Faith, 37
Asaph, 107

B

Baptismal prayer, 184
Beatitudes. *See* Sermon on the Mount
Bent, Samuel, 32
Bernhisel, John M., 35
Bernhisel Manuscript (1845), 35–36, 40
Beulah, 132
Bible, authenticity, 11
  editions, 25
  future perfection, 15–16
  imperfection, 9–10, 44–45
  incomplete, 16, 20, 27, 275
  LDS edition, 41–42, 72–74, 300–302
  manuscripts, 285–86
  new translations, 26
  perverted, 12–13
  Phinney 1828 ed., 76
  reservations in belief about, 14
  secular translations, 218–19
  textual history, 273–75
Bible Aids Committee, 41
Bible (Inspired Version). *See* Joseph Smith Translation
Bible (King James Version). *See* King James Version
Bible (New Testament). *See* New Testament
Bible (Old Testament). *See* Old Testament
Bidamon, Emma Smith, 38
Book of Abraham, 15, 21, 303
Book of Mormon, incompleteness, 20
  importance, 10–12
  Isaiah text, 121–27, 130–32
  prophetic forthcoming, 114–15
  sealed portion, 15, 20
  Sermon on the Mount, 164–65
  unchangeable, 12
  veracity, 21
Book of Moses, 52–53, 278, 299–300
Book of remembrance, 64
Brass plates of Laban, 15–17, 20, 282–83
Broken heart and contrite spirit, 180

C

Cain, 61, 64, 283
"Calling and election sure," 127
Cannon, George Q., 34
Celestial marriage, 67–68
Charity, 225
Chazak (Hebrew word), 90
"Cheek, turning other," 182
Chronicles 1 and 2 (Old Testament books), 89–90, 98–100
Church (term), 148
City of Enoch, 28–29
City of Zion, 6–7
Commandment-breakers, 176–77
Commandments, 149–50
Commentary, 43
Confirmation prayer, 184
Consecration, law of, 232
Content restoration, of JST, 43
Councils of heaven, 115–17
Covenant (word), 278
Covenants, 62–63
Cowdery, Oliver, 30
Creation, 54–55
"Cross, take up" (phrase), 181

D

Daniel (Old Testament book), 138–39
Dark Ages, 13
Daughters of God, 61
Daughters of men, 61
David, king, 93, 96–97, 107
Deuteronomy (Old Testament book), 82–83
Disciples, 167
Discipleship, covenant, 172–74
Dispensation of the fulness of times, 19–20
Doctrine, establishment, 117
  restoration, 7–10, 21, 161
Doctrine and Covenants, Bible translation outgrowth, 28–29
  section 77, 257–58
  section 107, 66–67
  section 132, 67–68
  veracity, 21
Durham, Reed C., 40

E

Earth, 6, 261
Ecclesiastes (Old Testament book), 104
Elias, 263
End of the world, 239
Enduring to the end, 197
Enoch, 283–84
Ephraim, 65
Essenes, 209
Evil spirits, 92
Exodus (Old Testament book), 79–81
Eye, offensive, 181
Ezekiel (Old Testament book), 138–39

F

Faith, Paul's teachings, 223–24
Fall of Adam, 58–59
False prophets, 92–93
Familiar spirits, 92
Family prayer, 184
"Foundation of the Church," 2
"Fulness of time," 158

G

Gathering of Israel, 109–11, 131
Genesis (JST), extra-textual sources, 66–68
  fundamental message, 53–55
  gospel themes, 55–63
  relation to book of Moses, 52–53
  translation period, 66
  unique contributions, 63–65, 75
Genesis (Old Testament book), 27–28, 56–57, 60, 252
God, attributes, 90–91
  privilege of seeing, 73, 86, 112–13, 230
Golden Rule, 195
Gospel, Church administration, 148–49
  taught from beginning, 60, 276–78
Grace, Paul's teachings, 223–24
Grandin, E. B., 25

H

Hand, offensive, 181
Harmonization, 43
Harris, George W., 32
Hearts, 181
"Hearts, hardened," 78, 86
Heavenly councils, 115–17
Hephzibah, 132
Hezekiah, 129
Hosea (Old Testament book), 139–40
House of Israel, 134
Hypocrisy, 185, 191

I

"Inspired prophetic commentary," 43
Inspired Version. *See* Joseph Smith Translation
Isaiah (Old Testament book), 121–34
Isaiah (Old Testament prophet), 17

J

Jaques, John, 37
Jehovah. *See* Jesus Christ
Jeremiah (Old Testament book), 134–38
Jerusalem, 125–26, 240
Jesus Christ, character, 228, 284
  in Old Testament, 76–78
  lawgiver, 178
  light, 173–74
  ministerial counsel, 189–95
  perfection, 93, 134, 139–40, 145
  preexistent Lord, 78, 86
  prophetic fulfillment, 152–53
  role and mission, 56–57
  Second Coming, 226–27, 237–48
Jethro, 84–85

Subject Index

Jews, 151, 190, 202–13
Joel (Old Testament book), 140–41
Joseph Smith Translation (herein
　referred to as JST)
　advantages, 272–73
　brass plates and, 282
　doctrinal contributions, 276–88
　editorial revision, 31
　historical overview, 23–25
　incomplete, 33–35, 293–94
　manuscripts, 35–36, 38, 291
　negative attitudes about, 14, 39–40,
　　42, 294–95, 303
　prophesied, 54
　publication, 31–33, 37–38, 297,
　　302
　purpose, 292
　secular translations and, 218–19
　teaching methods, 298–99, 301
　title, 295
　translation process, 25–29, 293
　verity, 14–15, 21
Joshua (Old Testament book), 90–91
Judaism. *See* Jews
Judas Iscariot, 108
Judges (Old Testament book), 91

K

King Follett Sermon, 20
King James Version, 24
　LDS edition, 41–42
Kingdom of God, 188, 267
Kingdoms of glory, 232
Kings, 1 and 2 (Old Testament books),
　89–90, 96–98
Korah, 83

L

Law, 175–79
Law of Moses. *See* Mosaic law
Law, William, 32, 297–98
Lectures on Faith, 31
Lee, Harold B., 41
Leviticus (Old Testament book), 81–82
Light (symbol), 172–75
Literalism, 141
Lord's Prayer, 184–85
Lord's will, 196
Luke (New Testament book), 148,
　155–58
Lundwall, N. B., 39
Lust, 181

M

McConkie, Bruce R., 34–35, 41–42,
　300
M'Lellin, William E., 44
Malachi (Old Testament book), 144–45
Man, nature, 59
"Man child," 266
Manasseh, 65
Mark (New Testament book), 148,
　154–55
Marriage, Paul's teachings, 221–23
Matthew (New Testament book), 28,
　148–54, 252
Matthews, Robert J., 38–39, 41
Mediators, 233
Meekness, 181
Melchizedek, 62, 65, 229–30, 284
Melchizedek Priesthood, during Penta-
　teuch period, 74–75, 83–84
Millennium, doctrinal restoration, 21
Ministry, full-time, 187, 189
Missionaries, JST usage by, 299
Monson, Thomas S., 41
Mosaic law, 168, 173, 177–78, 203, 223
Moses, authorship, 107
　rebellion against, 83
　tables of stone, 73–74
　visions of, 32
Moses, book of. *See* Book of Moses
"Motes and beams" teachings, 191
Mulekites, 128
Mysteries, 192–93, 301

N

Nehemiah (Old Testament book), 89–90,
　100
Neum, 17
New Testament
　Epistles, 216–17
　Greek texts, 217–18
　translation, 28–29, 215–16
"New Translation of the Bible," 295
Noah, 64
Numbers (Old Testament book), 82

O

"Offending body part," 181
"Oh Say, What Is Truth?," 37
Old Testament
　continuity, 278–82
　Jesus Christ in, 76–78

310 — Subject Index

revisions, 75—76
translation, 27—28
Oppressed, redemption, 113—14
Oral law, 179
Original sin, 58

P

Packer, Boyd K., 41—42
Patch, Robert C., 41
Paul (apostle), 158, 219—21
Pearl of Great Price, 36—37, 299
Pentateuch, revision, 75—76
Perfection, 183
Persecution, 171, 182
Peter (apostle), 3—4
Pharaoh, 78—79
Pharisees, 208
Pratt, Orson, 38, 75
Prayer, 184—85
Predestination, 232
Premortal life, 115—17
Priesthood, 62
Prophecy, gift of, 2
Prophetic documents, 43
Prophets, 2, 17—18, 294
Proverbs (Old Testament book), 104
Psalms (Old Testament book), 107—17

R

Rasmussen, Ellis T., 41
Reconciliation, 179—80
Records, sacred, 126
Redemption, 113—14
Redemption of Israel, 109—11
Re'em (Hebrew word), 127
Reorganized Church, 14, 35, 38, 291, 302—3
Repentance, 91, 195
Restitution, times of, 5
Restoration of all things, 19—21
Revelation, 2, 20
Revelation (New Testament book), 13, 251—68
Revised Standard Version, 218—19
Richards, Franklin D., 36—37, 299—300
Rigdon, Sidney, 30, 46
"Rock of revelation," 2

S

Sacramental prayer, 184
Sadducees, 207—8
Salt (symbol), 172—74
Salvation for the dead, 231
Samuel, 1 and 2 (Old Testament books), 89—91, 93
Satan, 57—58, 60
Scribes, 29—31
Scripture, 12
 interpretation, 117—18
 of unequal value, 117
Scriptures Publications Committee, 41, 296, 300
Second Coming, 226—27
Sermon on the Mount, accounts and versions, 165—66
 audience and setting, 166—68, 187
 Book of Mormon contributions, 164—65
 disciples and beatitudes, 168—72
 hearing and doing admonitions, 195—98
 JST contributions, 163—64
 law discussion, 175—78
 laws unto perfection, 178—83
 ministerial counsel, 189—95
 ministry teachings, 186—89
 salt and light symbols, 172—75
 significance, 198—99
 worship teachings, 183—86
Seth, 118
"Seven seals," 262
Shiloh, 135
Sin, 114, 224—26
Sins of the heart, 181
Sleep, 135
Smith, Emma, 29. *See also* Bidamon, Emma Smith
Smith, George A., 34
Smith, Joseph, Bible translator, 23—31, 54
 biblical knowledge, 118
 integrity, 43
 received revelation, 201, 287
 scripture teaching methods, 296
Smith, Joseph Fielding, 34, 39—40
Solomon, 94—95, 107
Song of Solomon (Old Testament book), 104—6
Sons of God, 61
Sons of men, 61
Spiritual understanding, 118
Sufferings, 231
Sun, 123
Symbolism, 141
Synoptic Gospels, 147—48
 settings and backgrounds, 158—61

Subject Index

T

"Take up your cross" (phrase), 181
Talmage, James E., on Genesis, 54
Taylor, John, on tables of commandments, 74–75
Teachers, 2–3
Temptation, 185, 224–26
Ten Commandments, 75
Ten tribes of Israel, 264
Textual variants, 44
Theophilus, 155
"Thief in the night," 158
Topical Guide, 41
Transgressions, 114
Translation (terminology), 26
"Triple combination," 41
Twelve Apostles, 167–68, 187, 189

U

Ungodliness, 181

W

Whitmer, John, 30
Will of the Lord, 196
Works, Paul's teachings, 223–24

Y

Young, Brigham, 34, 271–72

Z

Zechariah (Old Testament book), 143–44
Zenock, 17
Zenos, 17–18

Scripture Index

OLD TESTAMENT

Genesis
1:2	33
1:26–27	64
1:27, 29 (JST)	64
1:30	64
1:32 (JST)	64
2:4	77
2:5 (JST)	64
2:20–22 (JST)	58
2:24	222
3:1–5 (JST)	282–83
4:1	61
4:1–8	64
4:2–5:13 (JST)	64
4:10 (JST)	58
4:11 (JST)	58–59
4:12–13 (JST)	58–59, 61
5:1	64
5:4, 6 (JST)	61
5:11 (JST)	61, 282
5:22–23	64
5:44 (JST)	60, 279
5:45 (JST)	63
6:2	61
6:5–8 (JST)	61–64, 279
6:6	64, 91
6:12, 22, 43 (JST)	61
6:18	278
6:21–7:78 (JST)	64
6:36 (JST)	61
6:38 (JST)	161
6:47–50 (JST)	59, 279
6:51–56, 59–65, 67–71 (JST)	58–59, 276–78, 284
7:58 (JST)	63
7:70 (JST)	114–15
8:1 (JST)	61
8:3 (JST)	61
8:7 (JST)	62
8:15 (JST)	64, 284
8:23–24 (JST)	63, 280
9:14–15, 17, 21–25 (JST)	63, 280
13:13 (JST)	63, 280
14:16–40 (JST)	284
14:18–20	62–63
14:24	65
14:25–40 (JST)	52, 65
14:26–28 (JST)	62, 281
14:37–38 (JST)	62
15:16	142
17:1	68, 77
17:3–8, 11–12 (JST)	63, 281
17:17	65
17:23 (JST)	65
18:1	230
18:23 (JST)	62
19:8	65
19:11 (JST)	65
19:31–33	65
19:37–39 (JST)	65
21:31 (JST)	65
21:33	65
24:2, 8 (JST)	65
24:2, 9	65
28:22 (JST)	65
41:43	77
48:5–11	65
50:24–36	63, 65

Exodus
3:2 (JST)	80
4:10	80
4:21	78, 90
5:4 (JST)	80
5:11	76
6:1–3	76, 77
6:3 (JST)	77
6:29–30 (JST)	80
7:1 (JST)	80
7:3	78, 90
7:3, 13 (JST)	79, 284
7:13–14, 22	78–79
7:22	79
8:32	79
9:12	78, 90
9:34	79
10:1, 20, 27	78, 90
11:10	78, 90
12:37 (JST)	80
14: 8, 17	78
14:20 (JST)	80
18:1 (JST)	84

21:20 (JST)	80	28:11–13 (JST)	92
22:18 (JST)	80	28:15 (JST)	92
22:28 (JST)	80		
23:3 (JST)	80	2 Samuel	
24:9–10	230	12:11–12	93
32:1	76	12:13 (JST)	93
32:12 (JST)	80–81	24:16–17 (JST)	93
32:12, 14	91		
32:14 (JST)	81	1 Kings	
32:35 (JST)	81	3:2–4 (JST)	94
33:20 (JST)	72–73	3:6 (JST)	95
33:23 (JST)	73	3:9 (JST)	95
34:1	74	3:12 (JST)	95
34:1–2 (JST)	74, 84	3:14 (JST)	95
34:14 (JST)	78	11:4 (JST)	96
		11:6 (JST)	96
Leviticus		11:33–35 (JST)	96
12:3–5 (JST)	81	11:38–39 (JST)	96–97
21:1 (JST)	82	14:8 (JST)	97
21:11 (JST)	82	15:3 (JST)	97
22:6	76	15:5 (JST)	97
		15:11–12 (JST)	97
Numbers			
11:10–16	83	2 Kings	
16:3	83	8:26	99
16:9–10	82–83	18–20	128
16:10 (JST)	84	18:20	128
22:20–22 (JST)	82	19:35 (JST)	98
23:19	81		
		1 Chronicles	
Deuteronomy		21:1	57
2:30 (JST)	82	21:15 (JST)	98
10:1 (JST)	74, 84	21:20 (JST)	99
10:2 (JST)	82		
14:21 (JST)	82	2 Chronicles	
16:22 (JST)	83	18:20–22 (JST)	99
18:15–19	229	22:2 (JST)	99
23:15	208–9	25:18 (JST)	100
25:4	158	34:16	100
32:4	81		
34:6	83	Nehemiah	
		10:29–30 (JST)	100
Joshua			
11:20 (JST)	90	Psalms	
		11 (JST)	111
Judges		11:7	113
2:18 (JST)	91	12:1	113
		13:1 (JST)	112
1 Samuel		14 (JST)	111–12
15:11 (JST)	91	16:10	93
15:35 (JST)	91	24:8, 10 (JST)	114
16:14–16, 23 (JST)	92	27:8	113
18:10 (JST)	92	29:1–2	116
19:9 (JST)	92	32:1 (JST)	114
28:9 (JST)	92	33:4 (JST)	114

Scripture Index

36:5 (JST)	114	42:19–25 (JST)	129–30
37:11, 22, 29	113	43:11	78
42:2 (JST)	112	43:14–15	78
46:10	111	45:7	142
68:4	77	48:1, 12, 15 (JST)	131
69:8–9	108	48:8 (JST)	131
69:21–23, 25	108	50:5 (JST)	131
82:1	115–16	52:15 (JST)	131
82:6	116	53:2	202
83:18	77	53:9	132
85:11 (JST)	114	55:1–2 (JST)	132
89:5–8 (JST)	116	60:1–2, 14	139
90:13 (JST)	112–13	60:22 (JST)	132
91:6	109–10	62:4–5 (JST)	132
95:3	117	63:17 (JST)	132, 284
96:4	117	64:4 (JST)	133
97:7	116	64:5–6 (JST)	132
97:9	117	65:1–2 (JST)	133
100	110	65:20 (JST)	133
102:18 (JST)	113		
103:20–21	116	Jeremiah	
107	110–11	2:24 (JST)	136–37
138:8 (JST)	114	3:14	140
144:11–12	111	7:20	255
148:2	116–17	8:8	138
		18:8, 10 (JST)	134
Proverbs		18:14 (JST)	135
18:22 (JST)	104	26:3–6 (JST)	135
		26:13 (JST)	135
Song of Solomon		26:18–20 (JST)	136
6:10	106	29:19	135
		30:12–15 (JST)	137
Isaiah		30:16 (JST)	138
4:1	122	35:14 (JST)	135
6:1	230	35:14–15	135
6:13	140	42:10 (JST)	136
9:6	78	44:4	135
11:16	128		
12:2	77	Ezekiel	
13:2 (JST)	123	6:8–10	140
13:10	123, 243	14:9 (JST)	138–39
14:12	57	23:17, 23, 28 (JST)	139
16:6 (JST)	123	31:3	255
24:20	110	32:7	243
28:13	124	48:35 (JST)	139
29:1–8	125–26		
32:14 (JST)	127	Daniel	
34:7 (JST)	127	5:25–28 (JST)	139
34:16–17 (JST)	127	9:27	243
35:8 (JST)	128	11:31	243
36:5 (JST)	128	12:11	243
37:32 (JST)	128		
37:36 (JST)	98	Hosea	
38:15–17 (JST)	129	1:10–11	140
40:3 (JST)	127	2:23	140

Scripture Index

3:4—5	140	Jonah	
11:8 (JST)	140	3:9—10 (JST)	143, 284
Joel		Micah	
1:6 (JST)	140—41	2:12	140
2:13—14 (JST)	140		
2:31	110, 243	Zechariah	
		4:10 (JST)	143—44
		4:14 (JST)	144
Amos		6:5 (JST)	144
3:6 (JST)	141	8:7, 13 (JST)	144
3:7 (JST)	142	14:6—7	244
4:3 (JST)	142—43		
4:5—6 (JST)	143	Malachi	
7:3, 6	141	4:5—6	144, 296
9:8—9	140	4:5—6 (JST)	144

NEW TESTAMENT

Matthew		5:48	183
3:2	192	5:50 (JST)	149, 183, 195
3:2 (JST)	153		
3:22—27 (JST)	153—54, 238	6:1 (JST)	183—84
		6:2, 5, 17 (JST)	185
4:17	192	6:3 (JST)	184
4:18 (JST)	153	6:7 (JST)	184—85
4:22 (JST)	190	6:9—16 (JST)	184
5:1—2	166	6:13	200
5:1—4 (JST)	150, 169	6:13 (JST)	185
5:3—7:35 (JST)	165	6:14 (JST)	185
5:5	113	6:15 (JST)	200
5:5 (JST)	170	6:16 (JST)	185
5:8 (JST)	170	6:22 (JST)	185
5:12	171	6:24—28 (JST)	186—88
5:12 (JST)	170	6:29—30	149
5:13	173, 174	6:32—33	188
5:13 (JST)	170	6:36—39 (JST)	188—89
5:14	173	7:1—5, 14, 16 (JST)	187, 189—90
5:14 (JST)	171		
5:15—16 (JST)	173—74	7:3—5	191, 206—7
5:17—18	175—76	7:4—8 (JST)	206—7
5:19—20	176, 200	7:6	192
5:19—20 (JST)	175—76	7:6—9 (JST)	191, 194
5:20—21 (JST)	203	7:7—10	193, 210
5:21—22 (JST)	173, 176, 183	7:9—11	194
		7:10—19 (JST)	192—93, 210
5:22	200		
5:24—26 (JST)	179	7:14—15 (JST)	193, 195
5:27—28	180	7:16—21	196
5:29—31 (JST)	180	7:16—21 (JST)	194—95
5:34 (JST)	181	7:22	197
5:40—41	181—82	7:24	178
5:42—43 (JST)	181—82	7:28	167

Scripture Index

7:30–33	196–97	12:28 (JST)	207–8
7:36–37 (JST)	151, 167, 207	12:44 (JST)	154
		13:14	240
8:1	166	13:32	245–46
9:14	167	13:47 (JST)	246
9:15–16	159, 204	14:31 (JST)	154
9:16–22 (JST)	159, 204	14:36–38 (JST)	155
9:35–36	150	15:23	108
10:1	167		
10:5–6	190	Luke	
10:14 (JST)	196	2:51–52	237
10:16	196	3:2–11 (JST)	156–58
10:19–20	189	3:13	157
11:1–2	167	3:19–20 (JST)	155, 157
13:47	192	6:6–11	190
15:1–9	206	6:13–20	167
15:8 (JST)	205	6:20–23	171
16:3	202	6:20–49 (JST)	166, 182, 198
16:13–19	148		
16:24	181	6:27–35	182
16:25–29 (JST)	150, 181	6:43–46	196
18:1–5, 7–9	148	7:1	167
18:6–9 (JST)	150–51	9:20–21	148
18:10–11 (JST)	150, 284	11:1–4 (JST)	184–85
18:12–17	148–49	11:4	185, 200
18:21–35	148	11:14 (JST)	194
19:13 (JST)	284	11:53 (JST)	212
23:1–2, 12, 21, 28–29, 33–37	151–52	12:9–14 (JST)	189
		12:33 (JST)	158, 200
23:21 (JST)	206	12:34 (JST)	188
23:38–41 (JST)	154	12:41–42 (JST)	246
25:1–13	244	12:44 (JST)	158
25:1–12 (JST)	200	13:25 (JST)	197
25:21	248	13:26	197
27:9	138	14:33–35	159, 172, 205
27:34, 48	108		
28:18–20	183	14:34–38 (JST)	159–60, 172, 205
36 (JST)	187		
		16:13–19 (JST)	283
Mark		16:19–24 (JST)	160, 212
1:1–6 (JST)	285	17:32	240
3:1–7	190	17:35–38 (JST)	157–58, 245
3:14	168		
7:1–9	206	19:11 (JST)	202
7:6–7 (JST)	205	19:43–44	240
7:9–12 (JST)	207	21:12	239
8:29–30	148	21:16	239
9:6 (JST)	154	21:18–20	239–40
9:31 (JST)	154	21:25, 32 (JST)	243
9:40–48 (JST)	150–51, 181	21:37 (JST)	244
10:7–9	222	John	
10:30–31 (JST)	155	1:19 (JST)	39
11:34 (JST)	154	2:17	108

3:5	170	Galatians	
4:22	204	3:19—20	233
6:46	230	3:24 (JST)	183
7:5	108	1:10	5, 158
8:1—11	283	4:10 (JST)	228
19:29	108	4:26 (JST)	225
21:22—23	265		
Acts		1 Thessalonians	
1:1	155	4:15 (JST)	227
1:8	155	5:2—6	158, 245
1:20	108	2 Thessalonians	
2:27, 31	93	1:7—10	247
3:1—21	4	2:2—3 (JST)	227
3:22—23	229	2:7 (JST)	227
7:22	80	2:9 (JST)	227
7:55—56	230		
18:24—26, 28	288	1 Timothy	
		1:1 (JST)	228
Romans		5:18	158
1:5 (JST)	232	6:16 (JST)	230
1:6	232		
3:8 (JST)	220	2 Timothy	
3:24	223	1:10	148
3:28 (JST)	223	3:15—17	212—13, 223
4:16 (JST)	224		
6:7 (JST)	224	Titus	
6:14 (JST)	224	1:15—16	223
6:17 (JST)	225	2:11 (JST)	218
7:14—19 (JST)	220, 228		
7:14—15, 17—20	219—20	Hebrews	
7:22 (JST)	220	3:8	86
8:1—10	220	4:2	86
8:20 (JST)	225	4:15	132, 228
9:3 (JST)	221	5:7—8 (JST)	229
11:9—11	108	6:1	228
13:2 (JST)	219	7:3	229
13:6—7 (JST)	232	7:3 (JST)	62, 229—30
		7:11	86
1 Corinthians		7:13	284
1:23 (JST)	232	7:26 (JST)	228
2:11 (JST)	118, 230	7:27	228
4:4 (JST)	219	9:15, 18, 20 (JST)	218
5:9	221	9:23—24, 28	86
6:12 (JST)	220	9:26 (JST)	226
7:1 (JST)	222	10:1	86
7:6, 25	222	11:1 (JST)	218
7:26—33	222	11:40	231, 296
7:26, 29, 32—33 (JST)	222—23	13:4	223
9:9	158	13:5 (JST)	232
10:11 (JST)	226	13:8	60
11:11	222		
12:3	33	James	
12:28	1	1:2 (JST)	225
14:34—35 (JST)	223	1:5—6	195
15:41	232		

Scripture Index

1:12 (JST)	225	Revelation	
1:17	142	1:1–2, 4–5 (JST)	259
2:4 (JST)	219	1:7 (JST)	260
2:19 (JST)	224	2:17	256
		2:22 (JST)	260
1 Peter		2:26–27 (JST)	260
2:12 (JST)	218	4:1–2	230, 260–61
2:22	228		
3:1, 2, 16 (JST)	218	4:5 (JST)	261
3:19–20 (JST)	233	4:6	256
4:6 (JST)	233	5:1	261–62
4:7–8 (JST)	225, 226	6:1–11	262–63
		6:12–7:17	243, 262–63
2 Peter		9:1–5	254
1:19 (JST)	231–32	11:3–13	243
1:20–21 (JST)	256	11:15 (JST)	265
3:4 (JST)	227	12:1 (JST)	266
3:8–9 (JST)	227	12:3 (JST)	266
3:10	158	12:6–10 (JST)	266–67, 283
3:10 (JST)	227		
3:12–13 (JST)	227	12:7	256
		12:14 (JST)	267
1 John		14:1–5	264
3:6–9 (JST)	226	19:10–11	2, 262
4:12 (JST)	230	21:2–3	139
3 John			
1:11	142, 230		

BOOK OF MORMON

		25:9	135, 142
1 Nephi		25:23–30	179, 183
5:18–19	15	27:15–20	27
13:23	16, 24, 282	28:30–31	124, 208
13:24–34	13, 24, 58, 218, 252	30:15–18	21
13:35–40	24	Jacob	
14:12	268	4:4	278
14:20–21, 25	268	4:14	203
14:23	13, 252	7:11	153, 278
14:27	268		
15:8–9	211	Mosiah	
15:23–24	260	3:19	59
17:35	142	13:30	183
19:10–17	17		
19:23–24	43, 126	Alma	
21–22	126	17:2–3	207
		30:3	183
2 Nephi		37:4–5	16
2:17	282	40:23	239
2:22–25	282	45:19	83
6:5	126		
6:18	131	3 Nephi	
11:8	43	8–11	244

9:19—20	180	16:17—20	126
10:12	168	18:16, 22—25, 30	173
11:11	196	18:24	174
11:41	168	20:11	121
12:1—2	168, 169	20:32—34	126
12:3	170	21:1	131
12:6	170	21:2	198
12:12—14	171, 173, 174	23:1	121
		23:4	199
12:16—20	174—77	23:7	166
12:22—24	179	25:2	144
12:27—30	180	26:6—12	163, 166
12:48	183	27:20, 23	192
13:1	183—84	27:26	163
13:22	185	27:27	183
13:24—25	186—87	29:1	199
13:33	188	30:23	229
14:1	189		
14:16—20	196	Mormon	
14:22—23	197	9:34	45
15:1	166		
15:5—6, 9	121, 173	Moroni	
16:4—7	199	7:12	92, 141
16:6—15	175	7:45, 47	225

DOCTRINE AND COVENANTS

1:17	23	84:19—25	85, 112
4:5	186	84:26—27	85
5:10	23, 106, 163	84:54—57	46
18:15—16	172	86:3	267
20:11	11	86:11	173
20:25—28	278	88:17—20	114
25:6	30	88:68	113
35:17—20	46, 161, 283	88:87	243
42:12—16	3	93:1	113
42:56—58	101	93:16—28	183
42:84—92	149	93:38	59
45:39, 44	244	93:53	293
45:42	243	101:32—34	5
45:57	244	101:38	113
45:60—62	28, 215, 284	101:39	173
46:13	2	103:9—10	175
47:1	30	105:31	106
50:17—18	2	106:4—5	245
68:3—4	213	107:3	62, 230
76:15	292	107:40—52	66—67, 118
76:25—30	256	107:57	67
77:1—5	261	109:73—74, 76	106
77:6—7	262	124:89	297
77:9—15	263—65	128:18	144, 296
84:5—6	85	130:7—11	256, 261

Scripture Index 321

130:20—21	95	133:18	264
131:5	232	133:23—24	6
132:1—2	67	133:27—28	128
132:39	97	133:50—52	246—47

PEARL OF GREAT PRICE

Moses		7:18	29
1:1—2, 6—8, 26, 40	53—54, 72	7:51	63
1:11	72	7:60, 63, 64	248
1:40—41	23, 46, 54, 275	7:62	114—15
		8:13, 15	61
2:26—27	64	8:19	62
2:30	64	8:25	64
3:5	64		
3:17	58	Abraham	
4:1—4	256	1:16	77
5:2—28	64	2:8	77
5:4	61	2:11	233
5:10—13	58—59, 61	3:22—28	116
5:16, 18	61		
5:26	61	Joseph Smith-Matthew	
5:58	60	1:12—15	240
5:59	63	1:16—18	241
6:3	61	1:22—27, 29—31	242
6:5	64	1:33—34	243
6:7	62—63	1:36—37	244
6:13, 21, 41	61	1:39, 43	245
6:21—7:69	64	1:44—45	244
6:34	61	1:47	245
6:36	161, 201		
6:49	59	Joseph Smith-History	
6:52	63	1:36	24
6:54—55	58—59	1:40	229
6:62	58	1:68	25
6:67	62	1:74	25